BREATHING UNDERWATER

Soul Mates and Twin Flame Reunion
Guided by Angels to Heal the Past and Love in the Present

A TRUE STORY

JULIE HOPPER

Library of Congress Cataloging-in-Publication Data

FIRST EDITION

Cover by Shellie Z Design
Cover image photographer: David De Lossy: Collection: Photodisc/ Getty Images.
Edited by Nicole Bobbitt

Grateful acknowledgement is made to the following for permission to reprint previously published material:

The Joseph Campbell Companion, copyright 1991, The Joseph Campbell Foundation.

Reprinted by permission from *Black Elk Speaks: Being the Life Story of a Holy Man of the Oglala Sioux*. The Premiere Edition by John G.Niehardt, the State University of New York Press ©2008, State University of New York. All rights reserved.

The Elizabeth Kubler-Ross Foundation, permission granted by Ken Ross.

Literarische Rechteverwaltung von Erich Fromm, permission granted by Dr. Rainier Funk.

BreathingUnderwater.NET

ISBN-10: 1475275315
EAN-13: 9781475275315

For my Twin Flame ~ and for those who are afraid to love, and those who love with an open heart.

My deepest gratitude goes to all of my friends, who without their encouragement and support, this book may have never been written. And to my guides and mentors, who inspired me and kept me strong throughout the journey.

INTRODUCTION

I wish that I'd had a book like this to serve as a guide for myself twenty years ago. Everything in our story is true, except for those few names, dates and details that were necessary to change in order to protect the privacy of others, while describing the events as they occurred.

At this time, many Twin Flames are finding each other. Although everyone's journey is different, we can learn from each other by sharing our experiences. These lessons can be applied to any relationship. My hope is that our story will serve as a guide, validation, and inspiration to anyone who is trying to find their own path.

The world is full of walking wounded in some form or another and we all communicate that differently. If you first learn to recognize your own fears and insecurities, it will be easier for you to understand the language of others, as well as your own. You may discover that first impressions aren't always what they appear to be. This is especially true for those who are in relationships with adult survivors of child abuse. My heart and compassion goes out to you, as well as to those who have been the victims of abuse themselves.

This was not written for those who need to be convinced, but for those who seek to understand. You—yes you—have already had angelic encounters and messages from your guides. We all have magic surrounding us at every moment, if we only open our hearts and minds to be awake and aware enough to recognize it.

I wrote this as much to teach as to tell a story. I am not a writer, but if I waited until I became one, this book would have never been written. I hope this story will help you to find your own magic.

"*The thought manifests as the word. The word manifests as the deed. The deed develops into habit. And the habit hardens into character. So watch the thought and its ways with care. And let it spring from love, born out of concern for all beings.*"

~ Buddah

Table of Contents

To hold, you must first open your hand. Let go.

~ Lao Tzu

I

It was one of those eerily silent winter days, as my sisters and I stood on the porch of our trailer in stocking feet. The only sounds were those of the rain falling gently on the snow and muffled shouting coming from inside the house. We stood there quietly as our dogs circled around us, occasionally pausing to cock their heads and listen. Our parents had gotten into another one of their volatile arguments. When we found ourselves between the door and the large console TV that my father had just thrown against the wall—we chose the door.

Explosive arguments and violent posturing weren't unusual, but it was always horrifying to us as we stood by helplessly with no way to stop it. My father wasn't a wife beater, but their arguments always felt dangerously close, and real physical harm toward my mother was never more than a split-second lapse in my father's control over himself. Kids are like sponges, and no matter how we may rationalize as adults that our upbringing didn't leave an imprint on us, somehow it always does.

My mother was a runner, but not in the literal sense. After these fights she would disappear, threatening suicide, and we would spend the next hour trying to find her before she could hurt herself. As a child these episodes traumatized me, but as the years passed and they became routine, I began to resent her for it. Later on, I also became a runner in my own relationships, often creating some dramatic reason to cause my boyfriend to chase after me during an argument. Or I'd have the occasional, fleeting thought of suicide as a solution to my despair.

Aside from the dramatics in our family, we had plenty of love and nurturing from our parents, and they taught us good values. My father was an airline captain, and we moved to the Pacific Northwest because they wanted to raise their children in a more rural environment. They chose White Salmon, Washington, in the Columbia River Gorge, where they bought eight acres on a river to build their dream home. The double-wide trailer was only meant to be temporary until the house was built. But that would never happen because my father loved the planning of things far more than the end result.

It was 1975 and this was our second move in the last year. I was going into third grade, and not at all happy that we were moving again. Denver had been a rough transition for a southern kid from Dallas with a strong accent. And although I had been teased into losing most of it, I still wasn't sure what to expect in White Salmon. Eventually though, I adjusted as I grew to appreciate just how beautiful the Gorge truly is. Although many Americans don't even know that it exists, to me the Columbia River Gorge is like the smaller, green version of the Grand Canyon. Steep, rocky cliffs blanketed with fir trees rise up thousands of feet high in places, with beautiful white waterfalls spilling out every few miles, before flowing through the foothills of Oregon. The White Salmon and Hood River areas are particularly stunning; with an expansive green valley, and a mile-wide river separating the snow-capped mountains of Adams and Hood. At times when the sun is setting in just the right brilliant colors, the river appears as though it's on fire, and the green walls of the Gorge fade into a deep, purple hue.

Growing up, I never missed an episode of Julia Child's cooking show and I had thoughts of being a chef. But my real dream was to sail the Calypso with Jacques Cousteau or become a National Geographic photographer. Although it came naturally, I was a tomboy growing up because my father had wanted a son, and I was always trying to please him. We lived on the White Salmon River, so when I got home from school, I would either jump on my horse or grab my fishing pole. An avid hunter, my father taught me how to shoot a firearm. And when most little girls were getting skates or some other kind of girly thing, I got a 4-10 shot gun. Tromping around the dusty wheat fields of Central Oregon hunting pheasant in the heat of summer wouldn't have been my choice of things to do. But then — I had no choice.

My father was always coming up with some new business venture and because both of my parents had grown up poor, they wanted to instill a strong work ethic in their children. Our basic necessities were provided for, but spending money had to be earned by working in the family businesses. As early as my third grade year, I'd begun the hard, dirty work of setting irrigation pipes and picking rocks out of potato fields on a farm that my parents had partnered in. I bought my horse with the money, but it was our 72-acre apple and pear orchard that was the most grueling. While my friends had the freedom to take their summers off, most of my days were spent preparing for the harvest by pruning trees in the heat of the sun. And then there was our motel and country inn where I scrubbed toilets and did laundry. At the time, I resented my parents for it, but I would later realize how important it was in developing my drive to succeed.

I had a belief in God but it wasn't central in our household. I watched "Davey and Goliath" on Sunday mornings and the religious movies during the holidays, but that was pretty much all that I knew. I can only remember going to church a few times: once when my Catholic grandmother died and another when my oldest sister was baptized a born-again Christian, after which she burned her records and marijuana paraphernalia. I attended services one or two other times with the occasional neighbor, but to me it all seemed a little rehearsed. Like everyone was on their best behavior, but not really being themselves.

In some strange way though, I believe there may have been a past memory that was kindled, providing a clue as to where my spiritual beliefs would later develop. I couldn't have been more than nine or ten years old when the thought first came to me. I remember sitting under the stars watching the moon, and thinking that if the moon controls the tides, and our bodies are comprised mostly of water, then surely it would affect us too. I don't know where the thought came from because it wasn't a theory that I had ever heard discussed. It wouldn't be until much later that I learned about Astrology.

As a teenager I was tall and pretty, with long blond hair and a beautiful smile. But like many other teenagers, I was also very shy and insecure. They were traits that people often mistook as being aloof, or unapproachable. So I didn't date much in high school until my senior year, when I had my first significant relationship. That lasted for two years until we drifted apart when he went to college. I remember wanting nothing more than to have a family and a relationship, with the stability that I didn't have growing up.

I graduated from high school in 1984 and was living on my own for the first time. I didn't go to college because I wasn't into academics, and I felt as though I learned so much more when I traveled than I ever did in books. The windsurfing scene was just taking off in the Gorge, and I was working as a waitress in a local restaurant. People came from all over the world to sail there, and it had suddenly become an explosion of neon colored windsurfing sails and clothing.

During the summers, every night was a party in Hood River, and I spent most of them out on the town with my fake ID and two older sisters. Jack's was a popular bar at the local Chinese restaurant, where we usually began our nights drinking Scorpions; large bowls of rum infused orange juice, that we shared through three-foot-long straws. A group of Canadian bachelors living in a house they called The Heartbreak Hotel were regulars too. But as wild as things could get at Jack's, the most outrageous times to be had were at the occasional Pink Party. Thrown at random locations around Hood River, Pink Parties were an overcrowded, sea of hot, sweaty drunk people dressed in the craziest bright pink outfits imaginable; often dancing to live music from the local surf-rock band, The Ultronz. The one party in the Gorge that was not to be missed though was Moe night at the River City Saloon. People waited in long lines to get in, and it was always so packed that the Fire Marshall frequently threatened to shut the place down. Moe Dixon was a regular in the summers, playing Jimmy Buffet songs and oldies dance tunes on his acoustic guitar. Fellow musicians often accompanied him on the banjo or mandolin when they happened to be in town for the week to sail. Moe usually ended each night by playing "Dancing in the streets" by Martha and the Vandellas, as everyone poured out of the bar and danced in the street. *Those days in the Gorge were magic!*

Although I still wanted nothing more than to get married and start a family, I continued to become involved in a string of brief, casual relationships. I found myself hopelessly in love with a much older man who had moved to the Gorge from Massachusetts. Tim was a cigar-smoking windsurfer with a Boston accent, who looked a lot like a young David Crosby. He wasn't tall, but he had a big personality and a characteristic walrus mustache mixed with gray, where the scent of sweet cigars lingered as he kissed me. We had a deep love and respect for each other, and yet we never really dated. As hard as I tried, I couldn't seem to get our relationship to develop beyond the occasional night spent together.

He drove an old blue and white VW van, and the River City Saloon was his regular watering hole. Although I could call him whenever I wanted to, he seemed to keep an invisible barrier up that kept me at the proper distance. My best strategy was to slowly wear him down by stopping in for a drink whenever I saw his van out in front. If he stayed to drink with me long enough, we usually ended up back at his house for the night, often doing silly things together, like stealing apples from his neighbor's orchard, naked in the moonlight. But no matter how comfortable we were with each other, our time together never seemed to begin before 5:00 pm.

I admired Tim's intelligence and sense of humor; he was well-respected in the community, so I may have felt a sense of validation from him. And although there was probably a little of the "looking for a father figure" in the relationship, I truly loved him for the connection that we had with each other. Reflecting back, I was just too young at the time to understand the complexity of it all. His wife had left him for another man shortly before I met him. Emotionally, he wasn't ready to allow himself to be vulnerable again, especially to a younger woman who might outgrow him.

The relationship wasn't coming together for us the way that I wanted it to, and the turning point for me began when he started dating someone else. He tried to convince me that I was too young for him, but I didn't want to believe or admit it. I was sure that if I had been more interesting, more beautiful, more … something, then he wouldn't have been able to turn away from me. But what I *was* finally admitting to myself was that I had been looking for someone else to make me happy when first, I needed to learn how to do it for myself.

I decided that I didn't have enough life experience, and so I got the idea of going to Sun Valley, Idaho, for the winter ski season. The next day I packed my bags and with my mother along for the ride, I headed to Idaho. My first stop was Sun Valley Lodge where I landed a job waitressing at Gretchen's, a four-star coffee shop located in the main lodge. We drove back home the following day, and then three days later I returned there to live.

I found a second job working in a Mexican restaurant in Elk Horn called Tequila Joe's. Between the two, I worked hard from early morning through late into the evening. Coming home only briefly enough to throw on fresh clothes, and then out again to Whisky Jacques to party and dance. Back home no later than 1:30 am, I was up by 5:00 the next morning for work, and then I did it all again the following day. I was still trying way too hard to find love and fill the void. Every guy that I developed a strong attraction to was going to be the next "one." And in the process, I did some really foolish and embarrassing things. I was a little too desperate at times and the alcohol made it worse. Still, I think that it was also just a part of growing and learning from my mistakes.

My mother and father separated while I was in Sun Valley, so when I returned to the Gorge the following summer, I moved in with her. At the time I think that it was as much to keep her company, as it was to save myself money. It wasn't long before I recognized that I was beginning to repeat my same old patterns. With that, I made the decision to take the next relationship slower than I ever had before, and let it develop into whatever came naturally. If it didn't work out that was fine. I would let it go without trying to control it or make it work.

Guido had big, brown eyes, a wide, toothy smile, and a mop of blonde curls that grew past his shoulders. He had come from Switzerland to windsurf, and was living in a van with a guy from Austria and another from Germany. Living in a car was common in the Gorge because most of the sailors were short on cash and only there for the season. I never did learn who invited them, but they showed up at a party being thrown at our house one night. At 6'1 Guido was hard to miss, and although he had a slightly goofy tone to his deep Swiss accent, he was charismatic and my attraction to him was instant. From that moment on, Guido, Charlie, and Reinhart became fixtures at our house, and we invited them to park their van in our driveway, so they had a place to shower and cook.

I took my relationship with Guido more slowly than he wanted to, but in a way I was testing myself as much as I was testing him. I wanted to be sure that I was breaking my habit of automatically assuming that the intent for a long-term relationship was mutual. After weeks of not sleeping together, it still seemed too early for either of us to make that decision. So I considered his continued interest sufficient proof that he had serious intentions towards me.

Guido began staying in the house with me, but it didn't feel as though we were living together. It was more like we were just spending our nights together. During the day he windsurfed while I worked, and the evenings were usually spent hanging out in Hood River. Sailors followed the wind up and down the Gorge, so if he and his friends decided to camp overnight wherever they sailed that day, it was fine with me.

To some degree, I was ready to settle down, or at least be in a full time relationship. Guido and I got along really well and we cared about each other, so for me I thought that it was enough. And although I would have happily followed him back to Europe, he was a full-time traveler and wasn't ready to settle down. I tried to convince him that he was, but it didn't work. I thought that I had played this one safe, but the rejection from the men in my life was beginning to mount. I couldn't make sense of how they could seem to care so much about me, but not want to be with me for the long-term.

It was around this time, in the fall of 1988, that I was relieved to learn that after 25 years of marriage, my parents had finally decided on a long-overdue divorce. With yet another failed relationship of my own, I decided that it was time to go on another adventure. It was my way of running from the pain and clearing the slate. But I was also developing a firm belief that you can't rely on other people to make your life happy or interesting, you have to create it for yourself. With that, I chose Vail, Colorado, because the World Alpine Ski Championships were taking place there. I loaded up my car and brought my mother along with me to give her a break from the divorce and family business. I ended up getting a job at the Manor Vail Lodge working and supervising banquets for several of the international ski teams. Vail was more hard work and hard partying.

The Italian men's team was staying at the lodge and I had become friendly with many of them. After one of our nights out together, we came back to the lodge early in the morning to find close to 100 drunk Italians singing in the dark, snowy parking lot. Security arrived soon thereafter, and everyone dispersed into the banquet room that they called Casa Italia. After more singing and drinking, the men decided that the women in the room should get on top of the tables so they could have a beauty contest. Several of the men that I was sitting with insisted that I go up to be one of the contestants, but I politely refused. With that, I felt a sudden wobble and before I knew what was happening, I found myself sitting in my chair above them, as they carried me around the room singing. I was embarrassed and flattered at the same time. I didn't know how to react, but it didn't matter because there was no escaping. By the looks of disapproval on the faces of the Italian women, I gathered that I had been proclaimed the winner.

During my time in Vail, one of my favorite hangouts was at the Altitude Club, which was aptly nicknamed the "all dudes club" for its three-to-one ratio of men to women. Dark and loud with pounding

Techno music, fog machines, and laser lights, it was one of the most popular dance spots in town. It was there that I met Mats, who had come from Sweden to live in Vail for the winter ski season. He was tall, attractive, and a little on the pudgy side with spiky blonde hair. His blue eyes twinkled when he smiled, and he had a cheerful spirit and sense of humor.

I'm not sure that I realized it at the time, but I was beginning to develop a preference for European men. Their accents made them intriguing—yes. But they also seemed to be more cultured, and took themselves less seriously than the American men I knew. They had a feminine quality to their masculinity that they didn't seem to feel the need to hide, and I liked that about them.

Mats and I were together for most of the winter, but my long work hours were getting in the way of our relationship and we began to argue a lot. Money wasn't everything to me, but at the time I had to work hard in order to be able to travel and get ahead on a waitress' income. So although we truly cared for each other, we ended our relationship.

It was around this time that I had been reading the local paper and recognized a Rockabilly band from San Francisco that was going to be playing at one of the clubs. I had met them the winter before in Sun Valley, and I had a thing for the saxophone player. At the club, I met Tony again for the second time. Short and wiry with big, sexy, bedroom eyes and a shiny black pompadour, he looked a little like a young Tony Curtis. He was only in Vail for a couple of days and we had a brief relationship. Foolishly thinking that there could be more between us, I returned to the Gorge, packed up my car, and moved to San Francisco where he lived. I wasn't invited, but I thought that if nothing else, this would be another great adventure. I saw him once or twice, but he wasn't as happy to see me as I was to see him. San Francisco was expensive, so two months later I returned to the Gorge.

The Columbia River Gorge was my summer home base and jumping-off point for winter adventures. It was there that a mutual friend introduced me to Julie, who had come to the Gorge for a week to sail in a windsurfing competition. She was working as a windsurfing instructor in Aruba, and invited me to come to stay with her for a while. In exchange, all I would have to do is work a few hours each day in the company-owned gift shop and help out at the weekly barbeques. As a struggling waitress, I scraped together every last dime that I could save to maximize my time there. The ticket alone to get to Aruba was close to $900, and above that I needed money to live on.

It was 10:00 at night when I stepped off of the plane in Aruba, and the sudden rush of heat and humidity nearly took my breath away. I made my way down the metal stairs and onto the tarmac, where ground crews were already unloading luggage onto a cart. The air-conditioned terminal with its white tile floors was a big relief, as I breathed in the cool, mildew-scented air that's common for buildings in the tropics. Julie was a welcome sight after such a long flight, and it felt good to have finally arrived.

Located off of the Northern coast of Venezuela in the Lesser Antilles, Aruba is a territory of the Netherlands. The capital of the 69-square-mile island is Oranjestad, with pastel colored buildings similar to those you might find in Key West or San Francisco. My days were spent on beaches with sand as white and fine as baby powder, practicing my windsurfing skills, or lack thereof. When I got tired of sailing, I floated around the warm, clear water, snorkeling for lobsters and dodging the teeth of the occasional moray eel that I disturbed. Depending on the night, evenings were spent at impromptu parties at the light house, dancing to Meringue music while we watched the sun set. Or sometimes it was dinner out at La Petite Café or Boonoonoonoos, followed by dancing at the local disco. I had a fling or two, scuba dived for the first time, and got my water starts mastered. I spent a month of sun and sand in Aruba before my money ran out and it was time to return home again.

Life was great, but it wasn't rewarding. I was still missing that all important piece in my life: the love of a good man to share it all with. At times I wished that I had gone to college after high school. So many of my friends met their spouses in school, and I still wanted a family more than anything. But love and marriage seemed elusive to me. Like something in the wind that I was trying to catch, but was always just out of reach. Looking back now, I can see that what we want may not always be what's best for us. Had I started a family at an early age, I would have missed all of the adventure and interesting people that I met along the way. I'm a firm believer that life is short and it's never too late to live it. A friend of mine is always telling me, "You could fall face first in your mashed potatoes tomorrow, Julie." And he's right. I talk to people all the time who say that they wish that they could go do this or that. And then years later, they still haven't done it. All it takes is an idea, and a little creativity. I was inspired by the movie *Shirley Valentine* because she was a forty something British housewife who decided to go on a Greek adventure and ended up staying. She did come home eventually, but she broke the monotony of her daily routine, and found her true self in the process. I felt that transition happening to me — I was discovering my true self.

Through all of my travels I had been working hard and usually held the equivalent of two full-time jobs. With money saved when I came back to the Gorge, I decided to travel through Europe by train for a couple of months and stay in youth hostels. I had remained in contact with Mats and another friend that I knew in Germany, so I wouldn't be alone the entire time that I was there. My mother was still having some emotional difficulty with the divorce and had been working too hard at the family business. So I decided that I had just enough money to take her along with me for a couple of weeks.

We hadn't been to Europe for years and it would be a great escape and adventure for both of us. I had gotten my height and coloring from my father, but the Eastern European bone structure from my mother. Her side of the family was Polish, and she's much shorter and darker than me. I had a strong bond with her because I knew that she didn't have it easy at any point in her life. That included being married to a man whose income should have allowed her some luxury, but instead the money was invested in one unsuccessful business after another. My mother had her own set of issues, most of which were as a result of her own childhood, but one of her biggest flaws was trying to do too much for other people.

After two weeks of traveling through Switzerland, Italy, and France, it was time for her to return home. We made our way to the train station in Frankfurt, Germany, where we hugged and said a tearful good-bye. She would take the train to the airport alone, and I would board yet another that would take me north to see Mats in Sweden. Just as I turned to leave, the bottle of wine that I had picked up for the trip slipped out of my hand and exploded on the train platform. I heard gasps and words of disappointment for losing a good bottle of wine from passersby, as I picked up the broken glass.

My head still focused on my mother who I wouldn't see for months, and the embarrassment of the broken wine bottle, I boarded the car closest to me for the train headed north. Dimly lit with red vinyl seat cushions, and painted metal walls, it was one of the older train cars that gave the impression of being in a 1940s war movie. As I sat there gazing out the window, I reflected on our good bye and began to feel alone for the first time. The car was unusually noisy, so I looked up briefly to see what was going on. When I did, I realized that I was the only woman in the crowded train car. As it continued to register with me, I noticed that all of the men were wearing uniforms and they seemed to be celebrating. I was suddenly aware that I was in a train car filled with German sailors who had just gotten off of the ship! I shrank in my seat with the awareness of it, trying to make myself as small and inconspicuous as possible. The train would be leaving soon, and I had to make the decision whether to grab my bag and make a break for it, or hope that I might go unnoticed. With a sudden shift forward, I realized it was too late.

As the train pulled away from the station, the sailors began to sing as they slid a square, plastic jug of wine back and forth down the aisle. The drunker they got, the louder and more boisterous they were.

Oh, how I wish that I was invisible!

I tried not to make eye contact, but I glanced up quickly to see one of them looking directly at me. He held up a glass of wine and waved me over to his table.

OK, I thought. *What do I do?* I had to think quickly. *I don't want to join him, but I don't think that I can refuse him either.*

Although the question still remained in my mind as to whether or not I was safe, I was no safer in my seat than at his table, so I accepted his invitation.

He introduced himself as Karl, and poured me a glass of champagne from a bottle that was labeled to commemorate the ship they had served on. As we began to talk, I realized that his impression of Americans was clearly that of "Rambo" and the TV show "Dallas"—in a negative way. I hoped that after spending some time together talking with him, he was left with a much more favorable opinion of Americans. There had been several uncomfortable moments when drunk sailors decided that they would steal my attention from him. But when they got too close to me, he pushed them back to a safe distance and I arrived in Hamburg unharmed and with an unforgettable experience.

The next train that I boarded would take me to Mats' hometown of Gavle, Sweden. And again I found myself passing the time over conversation and drinks. But now it was with Per and Michael, a couple of goofy, beer-smuggling Swedes returning from a drunken weekend at the Oktoberfest in Germany. Alcohol was expensive in Sweden and the laws only allowed you to bring in a small amount of beer tax-free. And these guys were definitely over their limit, in more ways than one. Before the customs officer was due to come by, they asked if I would claim some of the beer that they carried in a milk crate as my own. Without hesitation, I agreed. Once the customs agent checked us and moved on, we let out a devious giggle of relief, because the officer didn't check the two bags hidden under their seats, or the duffle bag filled with beer in the overhead bin. As we approached the train station in Gavle, we said our good-byes and promised to stay in touch.

As I pulled my bag from the overhead bin, I could see Mats pacing the platform waiting for me. His spiky blonde hair and yellow ski coat with red, plaid collar were just as I remembered. I began to feel the same love and excitement well up inside of me that I had felt for him in

Colorado. And as soon as we embraced, it was as though we had never been apart. Mats lived alone, but his family was excited that he had an American friend coming to visit. He said that his grandparents told him that they "purchased a special cake from the bakery with real whipped cream and strawberries." The way that he explained it was childlike and endearing. We would meet them the following day, but that evening was promised to his mother who was making dinner for us.

There was no time to pick up flowers and I didn't want to arrive for dinner empty handed. When we passed a liquor store, I asked Mats to pull over so that I could buy some wine to bring as a gift. Double parked, he waited in the car for me while I went into the store alone. A few minutes later I reappeared with a bottle of wine in hand, and quickly slid back into the car. I proudly pulled the bottle from the paper sleeve to show him the wine that I had so thoughtfully chosen. He had a blank look on his face for a second or two before bursting into laughter. Hardly able to contain himself, he said that it was the same wine that the drunks and winos buy. I felt my face flush with disappointment and embarrassment at my mistake. I spent almost a full day's traveling money on that bottle.

In my defense I replied, "Well, at $12.00 a bottle, I wouldn't have guessed it!"

Still amused at my mistake, Mats smirked playfully as he said, "I told you that alcohol is expensive here! That's OK ... we won't take it in with us. My mom has been excited all week and she'll be happy just to meet you."

It was early evening when we arrived at her house, and I could smell something delicious cooking as we approached the front door. The warm yellow glow from the windows was welcoming. But I felt my grasp on Mats' hand become tighter, as I grew more nervous about meeting his mother for the first time. I tried to reassure myself that if she and Mats were anything alike, it would be just fine. Gunn-Britt was a small framed woman with brown hair and big blue eyes. She had an air about her that was tough as nails—in a good way. She spoke broken English with a husky voice that was still soft and feminine. I adored her from the moment that I met her, and she seemed to feel the same way about me. It was a sentiment that would continue through the years to come.

She greeted us with enthusiastic hugs and then, as is customary in Sweden, we removed our shoes at the door. It was a nice, but modest home with the living room open to the kitchen and dining area. Mats' older brother was there too, but he remained strangely silent as he sat on the couch. Just giving a slight nod as Mats introduced me to him. Gunn-Britt poured us both a glass of wine, and then guided us over to the dining table, where she proudly showed us what she had made for dinner. I was surprised to see the table covered with so many serving dishes, that there was hardly room for dinner plates. She had made a virtual Smorgasbord for just the four of us. The Swedish meatballs were still in the oven, but the table was colorful with ruby-red lingonberry sauce, assorted pickled vegetables, and other dishes that I didn't recognize. It was obvious that she must have spent a good part of the day cooking, and I knew that I would taste every bit of love that she put into it.

Dinner was delicious, and so was the wine. I planned to make dinner for Mats the following night, so I asked Gunn-Britt where I could purchase the wine that she served. With a big grin, she took me by the hand and led me to the bathroom. On the floor were three large plastic containers that must have been five to eight gallons each. One was red wine, and the other two were white. It was her illegal stash of homemade wine, and we had a good laugh at what a little rebel she was.

The next day Mats was taking me sightseeing in Stockholm, so we stopped by his grandparents home which was on the way. They lived in a little red house with white trim, the traditional color of Swedish homes. They spoke no English and appeared to be very frail. We only stayed long enough to have a piece of the special cake that they had purchased for my visit, before continuing on to Stockholm.

During the rest of my time in Gavle, I went shopping during the day and had dinner ready for Mats when he got home from work. I spent close to a week and a half with him before it was time for me to move on to my next destination. My time in Europe was limited by the money that I brought with me, and I wanted to experience as much of it as I possibly could. The thought did cross my mind to stay in Sweden and try to get a job, but Mats made no mention of it, so neither did I. We were so comfortable with each other, that at times it was hard to say if the relationship leaned more toward friendship or a romantic relationship. It didn't matter really, because although the love between us was still strong, neither of us was ready to make the commitment that it would take for us to be together full-time. But in the years to follow, we found that it was an unchanging relationship that would stand the tests of time.

I came home after two months in Europe with an increased sense of self-confidence. Years earlier when my relationship with Tim failed, I had made a conscience decision that I wanted to transform myself into someone who was knowledgeable about the world in general, and who could carry on an intelligent conversation with just about anyone. Now I felt as though I had finally become that person. Over the last several years, I had lived and traveled in many interesting places. I met wonderful people and had amazing experiences along the way. And although my deepest desire was still to fall in love and start a family, the need to fill the void was no longer as urgent. From the beginning, I knew what my strengths and weaknesses were. And at times I had to push myself to go beyond my own comfort level in order to grow into the person that I wanted to be. I was feeling more complete now, and although I was still making plenty of mistakes along the way, I was beginning to learn from them.

"There are no chance meetings"

~ Unknown

2

In July 1990, my newly divorced father fancied himself an expert on relationships. He had been on strike from Continental Airlines for several years, and suddenly began bouncing around ideas to showcase his new-found wisdom. One of many was to develop a *Northwest Men Magazine.* The concept would be nearly identical to that of *Alaskan Men Magazine,* with photos and bios of eligible bachelors, who were looking to meet women. Doing research for the project, he asked me to choose a guy from *Alaskan Men,* contact him, and then let him know what I thought. I had no idea that it would be the beginning of my journey, and a meeting that would forever change my life.

I picked up the magazine and began flipping through the pages with mild disinterest, all the while reminding myself that I hadn't had a winning track record with men for the last several years. Not to mention that these guys were probably getting more letters from women than they could ever possibly answer. Whenever I saw a face that caught my eye, I scrutinized the bio for every lame and incompatible statement that I could possibly find. Eventually, I came across one that, hard as I tried, I couldn't find fault with—almost.

Duff McLaren: 32 years old, 5'7", Scottish/Italian, Learjet pilot.
Pilot! God, pleeease don't let me like this one!
Ex-Marine flying Learjets in aerial combat maneuvers against F-15s.
Hmmm—sexy! And a little reminiscent of Top Gun.

In the photo, he was looking over his left shoulder and wearing a brown leather bomber jacket with a white fleece collar. He had an olive complexion with light brown hair and a great smile. I found myself intrigued by him, analyzing every detail of his appearance, from the way that he posed, to the stitches in his clothing.

There's got to be something wrong with this guy.

And then I saw it—a statement in his bio that said, "Family and friends are more important to me than any career."

Shit! This guy flies combat maneuvers against F-15s and he's got his priorities straight? Do I really want to go there? It doesn't matter. This is simply research and even if I write to him, there's little or no chance that I would ever get a reply—no danger.

Duff wasn't my usual type. He was clean cut and professional, so I had to convince myself that was OK. I had been dating windsurfers with hair down below their shoulders who lived in their cars. But "type" wasn't the real issue—he was a pilot! I swore that I would never date one. My father was a pilot and, in my experience, they generally do live up to their reputations as womanizers. But I liked what he said in his bio, which gave me some measure of hope—or perhaps insanity.

I decided to write to him rather than choosing some other random bachelor who would never be more than research. Certain that he must be getting mountains of mail, I went to the store to purchase stationary so that my letter would stand out. After much careful consideration, I chose lavender—still feminine, but not too girly.

As my excitement to put pen to paper grew, I became aware that I actually wanted this to happen. Before I knew it, a three-page letter flowed out of me without the least bit of effort. My words attempted to gain his interest and respect, even though part of me was saying that it was all a crazy idea. I had a thing for older men, so age wasn't an issue for me. But at 32, would he take a 23-year-old seriously? Although I was about to turn 24 in a couple of months, I wrote that I was 25. It sounded more established to me, and I wanted to bridge the age gap. In his bio he said that he liked a woman who could wear jeans during the day, and then dress up for an evening out. So I popped the letter in the mail with a photo of myself wearing something in between, and didn't give it a second thought. I figured that it would likely take months before I got a reply, if I ever got one at all.

Two weeks later, I arrived home around midnight and decided to check the answering machine before going to bed. On the recorder I heard an unfamiliar male voice saying that he had just moved to Medford, Oregon for a flying job, and he would be up until midnight if I wanted to give him a call. It was Duff. Listening to the message made me both nervous and excited! He had a beautiful voice and although it was now just past midnight, I decided to risk that I might wake him up.

When he answered, it was as if I was talking to someone who I had known all of my life. We talked about anything and everything with no uncomfortable silences. Two and a half hours later, he said that he had to be up at 6:00 am for a flight, and he would call me when he got home. We said good night, but I was too excited to sleep. I sat beside the answering machine like it was my most treasured possession, sipping wine and pressing the play/repeat button over and over again. There was something in his voice that resonated with me. It was soothing and felt like home. When he called the next day, we agreed that he would fly up for the weekend so we could meet in person. The next few days were filled with excitement and anticipation, as I cleaned house and anguished over what to wear.

Driving through the Gorge on my way to pick him up at the airport, I felt my anxiety and uncertainty begin to grow.

Will a weekend with a total stranger be awkward? Will he still be interested in me after meeting in person? This could all go terribly wrong!

I held onto the steering wheel tightly, as I painted the last coat of polish onto my fingernails; hoping that I wouldn't spill the bottle or get into an accident.

Standing anxiously at the tall windows of his arrival gate, I tried to guess which plane landing might be his. Eventually I caught glimpses of one that grew closer, then turned slowly toward the gate where I was waiting. A conversation kept playing through my mind:

He's on that plane. Duff has actually flown to Portland to see me and now he's here!

When the plane came to a stop, the ramp slowly extended until it fully encompassed the door. The hollow sound of the passenger's heavy footsteps walking through ramp's corridor caused my anxiety to grow, realizing that at any moment I could see him for the first time. The more people that came off the flight, the more my anxiety grew. And just when I began to feel a sense of relief and wonder if he had made it on the flight at all—there he was.

Dressed in a dark blue pinstriped suit with cream colored snake skin cowboy boots; he was grinning so wide that it caused a vein to show in his forehead. He looked nothing like his photo. His complexion was fair, his hair was blonde, and he was shorter than I expected. Then there was his outfit screaming "Surprise! This is my real personality, and we're going to be spending the entire weekend together!"

My body tensed and I didn't know how to react. As he approached me, I tried to quickly reason with myself to relax; but there was nothing I could do to disguise it. I knew that he could sense my tension. After some awkward pleasantries, we began the semi-silent walk to my car, which would then lead to an hour-long drive through the Gorge. The uncomfortable silences were now abundant and almost unbearable.

At one point he said, "You know... my uncle lives in Portland if you don't want me to stay."

"No," I replied. "I've just never done this before, so I'm kind of nervous."

In my mind though, I was thinking that this was all going to be a disaster, and my facade was going to collapse at any moment. I had several different conversations going on in my head at the same time. One of which was: *I really liked him over the phone, why am I so un-attracted to him just because he looks a lot different than I expected? He's still a good looking man. Maybe it's the pinstripes, or those hideous snakeskin cowboy boots!*

At the time, I was living with my mother who owned a modest home on the bluff, overlooking the Columbia River and Mt. Hood. Finally pulling into the driveway was a welcome relief, because I knew there would be other people inside who could play interference for me. My mother could talk the paint off of a wall, and I had run out of stories about my travels and what it was like to live in the Gorge.

The day was hot, and we had just spent a long time driving in my car without air conditioning. After a brief introduction to my mother and smirking sister, Duff asked if he could find a place to change out of his suit, and into something cooler. I was happy that he would be changing clothes, but also a little apprehensive about what I might see him in next.

I got Duff settled in my bedroom, which was more comfortable than the one that I would be staying in. A few minutes later, we bumped into each other in the hallway. Polo shirt and khaki shorts: big improvement. He must have sensed the need to break the ice, or maybe he realized that his suit may have caused him to appear too conservative for me.

"Did you know that I have a tattoo on my leg?" he asked.

In my mind I wanted to answer, *Now that's a stupid question! How could I possibly know you have a tattoo on your leg?* But I didn't.

"What is it?" I replied sarcastically. "A snake?"

"No, it's a dragon," he said as he lifted the leg of his shorts to reveal a beautifully intricate tattoo of a dragon on his right outer thigh, which was about the size of a small football.

OK, I find that a little sexy, I thought to myself. Mr. Clean Cut was now becoming the Top Gun Pilot to me again, and as it happened, I had a thing for dragons. But it was still only a mild relief to my anguish and discomfort.

I offered to take Duff for a walk down to the bluff to show him the view, happy at the opportunity to create a new distraction. My mother laughs to this day that she could feel the icicles from my tension, all the way up to the house. We sat on the stone balcony overlooking the Gorge while we talked and I pointed to several landmarks in the distance. Although the mood still remained awkward, it was slowly becoming lighter. Duff told me that he had spent some time in Asia when he was in the Marines. Grasping for some sort of common ground, I replied that my favorite restaurant was Kampai, a Japanese restaurant in Hood

River. We both jumped at the chance to keep the momentum going, and agreed that it may be a good time to go to dinner.

Located in a cellar below another business, Kampai is dimly lit with private booths, rice paper wall dividers, and an exotic fish tank that bubbles softly in the background. It couldn't have been a more perfect spot for a first date. The décor and food alone would provide plenty of opportunity for conversation starters. After settling into our booth, I explained that I didn't eat sushi.

"Have you tried it before?" he asked with surprise.

"No, actually I haven't. But I'm just not much of a fish eater, so the idea of eating it raw…" I replied, as my expression of fear and disgust finished my sentence. "I really don't think that I could get past the idea that it's raw," I added.

That statement launched Duff into a lengthy and amusing dialogue about the joys of eating sushi. All the while demonstrating how to fold chopstick rests out of the red paper sleeves that they come wrapped in. He was fascinating to listen to—not only because he had a great sense of humor, but he had a degree in physics and could talk about everything from how a supernova is formed to the origins of sushi. When the waitress came by to take our order, Duff made a joke to her in Japanese; and they began to laugh privately at something only the two of them could understand. In my mind, I was the quiet observer analyzing their interaction.

I thought to myself, *He's funny, intelligent and worldly. A man like that is a direct reflection on the woman he chooses to spend time with. If he's trying to impress me, then it's beginning to work.* I felt my walls begin to withdraw.

We laughed and drank hot sake from little cups while we waited for our food. It wasn't long before the conversation began to flow again, just like it had when we first spoke on the phone. While we were eating, he asked me a question and when I turned to answer him, he kissed me quickly on the lips.

Tilting his chin down with a big grin as if to be coy, he said, "I hope that was OK."

I felt a sudden wave of warmth and desire for him wash over me. I don't know why I had been so rigid when we first met, but now I was feeling very connected again, and I wanted more of him.

We took our time making love, lost in each other's eyes as if the intent was to fuse our two bodies into one, responding naturally to every movement, like we had always known and belonged to the other. It had been less than twelve hours since we first met, and yet looking into his eyes was like seeing into his soul.

The next morning we walked down to the bluff to have coffee, the air still crisp as the sun continued to rise. Duff held me in his arms, while we talked and watched the colors in the sky fade into blue.

"Will you move to Medford so that we can be together?" he asked.

In my head I wondered if I had misunderstood what he had just said. "What did you ask me?"

"Will you move to Medford so that we can be together full time?"

The question took me by surprise, but then in some way it all made sense. Looking deeply into his eyes and searching for sincerity I asked, "Are you sure that's what you want?"

"Yes, I'm sure. That's why I'm asking." he replied with a slight smile.

With an expression of quiet conviction, I said "Of course I will..."

We pulled each other closer, quiet in the moment and absorbing our own thoughts.

This could be it—is this really happening? I thought to myself.

Over the next few weeks we talked by phone and he came up on the weekends. We hadn't made any definite plans, but then one day when we were talking, I told him that I was going to quit my job the following month, so I could move to Medford to be with him. He didn't tell me not to, and I was almost afraid to say much for fear that he would say that he had changed his mind. With no firm plan in place as to how this was all going to happen, a few weeks later I quit my job. I left Duff a voice mail with the happy news, but he didn't return my call.

I couldn't reach him by phone and now I was unemployed. A couple of weeks later I got a letter from him saying that he had flown to Virginia to transport some planes and that he would call me when he got back from his trip—but he didn't. Leaving me completely devastated. I truly believed in my heart that he was "the one." And now he had disappeared without so much as a good-bye.

"We are not human beings having a spiritual experience.
We are spiritual beings having a human experience."

~*Teilhard de Chardin*

3

My father switched gears from the magazine to opening up a dating service in Vancouver, Washington. He asked me if I wanted to come to work for him, and so with nothing else to do, I agreed. My plan was to commute an hour each way, so I could continue to live in the Gorge with my mother. I was still devastated at the loss of Duff and barely able to function. I just knew that there was something magical between us. *Soulmate* was a term that I had heard before, and I was certain that it described what we had experienced.

Shortly after his disappearance, I had a dream that I find difficult to explain, but I knew it had significance and meaning. It felt as if I was fully present and there, standing in a black void. The silhouettes of three men in shades of gray stood in front of me, and I could clearly see their forms, but they didn't have visible faces. In some unexplainable way though, I could faintly see the essence of their features and I knew who each of them was—except one. The first was a man who I had a brief romantic encounter with months earlier. Then next to him stood Duff and a couple of feet from Duff and closer to me stood another man, but I couldn't make out his face at all. I was startled when I realized that one of them ran past me, but I wasn't able to see which one it was.

When the dream was over, I didn't know what it all meant, but I knew that I was supposed to understand it. Turning it over and over in my mind made me crazy because I felt so strongly that it was supposed to mean something to me, but I just couldn't figure it out. It was one of those dreams that sticks with you, and I couldn't shake it— but I didn't want to either. I clung to it like it was my last and only hope, as I ran through every possible interpretation in order to try to understand what it could mean.

I started reading through the Bible and found the story of Joseph, who dreamed of seven withered stalks of grain, swallowing seven healthy stalks of grain. The interpretation meant that there would be seven years of healthy crops, followed by seven years of famine. He had other's in which the number of symbols also represented timelines. The metaphor seemed like it could be remotely similar to mine but it didn't entirely explain it. I wanted the dream to symbolize Duff coming back to me. But the man running past me could have symbolized Duff going away—I didn't know.

As I searched further in the Bible for meaning, I started noticing inconsistencies and contradictions in the stories. Reincarnation was only mentioned once that I found, and yet it was such an enormous concept in Eastern religions. I had never heard of it taught in Christianity, so it surprised me to find reference to it. I was on a mission, and the Bible was too wordy for me to understand clearly, so I switched to The Book. As much as I appreciated a simpler version of the Bible, I began to question just how much of it had been altered through translation and revisions throughout the centuries.

It was around this time that I began feeling energies running through my body. They would start mid-calf and, as they made their way upward, the hair on my arms would stand on end. When I laid down to sleep at night, the intensity increased and, as they moved into my groin area, it scared me and made me feel very uneasy. They were new and unfamiliar sensations, and I was afraid that it was some kind of ghost or spirit. I had never experienced anything like it before, and the only time that I had heard of something like it happening was in books about hauntings by amorous spirits.

Not knowing how to ease my concern, I tried to convince myself that it was probably just my angels letting me know that they were with me. Because around that same time, I also started noticing a feeling like cobwebs on my face at night, but there was never anything there. I would brush my face and then it would come right back again. Now that I understand, I believe that the cobweb sensation was their playful way of letting me know that they were around. But later I would learn that the other energies meant something entirely different.

In my un-daunting quest to understand my dream, I had been reading everything that I could get my hands on about spirituality, but nothing could explain it. In a moment of desperation, I decided to call the "700 Club" prayer line. A man answered and I explained the dream and the energies that I was feeling. I was hoping that someone who was more familiar with the Bible would take me lovingly under their wing and provide explanations to all of my questions.

Instead, in a southern, evangelical voice I heard, "Lord...let us pray for our sister Julie."

Suddenly feeling foolish, I quickly realized my mistake, said thanks, and then abruptly hung up. If I was to find answers, it wouldn't be with one-dimensional thinkers.

I started my new job working at my father's dating service, where I met Robin Taylor and Carla Hansen. They had worked together previously when Robin was a regional manager for a national weight loss company. A petite blonde, Robin had big blue eyes, a strong chin, and the presence to match. What she was doing working at my dad's start-up dating service was beyond me. But when I questioned her about it, she replied that she wanted a new challenge.

I spent my days at work going through the motions, uninterested, with my thoughts only on Duff, and all things spiritual. But Robin was one sharp business woman and if I was going to work with her, then I had to pull my head out of my ass and learn some sales techniques. She didn't literally tell me that, but she got her point across very clearly. My conviction was strong that Duff and I were destined to be together, and that my dream held the key. So strong that I was like a moth to a flame watching programs about spirituality on Oprah and other talk shows.

We had a little TV in the office and watching television did not go over well with Robin at all.

I had been reading as many books as I could find about spirituality, starting with other people's personal stories. Then I happened across *Life After Life* by Raymond Moody and several others about Near Death Experiences (NDEs). The stories struck a chord in me and I believed that they were true. Dr. Moody stumbled across NDEs in his own practice. It was not only adults that were having them, but also children who were far too young to make up some of the detail. They talked about the typical white light, tunnel, feeling of love and peace, and the meeting of relatives who had passed on. But in other similar books that I read there were also stories about souls waiting to be born. How they had chosen the parents that they would be born to for the lessons that they wanted to learn in this lifetime. That sometimes they had to work hard to help those parents get together.

The books went on to explain that some souls are only meant to be here for a short time, their purpose being to have some sort of impact on the parents and the people around them. That people and children with disabilities or illnesses chose their body prior to birth, because it was related to the lesson they came here to learn. No matter how briefly a child might be here, his or her birth and death has an impact on the parents in a way that would help them with the lessons and journey that they were here for. It was all so fascinating to me and a relief to think that the death of a child could actually serve a higher purpose.

Reincarnation was a concept that was still a little difficult for me to wrap my head around, but the stories that I was reading were clear and consistent. We are here to learn lessons that will assist in elevating our souls to a higher level of consciousness —to be closer to God. When our purpose has been served and our lessons have been learned, we may have what appears to be an accident or an illness. When it's our time, we are sometimes given the choice if we want to go or if we want to stay. Those who have a near-death experience prematurely often want to stay on the other side, but they are told that it isn't their time and they must return. My father had previously had a near death experience and his life flashed before him, and my maternal grandmother appeared to my mother shortly after her death. She was younger and more peaceful than she had been at the time that she died. Not long after that, my mother heard a man's voice say, "Don't be afraid to die, Loretta." And then a beautiful feeling of peace and comfort washed over her.

I began to read stories about children who recounted past lives in such great detail, their distraught parents researched what they were saying. The parents heard their children recall details that were later proven to be facts, about people who the child had no previous knowledge of, nor did the parents. Why children born to the same parents have completely different personalities from birth began to make sense. As well as children who displayed a passion, or amazing talent from a very early age—like being proficient on the piano and playing Mozart by the age of six. Although I had yet to put a label on it, I had begun to find my truths in Eastern Philosophy.

One morning, just as I was waking up but before I opened my eyes, I saw a deep, black void and suspended in it was a three-dimensional water lily blossom that was illuminated from within. It had multiple, deep purple petals and a white glow in the center shaped like a triangle. I could see that the outline glowed electric blue. Just as something illuminated in the darkness would be. The flower appeared to be made of stained glass and I remembered thinking that it was really beautiful before I opened my eyes. I didn't know what it meant, but I knew that I had really seen it and it didn't feel like a normal dream. It occurred to me later that when I was a kid imagining what the flowers in heaven would look like, I thought that they would look like stained glass.

I tucked the experience in the back of my mind and a couple of days later, Robin pulled me aside to ask me what was wrong with me. I told her about Duff and that I felt this soulmate connection to him. I also told her about the energies that I had been experiencing and then held my arm up for her to see the hair standing on end, but I didn't say anything more.

"Why don't you come over to my house for a glass of wine tomorrow and we'll talk." she replied.

The next day I went to her house and we got into a spiritual discussion. Robin seemed to know so much about everything, and she had a serenity and confidence in the way she explained it. I hadn't yet told her about the water lily vision that I had three days earlier when she handed me the book *Inner Reaches of Outer Space* by Joseph Campbell. Robin suggested that I might find some answers to my questions in it. We both felt as though we had a greater understanding of each other after our conversation. And agreed that I would lay off of the "Oprah" and "Montel" during work.

As I read *Inner Reaches*, I came across a section about Chakras, the seven energy centers in our bodies. My eyes grew wide when I read that the Chakra for spiritual effort was a lotus blossom with 16 smoky purple petals and a white triangle in the center. I hadn't counted the petals in my vision, but if I had to take a guess, then my guess would be 16.

Around the same time, I had been looking for another book in the library when I found, or it found me, *Spiritual Emergency* by Stanislav Grof. I read a line about Kundalini energies and decided quickly to check the book out. In it describes an energy that was similar to what I had been experiencing. It explained Kundalini, to be like a serpent that lays dormant at the base of your spine, and then rises up through your spinal column when activated, opening up the Chakras to awaken our inner knowledge and open the channels to a higher consciousness.

Inner Reaches also described these energies. For some people, the experience is described as painful or violent but for me, it wasn't that at all. I could just feel the tingle of energy begin and move gently up through the center of my body. Maybe it wasn't Kundalini that I had been experiencing, or maybe it's experienced differently by different people. But to me, it explained the energies that I was feeling in combination with my vision of the lotus blossom representing the Chakra for spiritual effort. I wondered why this was all happening to me. These were things that people spent years of great exercise and practice to experience, and sometimes never do. I had no idea what a Chakra was and now suddenly I had seven! Not only that, but the energies were happening to me without trying. But I realized that although I wasn't consciously trying, I was putting forth great effort to find the truth and a higher spiritual knowledge. So gifted or manifested, what I was experiencing was as a result of all that I had been working so hard to understand.

The reason that the book is called *Spiritual Emergency* is because there are many other stories about people having spontaneous spiritual experiences that are outside of their normal realm of understanding. Initially those people often think that they're imagining things and if they themselves don't, then other people around them think they are.

I don't remember what Robin said when I told her about my vision of the Chakra for spiritual effort, but she didn't disbelieve me either. Our experiences are personal and unique to us. Robin had a knack for having past life dreams and then recognizing the person in a crowd—in real life! She had also taken a trip to Greece and felt as though she was at home and that she knew her way around. I have never personally experienced that, but I don't doubt or disbelieve her either.

As my spiritual knowledge grew, I also learned about things like drumming, and using the energy of crystals for healing. Those things didn't resonate with me, but I don't discount them for other people. Maybe that person had a past life in which doing that was an important part of connecting to spirit. Just because I didn't need to drum, didn't mean that it wasn't significant for someone else. All of our paths and connections are unique to our own past and present experiences. Robin took me under her wing and mentored me, but all things spiritual weren't making the pain of losing Duff go away. I still believed in my heart that he would be back someday.

A few weeks later, just as I was waking up and about to open my eyes, I heard what I can only describe as what you might imagine the voice of God to sound like. The voice was ancient and wise, but speaking with love and compassion. He was speaking to me in a metaphor about nature and what I would later understand to be our path in life. As he spoke these beautiful words about nature, I acknowledged in my mind how beautiful that they were. But each line would slip away from my memory as soon as it was spoken. The only line that I can remember was one of the last:

"*A river cannot flow against its current.*"

In my single-minded frame of reference I replied, "That's so beautiful, but what does it have to do with Duff and me?"

There was no answer.

Several days later, it began to make sense to me, although I still think that I wanted to deny it. He was telling me that I needed to release my struggle to gain back the relationship that I had lost and continue where my life would take me. That was a very difficult thing for me to do and it didn't happen overnight. But as the years continued to pass and I began living my life by what he said, I realized that it made everything so much easier. It could be applied to every aspect of my life but for me, love relationships were the most difficult. I knew that I had been given the gift of remembering the one line that I could and should live my life by. "Follow the current to where your life takes you, because no matter how hard that you struggle against it, in the end the current will take you where it wants you to go."

The loss of Duff was still very difficult for me, so Carla, another woman in our office who also had a similar belief system to Robin's, suggested that I go see her psychic friend Margie. My only previous experience with a psychic was with a gypsy lady who had a sign in her window. She convinced me that if I gave her $250.00, she would bless the money and it would bring back the last man who I was in love with. I wasn't goin' down that road again. But Carla assured me that Margie was the real thing and she did a lot of police work on murder and missing person's cases.

Carla then related a personal story. She and her ex husband use to raise rabbits and they had one that was worth a lot of money. After coming home one night to find the rabbit gone, they became frantic. She called Margie who was not at all happy about being asked to track down a missing rabbit. Reluctantly though, she agreed and said that she saw the rabbit in three different suburbs of Vancouver. They couldn't solve the mystery until Carla's son came home and confessed that the night before, he and his friends had been drinking, got hungry, and butchered the wrong rabbit. Margie saw the rabbit in the three suburbs that the boys lived in and who had made it their dinner.

That was not only funny, it was also convincing. I was really excited to hear what she had to say and so I set up an appointment. Carla prepared me, although it wasn't necessary. Margie was in her late 40's, about 5' tall, with a mountain of red hair and big blue eyes. She wore all black and the contrast was striking. Her voice was soft and comforting, with a slight raspy quality from the Marlboros that she smoked, but it was her big smile that caused me to like her instantly. She was a gifted astrologer in addition to reading tarot and doing psychic work. That was 20 years ago and I've had so many readings with her that I don't remember the first. I do remember though that she nailed just about everything about my relationship with Duff. She did think that if we didn't come together at this point in our lives that we may come together when we were older. I would continue to value her guidance until she eventually retired.

Guardians of Hope was a book that I credit for helping me to transform my life. It was such a simple and easy-to-read book, and yet it had so much practical wisdom that resonated with me. The author suggested that in situations like mine, to meditate and visualize sending love, or angel light: rose pink colored light with gold flecks of God dust, as she put it. I had never meditated before and found it difficult to not only clear my mind, but to also create a mental image of Duff without losing it. The visual kept fading into other thoughts as they came swirling into my head, but I wanted this relationship so badly, that I exercised great effort and continued to practice.

I had no expectations as I settled into my pillow on the floor. Lighting the white candle on the small table in front of me, I said a prayer and picked up the bundle of sage leaves beside it, which were bound tightly with a red cotton cord. Burning sage, or smudging, was a way of creating a sacred space and clearing negative energy. Although the scent was very similar to marijuana, it had a light, expansive fragrance that brought forth a sense of peace and lightness of being. The smoke rose gently and I fanned it toward me as I had been taught to do by others. Placing the smoldering smudge stick in the abalone shell on the table, I began to take deep breaths of relaxation.

Just as I had done so many times before, I struggled to form a clear image of Duff in my mind but then, suddenly it was different. His image became clear to me—almost solid in appearance. And I could see the beautiful waves of translucent light flowing towards him—the edges dissipating into blackness that surrounded the illuminated image in front of me. My thoughts turned to how beautiful it was and I realized that I wasn't alone. I sensed a male presence sitting beside me. When I turned to look at him, I saw only that we were sitting beside each other cross-legged in white robes. I felt no surprise or hesitation that he was there, and turned my focus back to sending light to Duff. It was then that I became aware that the being beside me was very pleased with what I was doing. I didn't turn to look at him again, and still had no feeling of surprise that he was there. It felt perfectly natural that he was with me and I sensed very clearly that I knew him, so there was no reason for me to look at his face. I was beginning to play with the light and having fun with it. The being beside me seemed to take great joy in my amusement, and then the vision was gone.

My experience caused me to become even more open to the unknown. And I began frequenting a metaphysical book store in Portland to explore what other mysteries the universe might hold, that I had yet to discover. Walking through the door for the first time, meditation music and the scent of sage and incense permeated the air, creating a sense of somehow being closer in touch with the divine. I signed up for their newsletter, which said that they had an Empath on their schedule of events. I had never heard of one before, and it sounded interesting because he also read your soul's purpose and lessons for this lifetime. With great anticipation, I set up an appointment for both my mother and myself for the following week, certain that he would reaffirm that Duff and I were destined to be together.

We arrived at the book store for our scheduled appointment and went upstairs. Jon was an average looking guy and no different than I expected. My mother's reading was first so that I could judge whether he was the real deal or not. Being the skeptic that I am, I sat there critiquing his delivery and messages in my head and thinking, *Well, that's pretty general. Not much information being provided here. And that last statement could be about anyone.*

I was ready to leave without a reading for myself, but just as I was thinking that, a medium-size fluffy white feather floated slowly back and forth outside of the window until it finally disappeared. I wasn't sure, but I thought that I needed to pay attention because feathers are often a sign. And not only did this one seem to take longer than usual to float its way out of site, I couldn't think of a bird in our area that it could have belonged to based on its size and plumage.

It was now my turn.

OK, why not? I thought to myself. *I'm going to hear the same thing but with a slightly different spin.*

I sat in front of him and he started going through my past lives and what I had already learned. He said that he saw me sitting in a cave in tattered robes and because I had already experienced poverty, money probably wouldn't be much of an issue for me in this life. It didn't mean that I might not struggle at times, but somehow I would always pull through financially. He went on to tell me that he felt my soul and it was *very joyful.* The way that he described it was absolutely beautiful.

In my mind though, I thought, *That's really nice but it could still be applied to anyone.* I asked him about Duff and he didn't believe that he was the one that I was supposed to be with in this lifetime. *OK, I'm really not liking this guy now.*

Jon went on to say that the man that I would be with strokes my hair, and then he said, "You have an older female relative that's passed—a grandmother. And she touches you here." He held his fingers to his temples.

Tears started rolling down my cheeks because I instantly connected with what he said. Years before, my oldest sister dated a guy who had a natural gift as a medium. He told her that she had a grandmother who had passed and her name was Elizabeth. And that she watches over her. Our maternal grandmother's name was Elizabeth and since I don't remember when, I had been having strong energies and a tightening sensation primarily in my right temple. It usually happened when I was in need of comfort or reassurance. It became obvious to me late one night, when I was driving in a heavy snow storm through the Gorge with my mother.

We suddenly came up on a car that was sideways in the highway and there was no way that we could stop in time. If there was room to drive between the tail of the car and the barrier, it was literally by inches. I couldn't try to go around it on the opposite side because it would take too much of a correction. And if I slowed down too quickly, I would have slid into the car anyways. As my mom started to panic, I suddenly felt that familiar energy and tightening in my temple and calm washed completely over me. Without thinking, I took one hand off of the wheel and patted her on the leg and said that it was going to be OK. Everything happened in a split second and just 25 feet from the car ahead of us. I put my hand back on the wheel and drove safely between the car and the barrier as we watched the car behind us hit him. She was so shocked by it all that she tells that story to this day.

I've always wondered if that energy was my grandmother and now Jon was confirming that it was. Now—he had my attention and I was listening. He told me that my lesson to learn in this lifetime was to love without control. I didn't like it, but I think that our lessons truly are the ones that we don't want to accept. He was right—although the men in my past had truly loved me, they weren't ready for a commitment or the timing wasn't right for whatever reason. But I always found myself trying to convince them that they *were ready*. Even though their actions clearly told me they weren't.

It would take me several more relationships before I could finally let go, and be accepting if the person that I was with wanted to move on to someone else. I wish now that I would have found the strength to do that much sooner because it was the most empowering thing that I could have ever done. You can't convince someone they want something that they don't. The thought has crossed my mind that it might have changed the outcome of some of my past relationships had I not held on so tightly. But actually, I now believe that as much as I loved those men, they were only participants in my journey and meant to help me with my lessons—as I was with theirs.

Jon didn't think that Duff was "the one," although Margie believed that there may be a possibility. I had seen a psychic on local TV and decided to give her a try. Her name was Renee Madsen and when I arrived to the appointment, it wasn't at all what I expected. Her office was in an old three-story Karate studio in a questionable Portland neighborhood. Renee herself seemed nice enough though.

She was young with dark, straight hair and she giggled a lot. I can't remember everything that she told me other than she thought that I would have two sons and Duff wasn't the one that I was going to be with. It certainly wasn't what I wanted to hear, so I had no plans of going back. No matter what Jon and Renee said, I still believed that Duff and I would be together someday.

Not long after my reading, I was having an especially rough time. I loved Duff so much and felt so strongly that we were supposed to be together. But time was passing quickly with no word from him. I went to bed and closed my eyes—a flood of warm tears rolling down my cheeks and filling my ears. I don't remember why, but I was praying for hope and peace. With my eyes closed, a woman suddenly appeared in front of me in my mind's eye. She was three dimensional, and physically in front of me, like I could reach out and touch her. She had an expression of peace and serene confidence on her face, which was illuminated by a soft, gold glow that seemed to radiate from within. Her thick, golden, blond hair was long and wavy, and she wore a gold gown with a garland of flowers around her head and neck. She was sitting, although I didn't see a chair, and her arms were outstretched, with palms facing up and a gold disk on each hand. The vision was for only an instant, just long enough to watch as a white dove began to take flight from each disk and then she was gone. It was incredibly beautiful and to this day I'm not sure what it meant. I thought that the doves might represent the hope and peace that I was praying for. All I know is that she was beautiful beyond description, and I'm certain that it was a rare honor that I was allowed to see her.

"Should you shield the canyons from the windstorms, you would never see the beauty of their carvings."

~ *Elizabeth Kubler-Ross*

4

It came as no surprise to any of us when my father's dating service began to fail. For me it wasn't as much upsetting as it was a relief. I had finally had enough of the lonely hearts club, and was ready to move on with my life. As luck and timing would have it though, my car began to die just days before the business was to close the doors. I had to replace it quickly before I lost my job and could no longer qualify for financing.

After I sealed the deal on my new car purchase, I confided to my salesman that I was going to be in need of employment soon. Out of curiosity, I asked him what kind of money he made selling cars, and I was shocked by his reply. He added that women did very well in his business, and suggested that I fill out an application and talk to his boss. A couple of weeks later, I found myself re-employed in a new profession.

Selling cars was a tough business and everyone I worked with had a love/ hate relationship with it. Although I was a regular on the top ten list of sales people, the constant stress began to wear on me, and my emotional breakdowns were becoming far too frequent. Whenever I struggled to regain my composure, I'd walk the outer edge of the car lot, trying to appear busy. But on occasion when I was so overwhelmed that I couldn't regain control of my emotions, I would find a car to hide in until my eyes cleared and the redness in my face disappeared. Even with all of the stress, the money was so good that it was hard to walk away from, but the pain of Duff's disappearance was still fresh in my mind, and it was adding to the pressure. I had an absolute confidence that it was only a matter of time before we would be reunited, but logically I couldn't help but have a measure of uncertainty. Causing me to remain in a constant state of hope and heart break. My only coping agent was mass quantities of wine and solitude.

The first sign that I was making progress came in the form of a black 1994 Jeep Wrangler. It had been my dream car for years, and a sales manager at our car lot traded one in that was practically brand new. Knowing that my days at the dealership were numbered, I jumped at the chance to buy a new car at a big discount. It was just as much of a reward for all of the struggle that I had endured as it was a representation that the things I wanted most in life were starting to manifest. Much of my spiritual focus had begun to settle into the background, but when I received a job offer shortly after buying my jeep, I considered it another sign that I was moving in the right direction.

Gary and I worked at the car dealership together and he had just taken a job managing a new jewelry store that was opening. The mark up on the merchandise was ridiculously high, but the concept was to help people with little or damaged credit get established by opening revolving accounts for them. I wouldn't be making the money that I was used to, but what I would be gaining was management experience in a less stressful environment. I worked at the store for about an hour, before I realized that the job would go nowhere for me.

Glancing through the employment classifieds one day, I noticed an ad for a company hiring people to sell manufactured homes. I had always wanted to get into real estate, so I thought this might be my foot in the door. I interviewed with the owner of the company who was sharp but reminded me of a cross between a good ol' boy and used car salesman. He was one tough interviewer, making me justify the reasons that he should hire me; but my sales record at the car dealership was indisputable, and I managed to land the job. Not only did I enjoy manufactured home sales, but I excelled at it and was making far more money than I had been selling cars.

Carla Hansen and I had grown to be very close friends while working at the dating service; so when she found herself unemployed for a second time, I helped her to get hired as a salesperson with the company I was with. She seemed to love me like a daughter, so it made me happy to know that I helped her get a job that would finally give her some security and financial stability. Carla knew the deep pain that I still felt over my relationship with Duff; and although her intentions were good and she was only trying to help me heal, she became almost relentless in her attempts to convince me to date our assistant sales manager.

Ed was a cowboy with a weathered face, big brown eyes and a scruffy beard. He had a charismatic voice and a laugh that was contagious—he was one of those guys everyone wanted to be around. The only problem was that he was several years older than me and not my type whatsoever. His wife had recently left him for another man, so aside from my lack of romantic interest, I definitely didn't want to get involved with someone who was on the rebound.

Carla persisted, and Ed began to pursue a romantic relationship with me. After a company party that we had all attended together, we ended up back at my house for the evening. I offered to let Carla stay the night with me, rather than making the long drive back to her home; and after she went to bed, Ed and I stayed up late drinking. She was gone before we woke up the next morning, but by the clothes scattered on the living room floor, it was pretty clear what had happened.

Ed knew that I was still in love with Duff—I was honest with him from the beginning. But there was genuine love and affection growing between us. I stayed in bed to sleep off my hangover while he went in to work. It wasn't long before I got a call from him saying that Carla, my close friend of many years, had gone into the corporate office and filed a complaint against me for sleeping with Ed, who was my superior. My head still in a fog from the night before, I could hardly believe what I was hearing. Ed continued by saying, "It's serious—the shit has really hit the fan and they want to fire you."

At the time, Ed was so well liked that he probably had more job security than anyone else in the company. He tried to reassure me by saying that he assured them that if they did fire me, then he was going to leave along with me. Regardless of his intentions, the President and Vice President of the company wanted to talk to me, and I was to come into the corporate office immediately.

I wasn't sure how I felt when I walked through the doors of the lobby, but by the look on the faces of the office staff—I knew that it was serious. My head was spinning with all of the possible scenarios that might play out. As I walked into the office of the company president, the VP was sitting casually with one leg slung over the corner of his desk. They both seemed to be posed as if they were going to enjoy what was about to happen, and I was the sacrificial lamb being led to slaughter.

As nervous as I was, something inside me wanted to laugh out loud and say, *Are you freaking kidding me?* But in reality, I had just bought my first home and was terrified at the thought of losing my job.

While I sat there being scolded, my thoughts turned inward and their words dissolved into background noise. Although I gave the appearance that they had my full attention, in my mind I was thinking how ridiculous it was that the President and VP who were giving me this lecture, were both married and sleeping with any female employee whose panties they could get into. I returned my attention to them just in time to hear them say that they weren't going to fire me—yet. They went on to admit that Ed said he would leave the company if we weren't allowed to see each other, so for the time being they would move me to the sales center across the street and see how things progressed.

But as time passed, my relief was mixed with anger and concern as several people in the company began treating me like the scarlet woman. This—in a company filled with drunks, drug addicts and adulterers. I couldn't understand it. It didn't make sense. I was one of the top sales people and had previously been as highly respected as a woman could possibly be in that company.

Although I had been moved to the other location, I still felt as though I was under constant threat of termination. I was processing my worry one day, as I walked through the parking lot of the sales center to my car while considering the real possibility that I could get fired and lose the new home that I had just purchased.

In an instant, it was like someone turned off the light switch— everything went black and I found myself looking into the eyes of an Indian. His face was painted silver, and from just beyond each end of his eyebrows and down just below his cheekbones, were two U shapes painted solid indigo blue. He wore a thick, shiny black fur turban, and I could see every detail, as the light reflected a deep blue cast off of the smooth black fur.

Just as quickly as he appeared, I heard him say telepathically, but in a voice that was audible and sounded like a wise old Native American, "I am your warrior spirit."

And then he was gone. It was as though someone flipped the lights back on, and I was suddenly back in the parking lot, frozen in my steps. For several seconds, I tried to absorb the enormity of what I had just seen. It was broad daylight, I was fully awake, and he was as crystal clear as anyone else standing right in front of me.

I almost couldn't believe what had just happened, but I told myself that I had to, because it just did—*ten seconds ago!* It was strange that I wasn't scared or startled by him. Did it happen too quickly for me to feel fear, or did I somehow know him? I realized almost immediately that he was telling me that he was the one who was helping me to be strong through what was happening—the warrior guiding me and protecting me.

Tears began to well up in my eyes at the reality of what had just happened. I may have been too stunned at the time, but I hope that I thanked him. I won't forget that experience for the rest of my life and I couldn't if I tried. How do you describe suddenly being eye to eye with an Indian warrior in headdress and face paint? He was magnificent!

Fascinated by him, I began running my other experiences through my mind. I realized that the Indian must be one of my spirit guides, and the woman that I saw in gold with the doves must have been an angel; because aside from her having the appearance you might expect of an angel, the Indian didn't radiate the golden light that she did. It now caused me to wonder if the male presence who appeared in white robes with me during meditation, but who's face I didn't see, was a guide or an angel; and also the man whose voice I heard telling me that "A river cannot flow against its current."

It made me curious, but I realized that it really didn't matter. They were all messages meant to bring me peace, and to be reassured that there were guides on the other side watching over me and helping me through life. At the same time though, I realized that I wasn't always listening, or consciously living what they were trying to teach me. Although my life might not always be easy, or I may occasionally hit a rough patch in the road, it was all still likely part of the bigger plan.

I had learned to tap into my inner guidance, but I still tended to listen first to my fears and desires. There was the time when I desperately wanted to buy piece of property that I found with beautiful waterfalls, creeks, and a pond. When my financing to build a home on it fell through, I was completely devastated. But later I realized that it would have meant financial disaster for me had I gone through with it. The commute would have limited my job opportunities, and I certainly wouldn't have been able to take the job that I currently had. My Indian guide caused me to reflect on all of that and as time passed, it gradually became easier for me to let go of my fears, and the events in my life that I had no control over.

Although Ed and I had settled into a part time relationship, my thoughts and belief in eventually reuniting with Duff were still very present. My mother had been prodding me for weeks to have a phone reading with a celebrity psychic she watched on TV. The reading would be $400 for a half hour, and although I didn't personally feel compelled to do it, I figured that if I could be reassured that Duff was coming back into my life, then it would be worth every penny. After all, this was a famous psychic.

As chance would have it, I had something very major happening in my life on the day of the reading. I was sure that if the psychic was any good, then certainly they would pick up on it, which would validate the rest of the information. But shortly after getting on the phone with this person, I realized it was $400 worth of bullshit. The first ten or fifteen minutes were spent rambling about things that had nothing to do with me; and then this person went on to say that I would invest in ocean-front real estate with someone named Peter. I should have just set a match to my money and toasted marshmallows. Nothing in my life, past or present, was ever mentioned, and neither was the name of anyone who was actually in my life at the time. The major event that was happening to me on that day was never mentioned; and the answer on Duff was no, because someone named Michael would be coming into my life.

It became clear to me that this frequent guest of "The Montel Williams Show" was a fraud, who was profiting from the desperation of innocent people. The money motivation became even clearer to me when looking at the book store shelves, I noticed that she'd written more books than all of the other celebrity psychics and mediums combined. For me it didn't matter so much that the information that I was given was a load of crap, because I recognized it. But for desperate people who have lost a loved one, or had something tragic happen in their life, to be given false information is heartless and borderline criminal.

I continued to move on with my life, leaving Duff further and further behind me. I was just beginning to feel myself transition from loving, into being in love with Ed, when he sat me down on my back porch to talk. He began to cry as he told me that he wasn't ready to be in a serious relationship because he was still healing from his divorce—*my reason exactly for not wanting to get involved with him in the first place.* But as his tears turned into quiet sobs, I found myself comforting him, although still in disbelief at what he was saying to me.

I begged and pleaded with God nightly, asking why this was happening to me again. *Why can't I just meet and fall in love with a man who will never leave, and will love me forever?* But I didn't get an answer.

The next three years were as frustrating for me as they were painful. I was almost obsessed with trying to convince Ed that he was ready for a serious relationship—but it didn't work. I thought about what the Empath said to me years earlier: "Your lesson to learn in this lifetime is to love without control." What he said made perfect sense because I was trying to do everything that I could think of to try to fix something that was irreparable. And every time I started to heal and let go of our relationship, I put myself in a position to run into Ed and open the wound again—like I was picking the scab. Then there were the endless days and nights replaying every tearful conversation, and when I put myself in his position, I didn't always like what I heard. I knew that there was still a lot of love between us, and although I was beginning to find the strength to release it, I just wasn't quite there yet.

In 1999, I had grown tired of living in the city, and decided that I could use a fresh start and a new distraction. I was making enough money now that I could finally afford to buy a few acres of solitude in the country. Whether I ended up in Molalla because Ed used to live there, or if I just fell in love with the property that I found, I couldn't be sure. Either way, I had a small glimmer of hope that he would be drawn to the idea that I was there. He loved living in Molalla but he had lost his ranch in his divorce. To make matters worse, he was now living in town with his parents until he could get back on his feet financially.

My new mortgage was almost double what my last one had been, and it seemed like it was only few months later that the manufactured home business began to tank. Although I moved on to selling the bank repos, that wasn't going well either. My income had gone from $65,000 per year to around $25,000. My financial situation was beyond crisis, but somehow I was staying afloat.

I remembered something else that the Empath said years ago: "You've already experienced poverty in previous lives, so although you may struggle at times, you'll always manage and be okay."

As reassuring as that was, by 2001 I knew that I needed to get a real job, but it was just after 9/11 and there were no real jobs to be found. I wanted to get into real estate when I was younger and as it happened, real estate was the only industry that seemed to be doing well at the time. I was in credit card debt from trying to survive financially, so I decided that if I was going to do this, then I better crack the books and make it happen fast.

It was around this time that a friend of mine was going to go see a psychic that had done readings for one of the Portland Trail Blazer's wives, and she invited me to go along with her. I had been growing weary of life and what seemed to be an endless struggle, both personally and professionally. Maybe this psychic would have a new take on my situation. I was still having readings with Margie, but I thought that a second opinion couldn't hurt.

Aside from their height, Sophie was almost the complete opposite of Margie. In her early 70s and tiny, she looked like you might find her shushing you in a library. But there was wisdom in her eyes and she had great energy. She told me that I would do really well in real estate and within the next few years, I would be making more money than I ever had ever made before. She didn't have very positive news about Ed.

"Although he cares about you, I don't see that relationship coming together." She went on to say, "You'll meet a man who is about six feet tall with dark hair and eyes like you could see into his soul. He has a good ability to balance work with family life, and I think that you'll meet him within the next couple of years."

It all sounded really exciting to me, so I could only hope that she was right. I always felt like there was a piece of myself out there that was missing—yet to be found. But as the weeks and months passed, the promise of a new love was diminished by the ever present pain and loss of hope that Ed and I would be together. I found my thoughts often drifting into dark places.

Moles are almost impossible to exterminate, and I had tried everything. One day, I got the brilliant idea to plug as many holes

in my yard as I could find, connect a hose to the exhaust pipe of
my Jeep Wrangler, and put it down a hole. I thought that maybe
the carbon monoxide would kill them. As I worked to fasten the
hose to my exhaust pipe, I began to think about what an effort life
had become for me and how worn down and tired I was from it all.
Fastening a hose was easy, but as I looked around at the pile of gravel
that I needed to shovel, the fence that needed to be repaired, and
thought about my years of financial and romantic struggle, I started
thinking to myself, *What's the point of all of this anyways? This isn't fun
anymore.*

I stopped what I was doing and my eyes lost focus as I stared
blankly into space. My thoughts and sense of being turned inward and
I suddenly felt numb and empty inside. A dull wave of pain washed
briefly over my heart, and tears formed in my eyes. I felt myself slip into
a dead, emotionless place that I had never been to before, as I started
running through the events of my life, and what brought me to where
I was now. I was fast approaching 40 and all that I really ever wanted
was a family. I still had no children. Duff, the true love of my life, was
gone; Ed had just dumped me; and the prospects weren't looking good.
*It would be so easy to just put the hose from my exhaust pipe into the window and
climb in and close the door.*

I unzipped the side window of the soft top on my jeep and put the
end of the hose into passenger compartment, slowly zipping the gap
closed tightly around it. I paused to absorb what I had done, and then
walked to the door and slid into the driver's seat. As I closed the door
behind me, I felt another wave of pain cross my heart, and looked down
at the keys dangling from the ignition switch. I reached out and stroked
them, as I imagined what it would be like to turn the key. But I wasn't
serious—yet.

With the hose still in the side panel, I walked into the house, devoid
of any emotion and I Googled suicide. I read several stories about
people, *really good people*, who had killed themselves. One of the women
was forty and I thought, *I bet that she was just like me. . .single, never married,
forty or about to turn forty, and throwing in the towel.*

I was suddenly snapped back into reality when I remembered what I had learned about reincarnation and suicide popped into my head. "If you take your life before you've learned the lessons that you're here to learn, then you have to come back and live them again." *There is no way in HELL that I'm coming back to do this again! I've gotten this far and besides, before there was Duff there was Tim, and after Duff there was Ed—I loved them all.*

I started running through my mental check list of what would bring me the hope and will to get through this. *What would my mother do if I was gone? And no one would ever love my dog Gypsy the way that I did. I couldn't abandon her and leave her at the mercy of strangers, because if I was gone, my mother wouldn't be able to keep her.*

My father who I was now estranged from had told me, "No man will ever be faithful to you Julie." He also told my mother that there must be something wrong with me because I hadn't gotten married yet. I believed in true love, and there was nothing wrong with me. *Why is it more normal that I would have been divorced once or twice? Not everyone gets married at 30 and has 2.5 kids, or whatever the average is now. We all have our own timing, and I believe that there must be someone yet to come into my life. I deserve a true soulmate and not just someone who I love enough to settle for. What if I killed myself right before the right person was to come into my life? I'll roll the dice!*

I wasn't one to date a lot but in the past, I had always picked amazing guys with one or two exceptions. Although I still struggled at times feeling sorry for myself and was self-medicating with alcohol, I was pressed to be satisfied with the happiness that I found in the people and things that I loved. As lonely as I was, I reminded myself that I had to learn how to first make myself happy, before I could find true happiness with another person.

Shortly after my suicidal episode, a close family friend, Louis, who was an absolute joy and pure of heart, hanged himself in his ex-wife's garage. His 14-year-old son found him hanging there and tragically, Lou has left that imprint on his son for the rest of his life. Louis had been in love with a woman (not his wife) who toyed with his emotions and openly cheated on him. She wasn't a good person and no one liked her because everyone loved Lou and they could see what she was doing to him. But he loved her deeply and was so tormented by it that, unknowingly, she finally took the last thing that he had to give to her.

My sister Lynne, who was living at the Oregon coast, said that she met a guy there that she wanted to introduce me to. It had been a couple of years since Ed had said his final good-bye to me, and I was open to a new relationship, but not desperate. The next time that I was at her house, she and her boyfriend took me over to Kurt's for a drink.

Tall, good looking and mild mannered, he had an unexpected sense of humor that seemed to come from nowhere. As much as I grew to care about Kurt, I was in self denial because I wanted this relationship to work. I wanted someone to come home to and the security of a second income. The first time that I told him that I loved him, I literally choked as the words came out of my mouth, and hoped that he didn't notice. It wasn't that there was any reason not to love him, I just wasn't in love with him the way I tried to convince myself to be. The problem was though that I wasn't willing, or able, to admit it to myself at the time.

Kurt and I had been together for six months when we decided to take a scuba diving vacation to Honduras. There was no hiding from our differences on the trip and when we returned, I ended the relationship. But two weeks later the enormity of our differences had - suddenly lost all intensity and I wanted him back. *Thank god that he didn't agree to it!* That was the end of my insanity and I was now prepared to accept my fate. I wasn't going to settle for less than what I knew would make me happy. And even if it meant spending the rest of my life alone, I would no longer try to keep a relationship together that wasn't working. If I did get involved with someone again, then the door would always be open and they could choose to use it whenever they wanted to—*no hard feelings.* I finally understood why the Empath years ago told me that I needed to learn to love without control. Because what I had been doing all of these years wasn't working.

I was fast approaching forty and decided that it was probably time to start thinking about having a child on my own. I had a fear that I would get pregnant and then suddenly meet the right person, but I couldn't worry about that anymore. The clock was no longer just ticking; it was running out of time. But most of all, I was reaching a point where I needed something bigger and more important in my life than myself. I wasn't going to try to make another relationship fit if I didn't feel the same deep love that I felt for Duff.

Sophie suggested that I do something that she called "The Red Envelope." I hadn't heard of *The Secret*, or the laws of attraction yet, so it seemed a little woo woo to me at the time. I decided that I had absolutely nothing to lose and everything to gain; so I hand wrote everything that I wanted in a man and a relationship, listing only the positives. She explained to keep it simple, and "don't wants" were a big no no because by listing them, I might draw those qualities as well. After writing everything down, I was to put the letter into a red envelope, which represented love, and put it under my pillow. She went on to instruct me to read it out loud three times per day for three months. I knew that I wouldn't be able to follow through with that, but I did manage to read it at least once, sometimes two or three times per day. Then just over a year later—it happened.

"A person often meets his destiny, on the road he took to avoid it."

~ Jean de La Fontaine

5

Years earlier, Sophie had said to me, "You're going to meet a man who is six feet tall with dark hair, and eyes like you can see into his soul."

Whenever I found myself in crisis, whether it be business or personal, I often sought the advice of my psychic friends. While their style and delivery was different, the information that they gave me was almost always the same. And although I didn't live my life by every word they said, I often found that there was a glimmer of hope or a word of wisdom shared that would pull me through whatever it was that was happening at the time. I also knew that if they told me the same thing independently, their opinion was as reliable as anyone else's could possibly be.

My mother had been living with me for the last several years, and as much as I loved her, I just couldn't share the same four walls with her any longer. The plan was to buy a home that would allow her to have her own apartment; but when I sold my house before finding a replacement property, we were forced to move into a rental home. The crisis of the moment was that no matter how hard I searched, I just couldn't find a house that would work for the two of us. And when I did, the house didn't seem to "feel right."

It was that problem along with the ongoing failure of my romantic life. I had recently turned 39 and was releasing all hope of getting married, but I still wanted to have children. I was beginning to seriously consider the idea of using a sperm bank to become pregnant on my own—I even had the catalogue. But deep in my heart, I knew that I didn't feel totally committed to the plan.

A few days after my reading with Margie, I met with Sophie for my second opinion. Both of them assured me that I would find a house soon, and they saw me taking a vacation in the next six to nine months, on which I would meet a man who I would be romantically interested in.

Margie said, "Either he raises llamas, or you'll get into a conversation about llamas." As confident as I was in her abilities, *that was pretty specific.*

Sophie added, "The relationship will be on his terms." *His terms. . .?* I wasn't sure I liked the sound of that.

Always feeling a little short on cash, a vacation was the last thing on my mind when I had a house to buy and a pregnancy to consider. But several months later, my 15-year-old niece, Mikala, had been acting up, and I made a deal with her: if her grades and behavior improved, I would take her on a vacation so she could learn how to scuba dive. I thought that accomplishing something on that scale might generate some confidence and self-esteem. Her brother and I had taken a trip to New York the previous year, so it seemed only fair to offer her a trip as well.

Petite and busty with sparkling brown eyes, Mikala is cute and spunky with a great sense of humor. She started doing better at home, so I gave her the option to choose between Florida or Mexico. After much deliberation, the decision was made—she chose Florida. It did register to me briefly that I had been told months prior, that I would meet a man on a trip, but I really didn't put a lot of thought into it, and I certainly wasn't going to Florida to meet him.

It was late July 2006 when we left on our Florida scuba adventure. After a few days of diving the pristine, turquoise waters of Key Largo, we headed south to Key West. The author and adventurer Ernest Hemmingway had been one of the most beloved and colorful of Key

West's famous residents. And on the day of our arrival, the town was just kicking off its annual Hemmingway Days celebration. The streets were bustling with white haired and bearded men dressed in white shirts and trousers, wearing red berets and chomping on fat cigars—a tribute to Hemmingway and the traditional dress worn when he ran with the bulls in Pamplona, Spain.

As we explored Duval Street on our second day there, we heard someone shouting and looked in the distance to see a man leaning out of a doorway calling and waving at us to come into the bar for a drink. I was apprehensive at first, but then assumed that the guy waving us in worked there. Once inside though, he introduced himself and his wife. Duff and Michelle were in their mid-40s and were the kind of fun, hard-partying couple that let money flow freely. The name of the bar was "The Smallest Bar in Key West," *and they weren't kidding.* It was more reminiscent of an oversized closet, with colorfully painted walls and a pirate theme with odd bits and pieces. After a few drinks, it was time for us to move on to explore the rest of Key West. As we were saying our good-byes, Duff and Michelle asked if we'd like to join them for dinner—it would be their treat. We happily accepted their invitation, and agreed they would call us in a couple of hours to set up a time and place to meet.

By the time Mikala and I made it to the port where the cruise ships docked, the sun was just starting to set over the water, and the pier was becoming a carnival atmosphere of street performers. I was beginning to think that Duff may have forgotten us, when mid way through the Cat Man's performance of tight rope waking tabbies jumping through fiery hoops, my phone rang. Duff asked me if we were still on for dinner, and then gave me directions to the restaurant.

He added, "Michelle and I just met a guy that's staying at our hotel, and we think you should meet him. I hope that you don't mind, because we invited him to join us for dinner."

"I don't mind at all."

"Great! We'll see you there at 9:00!"

Night had fully set in when Mikala and I arrived at the open-air restaurant, with only lush tropical plants separating the white linen

covered tables from the festivities on Duval Street. Candlelight softly
illuminated the faces of the dinner guests, casting shadows and reflecting
the dark polished wood accents in the room. Duff and Michelle were
sitting at a table when he saw us and waved us over. As we talked
over dinner, I paused with a sense of surprise and recognition as he
mentioned that he used to raise llamas. I recalled my friend Margie
telling me that I would meet a man on my vacation who either raised
llamas or we would get into a conversation about them; I assumed that
she meant someone who I would be romantically interested in. Duff
was obviously married, so I reasoned with myself that it was just a
strange coincidence. But I also found it odd that he had the same name
as the pilot I was in love with years before. A curious thought crossed
my mind and I wondered if there might be more to our meeting than I
realized.

After we finished dinner, Duff mentioned that the man that they
had invited to dinner must have gotten delayed, and would I join them at
the night club upstairs for a drink. Apparently he forgot that my fifteen
year old niece was with me, and although minors could go into bars in
Florida, this wasn't one of them. I thanked them both for dinner and the
invitation, but politely explained that it had been a long day and I should
stay at the hotel with my niece.

I had just pulled the blanket under my chin when my phone rang.
It was Duff and I could barely hear him with all of the music and
background noise; all that I was able to make out was that they were at
the club, and the guy that they wanted to introduce me to was there.

He was half shouting as he said, *"He really wants to meet you. Why don't
you hop in a cab and come over for a drink?"*

"Thanks Duff, but it's after Midnight and I just got into bed."

"No Julie, I mean—*he really wants to meet you!"*

"But I don't feel like going out." I protested.

"We won't take no for an answer. We're sending a cab for you and it
will be there in ten minutes!"

"Why does he want to meet me so bad? He has no idea who I am."
I argued.

"We showed him your business card with your photo. When you get here, we'll ask you if you have friends in Hawaii or Oklahoma. If you don't like him, just say Oklahoma and you can go home—promise!"

My niece practically shoved me out the door and the next thing that I knew, I was in a cab going to meet someone I didn't know and couldn't really care less whether I ever did.

At Midnight it was still warm enough outside to perspire, and I could feel the uncomfortable wetness set in as I approached the club's entrance. The long, dark stair well was crowded with people who had chosen that place to stop and talk. A drop of sweat rolled down my cheek, and I carefully wiped it away with my finger. The pounding music grew louder with each step, and as I blotted my forehead and upper lip with the back of my hand, I kept asking myself: *Why did I get out of bed for this?*

I reached the top floor, which was open air like the restaurant below, and I saw Duff and Michelle sitting alone at a table. *Why did I do this?* I asked myself again. *I know that it's a waste of time and I'm going to regret it. The guy is probably a loser anyway. One drink and I'm out of here!*

I sat down and just as we began to make small talk, I suddenly felt myself falling backwards on my barstool. I panicked!

In a split second, I knew that I was going to fall and I tried to understand how it could be happening at the same time. I felt pressure at my shoulders and realized that someone had their hands on me. I wasn't falling, because they had control over me and then I felt a face close to mine. Lips brushed my cheek as I struggled to regain my balance and right myself. I grasped to get a hold on whoever it was and tried to push them off of me. I couldn't see who it was, but they still had me in their grip, and I felt lips brush my cheek again. One more hard push and I franticly grabbed at the edge of the table with both hands, trying to keep myself upright as I felt myself suddenly freed from their grasp.

My shock turned to anger—whoever it was, they were about to get the business end of me and I was pissed! I turned to see a young man standing there. Wide eyed and looking as though he didn't know if he had just insulted me, or if his ego had been severely bruised; not at all the reaction he expected, or was probably used to getting from women.

With head cocked and an expression of "who the hell do you think you are?" I said with disgust, *"I don't even know you!"*

"I'm sorry... I didn't mean..." he said softly, as if uncertain what to say next.

Shaking my head slightly, I turned my attention back to Duff and Michelle who looked very amused by what was playing out before them.

"Julie, Duff said, this is Brayden. The one that I wanted to introduce you to."

I nodded in acknowledgement while keeping my eyes on Duff.

Brayden came to stand beside me still wide eyed as though he had just committed some terrible offense and again, he said softly, *"I'm sorry."*

It wasn't until then that I noticed his big, beautiful green eyes—a color that I had never seen before. I was almost mesmerized by them. His lips were full and his dark hair trimmed short. His features were boyish, in a beautiful way. I wasn't sure if I was attracted to him, but the look of disappointment in his eyes drew me in. He asked if he could sit down beside me and I replied "yes" with indifference, ignoring any further attempts by him to get my attention.

I glanced back at him just quickly enough to see his big sad eyes again as he mouthed the words, *"I'm sorry"* without speaking.

I began to reason with myself—*How much do you really needed to punish this guy?*

I tried to redirect my focus on Duff and Michelle, but I was distracted by the feeling of his eyes on me. Brayden then began asking me some very personal questions about myself: If I had been married, if I wanted to have children, and among other things, when was the last time that I had been with a man!

I turned to him with an expression of disbelief. "You're asking me some pretty personal questions considering I don't even know you!" I replied.

He apologized again, but seemed undaunted. For some unexplainable reason, my tone turned soft, and I began to answer each one of his questions.

"I want to get married, but I guess that I haven't met the right one yet. I want to have children, and I've been thinking about having a child on my own. The last man that I was with was about two and a half years ago. I've had friends with benefits, but it got to the point that it didn't mean anything to me anymore, and so I haven't been with anyone since."

Brayden's voice had a sensual quality about it, as he began to tell me about himself. But part of me was still annoyed with our introduction and I wanted to dislike him. He began by saying that he was originally from Scotland.

"You sound Irish." I replied harshly.

I knew the difference, but I wasn't ready to trust him. I also wasn't drawn to a man just because he had an accent—although his was certainly beautiful and it did add to his charm. With all of my traveling, I had probably dated more men from other countries than I had from the United States. So it was more important that I look beyond the accent, and to the man behind it.

"No." he corrected. "I'm originally from Glasgow but I live in Florida now. I'm a private Learjet pilot."

"Oh my God not a pilot!" I thought to myself. *That was the worst thing that he could have possibly said to me!*

"I would rather that you were a garbage truck driver!" I replied with mild disdain.

His face held an expression of concern and mild amusement, as if uncertain how to respond. I'm sure that statement along with his Scottish accent usually cinched the deal with women but for me, it was the wrong answer.

"I'm sorry—I won't date pilots," I said flatly. "My father was a pilot and I know the mentality. I was in love with a Learjet pilot once, and I would never get involved with a pilot again." As if to drive the point home even further, I added, "It would never work for us anyways. I love Oregon and I would never leave there."

In my mind, I also knew as he did that Oregon was a very difficult state for a pilot to be based out of. Aside from that, his job was in Florida.

His expression changed and I thought that I may have seen pain in his eyes. Like that of a little boy who had just gotten his favorite thing taken away. I felt a pain in my heart for him, and I began to question why I was trying so hard to push him away. He seemed very genuine and sincere, although my logic still told me that he was a player. But then there were those beautiful green eyes filled with sadness and rejection staring back at me. As if asking me to take the pain away.

Without thinking I said, "Well…you're a pilot. So you can live anywhere."

His face lit up like it was Christmas morning and I think you could have stuck a fork in me because I was done—*but not ready to surrender.*

Watching the tension play out, Michelle asked me, "So Julie, do you have friends in Oklahoma or Hawaii?"

"*Both.*" I replied.

I just wasn't sure about him yet. His initial approach before we were introduced was overly confident and it annoyed me. But I also reasoned with myself that I needed to lighten up and take it as a playful hello gone awry. Because that hurt boyish look of apology drew me in and made him attractive. Before I allowed myself to indulge in any thoughts and possibilities, I needed to know more about him.

"What do you drive?" I asked. *A clear indication to me of a man's ego.*

"A 2000 Jeep Grand Cherokee." he replied.

"Really? That's what I drive—same year too."

I thought the coincidence was interesting, but it also told me that he wasn't into status symbols, which was important to me. Still looking for the weak point, I asked, "What did you drive before that?"

"A 95 Jeep Sahara."

OK—this is getting interesting, I thought to myself. My last car was a 94 Jeep Wrangler purchased in 95. I wanted the Sahara, but I couldn't afford it. They were basically the same car, but the Sahara had a few more standard features. He added that he had a white Great Dane, and so he got the Cherokee to have more room for his dog. This was all becoming eerily familiar. I sold my Wrangler for the same reason. My Hungarian Kuvasz, which happened to be white, weighed 120 lbs and

I needed the extra room for her. I couldn't think about it anymore—it was all just a strange coincidence!

As he continued to tell me more about himself, he said that he was separated.

There's my red flag! I thought to myself. *There is no way for him to prove that to me, at least for the time being. Besides, isn't every man that's out fooling around, 'separated'?* Still, I reasoned with myself that he could have just as easily said that he was single. *Maybe that shows honesty. I'll reserve judgment for now.*

Brayden went on to explain that his soon-to-be-ex was in real estate just like I was. He was 32 and had been living in Florida for the last few years.

"You're too young for me!" I protested. "How would you feel ten or twenty years from now when I'm so much older than you?"

"My ex is 18 years older," he replied, as if to convince me.

Interesting. . . I thought to myself. *He likes older women. I wonder what that means?*

Between the noise in the bar and Brayden's accent, I was only hearing bits and pieces of what he was saying. Then everything began to register to me in a strange, fragmented way and the undeniable similarities hit me: The first man that I was in love with and felt soul connected to, was a thirty- two year old Scottish/Italian Lear jet pilot, who was eight years older than me and lived in Alaska. Now, I've just met another thirty-two year old Scottish Lear jet pilot, but he's eight years younger than me and lives in Florida. In some ways, they were opposites because one was older and the other younger. They lived at the opposite ends of the country and one was tall, the other short. It would be like lightning striking me to meet two Scottish Lear jet pilots of the same age and age difference. *This has to be more than just coincidence—but what does it mean? Am I over thinking this?*

I knew that I had too many cocktails in me to contemplate the meaning of the Universe, so I decided to check it in the back of my mind to ponder later.

Duff and Michelle were arguing when Brayden's co-pilot showed up at our table. Hilary was in her late 20s or early 30s and although she herself was married, she was obviously "with" some guy she had met in the bar.

Brayden seemed annoyed by the drama playing out at our table and with a flash of excitement in his eyes, he quickly grabbed my hand and said, "*Come with me!*"

Pulling me off of my bar stool with such force, that I nearly tripped, his pace slowed as he scanned the room, and his grasp became gentle as he led me to a quiet hallway. I had no idea what he was doing, until he turned and pinned me up against the wall and began to kiss me. The intensity of emotion coming through his lips took me by surprise. And when he pulled away, I thought that I could see love in his eyes.

"I'm so happy that I met you." he said with genuine tenderness, as if looking into my soul and searching my eyes for agreement.

For the first time since we met, I was left speechless. And if I was resistant to him in the beginning, I was resistant no longer—I knew that I wanted more of him.

We held hands like a couple falling in love, as we walked back to the table. Duff and Michelle were still arguing, and said that they were going back to their hotel room. A few minutes later, I heard the song "Sweet Home Alabama" mixing faintly with the background noise. I looked around to see where it was coming from, as Brayden lifted his cell phone to his ear. It was his ringtone, and I suddenly began to wonder if someone had given this guy personal notes about me before we met. We had so many strange similarities, and now my all time favorite song was his ring tone? *How could that be?*

Brayden rolled his eyes as he held the phone to his ear and listened. When he pulled it away, he folded it closed as he said that it was Duff. The taxi driver kicked them out of the cab for arguing with each other, and would he come pick them up? Brayden asked if I would come with him, but it was late and I needed to get back to Mikala in the hotel room. Although I knew that I shouldn't go with him, I just wasn't ready to say good-bye yet.

We left the club to find Duff and Michelle in the dark by the side of the road. The arguing continued as we drove to their hotel, but it was just a bunch of loud rambling. It wasn't clear what started the argument, but apparently Duff had pulled the expensive diamond earrings that he had just bought for Michelle out of her ears.

We delivered them to their hotel room and Brayden tried to calm Duff down, while I tried to calm Michelle. They offered us a joint and when we politely declined, they said they had some pills.

Brayden and I looked at each other as if to say, *"Are these people crazy?"*

I saw a shift in Brayden's gaze from across the room and we communicated without speaking. *"Why are we wasting our time with these people, when we could be spending time alone?"*

There was a clarity and connectedness to it as I thought to myself, *I don't know this guy, so why do I feel like I've known him forever?*

We left their room and Brayden asked me back to his. I told him that it was late and that I needed to get back to my niece. He replied that it was already late and he probably shouldn't drive. A few hours of sleep wouldn't make any difference, he said, and I reluctantly agreed. He promised that nothing would happen, but I knew differently. I wasn't concerned; I felt safe—like I had always known him and had finally come home.

As we entered his room, he made sincere, but testing jokes about being a gentleman and not touching me.

Sliding his arms around my waist and gently pulling me close to him, he asked softly, "Can I kiss you again?"

I knew what that would lead to, but I hadn't been with a man for a long time and I wanted him. Part of me was still questioning how far I should let this go. He leaned into me, softly brushing his lips against mine. His hands moved up to the back of my neck and he began kissing me deeply as he felt the knot of my halter top in his hands. He slowly began to untie it when he stopped himself.

Pulling back and pausing to look tenderly into my eyes, both searching and hoping for the answer he wanted, he asked, "Is it okay?"

Holding his gaze, I nodded "Yes," in agreement, and he continued.

As we made love, he began whispering to me over and over again, "Tell me I'm your baby."

I felt a sudden quiet panic as I thought to myself, *I don't even know you. My baby?* It made me feel uneasy and I was suddenly wondering, *What the hell am I doing? I just met this guy and who is he really?* I processed my dilemma quickly and decided not to let my thoughts ruin the moment. I reasoned with myself that I was preparing to go to a sperm bank and have a child on my own, and here I was with a man who I wouldn't hesitate to be the donor. I reassured myself that if I was lucky—I would get pregnant.

My attention was drawn back to him as he kissed and caressed my body. I felt his emotions flow through every movement, like a dance between a couple who were already in love. And although my suspicions lingered, I was certain this was not casual for him.

The next morning I woke up to my phone ringing and I panicked when I realized what I had done. It was my sister. We hadn't slept for a few hours; it was now 10:00 in the morning!

"How could you leave my 15 yr old daughter alone in a hotel room in a different state?" she shouted, " Anything could have happened!".

I started to cry at the shock and horror of what I had done. I apologized profusely and said over and over again how inexcusable it was.

I hung up the phone and looked at Brayden who was wide eyed and said, "Get me back to my hotel room. Now!"

We drove in silence except for my mumblings about how awful and irresponsible I had been, and how bad this was. He stopped in front of my hotel. I gave him a quick kiss and ran to the room without looking back.

Once in the room, I hugged Mikala and apologized. She didn't seem to think that it was a big deal, but said that she had only been worried about me. I explained what had happened and how I felt about him, and when we decided to go to breakfast, she insisted that I call and invite him to join us. I called Brayden and it was obvious that I had woke him up. He said that he would love to, but that he needed to sleep.

With tenderness and purpose in his voice he said softly, "You do realize that I'm courting you don't you?"

A wave of warmth washed over me and I was speechless. It was the most romantic statement that had ever been said to me, and he seemed to be sincere about it. His words surprised me, but in other ways they didn't. I felt so connected with him but yet, I didn't want to hold too much hope that our relationship would go any further.

Before I could form my reply, Brayden went on to say, "The way that you were this morning!" and stopped there.

I didn't understand what he meant. He saw me at my worst that morning. I had done something terrible and inexcusable. I was in tears the entire ride back to my hotel, and I barely said good-bye to him. It wasn't until later that I realized that my reaction to what I had done meant something to him. My maternal instinct and need to make sure that Mikala was safe was really important to him.

He needed to get some rest because he was flying out that day, but asked if we would come by the airport and he would give us a tour of the plane. Although I wasn't impressed by a Lear Jet, I knew that Mikala would be and it was as good excuse as any to see him again. Even though he had said he was courting me, my heart didn't dare to think that our relationship would go beyond what had already been: a wonderful, vacation romance.

When we arrived at the airport, Brayden greeted us in his uniform. He looked so professional in his starched white shirt and tie. A stark contrast from the man I saw naked the night before. I felt a little nervous, not knowing if the connection I had felt to him was only my imagination misinterpreted through the fog and affect of alcohol. It was all very polite as I introduced him to Mikala. And just as a sense of awkwardness began to develop, he suggested that we go out onto the tarmac to see the plane. I sensed his pride and enthusiasm, so I tried to appear impressed as he gave us a tour of the small eight seat cabin. It was finished with leather seats and polished walnut accents. *It's a little worn and dated*, I thought to myself. But this was how the other 1% lived, and I tried to imagine what it must be like to have that kind of money.

Brayden suggested that I take a photo of him and Mikala together with the cockpit in the background.

Just as I started to put the camera away he said, "Oh no! We need one more!"

I passed the camera to Mikala and as I moved toward him, he pulled me quickly onto his lap with a big smile. He didn't seem to want to let me go, as he apologized and said that he had to do his pre-flight check list.

Walking toward the gate, he suddenly said with excitement, "Hey! How about a photo of Mikala on the wing?"

She wasn't going to miss her photo op on a private jet, so Brayden lifted her up onto the wing for one last picture. It hadn't occurred to either of us that the metal was scorching hot from the sun until, without saying a word, she quickly folded her hands under her bare thighs to protect them from the heat.

Brayden walked us to the car, and Mikala took her place on the passenger side, but she didn't get in, or seem to realize that we needed privacy.

As it became awkward, Brayden said quietly, with hesitation, "I want to kiss you, but..." as he nodded towards Mikala on the other side of the car.

"Then why don't you?" I whispered.

Moist from the heat and humidity, but soft as if our lips melted into one another's—I can still feel that kiss. With a promise, but never knowing if I would ever see or hear from him again, we said our good-byes.

"A soulmate is someone to whom we feel profoundly connected, as though the communicating and communing that takes place between us were not the product of intentional efforts, but rather a divine grace."

~Thomas Moore

6

"He's hot!" Mikala said, with a big, wide smile as we drove away from the airport. "And his accent is soooo sexy!" I laughed in agreement, and we talked about how strongly I felt for him. But I told her that it was better for me not to have any expectations. As much as we both adored Brayden, it was better that we turn our focus to our last day in Key West, and make the most of it.

The next day, we made the long drive back to Miami where I had a room reserved at one of the art deco hotels in South Beach. It would be our last night in Florida before catching our flight home in the morning, and I couldn't have chosen a better way to end our trip. The sun had already set when we arrived, and the brightly painted art deco hotels lining the beach were lit up with neon lights, accenting their architecture.

Brayden called me later that evening and we spoke just briefly enough for him to tell me that he was on his way to Kansas. The conversation seemed somewhat guarded, because I don't think either of us knew what to expect. The distance would make a relationship next to impossible, but we agreed that although we lived far apart, we would continue to talk.

Our plane had a short layover in Houston, which turned into a lengthy delay due to weather. I had time to kill, so I thought it might be a good opportunity to call Brayden and test the waters. I had no idea where he was flying to next, but after he answered, we were surprised to find that we were both in Houston on layovers.

Both excited and shocked by the coincidence, he said, "Change your ticket and spend the night with me!"

"OK I'll try, but I don't know if they'll let me."

"You'll be able to—I just know you will!"

Mikala was even more excited by the idea than I was, so I went to a ticket counter and asked to be put on a flight the following day. The woman at the counter was extremely rude and refused me. She insinuated that I was trying to pull something over on her, and I was angry with her tone. Why would trying to stay in Houston be underhanded? Our flight had an indefinite delay, and it wasn't like I was trying to spend another day in the Caribbean, for Christ's sake.

I returned to our departure gate and explained to Mikala that I couldn't change the ticket. But she wasn't going to take no for an answer and insisted that I try again. I went back to the counter and asked the woman for her name so I could report her treatment of me. She asked me a few questions that might justify the change and then handed me two tickets for a flight the next day. Mikala and I were ecstatic!

We wheeled our luggage out to the passenger pick up area just as Brayden raced up in a car with huge smile. As he began to help Mikala into the car with our bags, he looked at me from over the roof with an expression of, *"I should be opening the door for you and I want to, but what do I do? Because I'm already helping her."* I gave him a smile of acknowledgement, and slid into the passenger's seat. Crashing every toll booth without paying, it was as if he couldn't get back to the hotel fast enough to be together.

He rented a room next to his so Mikala could be close to us, and after we put our bags in the room, we all went down to the bar to have dinner together. When Brayden briefly excused himself from the table, I asked Mikala what she thought of him.

She enthusiastically approved, saying, "Not only is he *hot*, but he's really funny too!"

It didn't hurt that he mentioned that he had an interview the following week for a position as a private pilot for Kenny Chesney. An interview that I would later be relieved to find had been cancelled, because I knew that would take him on the road with less flexibility in his schedule for us to see each other.

It was unseasonably cold in Houston that day. So when we delivered Mikala to her room, I made myself busy figuring out how to turn on the heater; while Brayden put her pink Von Dutch baseball cap on sideways and started making rapper jokes. He had a wickedly funny sense of humor that I just loved about him, but our laughter was quickly interrupted as the heater started smoking. We began to panic just as the smoke alarm sounded. The front desk called to find out if everything was OK and I explained that there must have been lint built up on the coils, but everything seemed to be alright now.

Brayden and I hugged Mikala good night, and as we started out the door, she called to us with a smirk on her face, "Don't do anything I wouldn't do! On second thought—just kidding!" she added with a big smile.

I opened my eyes the next morning, and looked up to see that Brayden had been watching me while I slept. He was buttoning his crisp, white shirt with epaulets, and smiled down at me with a look of adoration.

He came to kneel down beside me and, with tenderness in his voice as if he could barely find the strength to leave, he said, "You know... I have to leave and go to work, but I don't want to."

He kissed me softly and then with a tilt of his head, he smiled before turning toward the door.

Wrapping myself in a sheet, I followed behind him. We kissed once more before he turned to walk down the hallway, neither of us knowing what to say, but not wanting to say good-bye.

Back in Portland, we started the long drive to the Oregon coast where Mikala lived. Stopping briefly at the McDonald's in Tillamook to use the bathroom, a woman struck up a conversation with me while we waited in line. She said that she had just arrived from Houston. I thought it was strange, but I didn't comment. *What are the chances that I would meet someone in the bathroom at the Tillamook McDonalds talking about Houston? And why did she decide to share that with me?*

I hadn't been home for more than a few days, when a friend invited me on a trip to Seattle August 4 and 5. I was reluctant to go out of town again, but I hadn't heard from Brayden, and decided it was best that I stay busy. We were having dinner in Seattle when my phone rang. I didn't recognize the number, and thought it might be a business call, so I let it go to voicemail.

As we walked back to the hotel, I checked my messages and in a soft, sensual Scottish voice I heard, "Julie Hopper... I can't get you out of my *head! You!* Were supposed to call me back. *Anyways...*I can't stop thinking about you. Hope all is well, honey. Hope to talk to you soon."

I had to listen to it a few times to understand him because I was still adjusting to his accent. It made me happy to hear from him, but I decided he needed to stew a little because he had kept me waiting for so long.

The next morning while we were walking though Seattle, I started getting nervous about calling him back. I felt so strongly for him, that I didn't want to make the same mistakes I had in the past by being too eager. I suddenly I felt something drop in my hair, and as I reached to pull it out, it felt moist. I pulled my hair forward to see a big grey and white smear. *Bird poop!* I was amused and disgusted by it at the same time. We were surrounded by office buildings, without a bathroom in site. I left my friend with the promise of returning quickly, but had to walk several blocks before finding a place to wash it out.

On my way back to her, and with Brayden still on my mind, I thought it may be a good time to call him while I was still distracted. I convinced myself it was all very casual as I pulled my phone out of my purse. I took a few deep breaths and pressed the call back button. Brayden answered and asked me what I was up to.

"Well...actually... I'm in Seattle and was walking down the street and a bird just pooped in my hair."

He laughed, and his accent turned thick and excited as he replied with the Scottish term for shit.

"You're telling me that a bird just shite in your hair? Oh!—That makes you all the more attractive!" now laughing uncontrollably, "You know, when you didn't return my call last night, it was all that I could do not to try you again. I miss you... But now I can't get this picture of you out of my head with bird shite in your hair!" he said laughing again. "I'm at the airport right now, hun, but I'll call you again when I land okay?"

When he called, I was at the top of the Space Needle. He told me how much he wanted me at that moment, and then asked me to tell him in a very personal way, that my lady parts were his and only his. He was relentless, so I whispered my answer quietly, hoping that no one would hear.

As the days passed, we talked at least three or four times a day. He would call me from the plane, or the hotel that he was staying at. I've never considered myself to be a prude, but now he was asking me to send him some very personal photos. I had never done anything like that before, so I kept refusing.

"Won't you do that for the man of your dreams?" he asked.

"Oh...is he there with you now?" I replied.

"Oh! I am SO going to club you over the head and drag you back to my cave!" he laughed.

Brayden's schedule was busy and unpredictable, so I told him if he was ever going to be in one place for a few days to let me know.

"How do you feel about Wichita?" he asked. "I'm going to be there on the 13th of August for three days."

"Sure! I like Wichita!" I replied enthusiastically.

We set about arranging the ticket and he offered to pay for half, but I had some air miles that I could use. As it worked out, it was going to be a long trip with and overnight in Vancouver, Canada.

"Don't do it Julie." His tone turned serious and convincing. "I'm not worth it."

"Yes you are!" I replied happily. "I just told the booking agent that I was using the miles to go see the man that I'm going to marry."

Silence.

"What did you say?"

"I said that I was using the miles to go see the man that I was going to marry."

Silence.

"When is that going to happen?" he asked.

"When you ask me—but it's not going to happen over the phone."

"You've got that right!" he laughed.

"Hey, guess who's here!"

"Who?"

He put Hilary on the phone, his co pilot that I met on the Key West trip. We made small talk and then I told her that I needed to ask her a question.

"Is he a good guy? Can I trust him?"

She paused for a moment. "You know that he's married right?"

"Yes."

"Well, all I can tell you is that he's the only guy that I can go get shit faced with and not have to worry about."

That was a good enough answer for me. Brayden told me that he was separated when we met and at this point, I just had to trust that he was telling me the truth. A marriage that is falling apart is still "married." But I needed to find a way to confirm that there was indeed a separation. Maybe I would be able to verify it while I was in Wichita with him. Marriage and fidelity were important to me and no matter how connected I felt to him, I had no intention of interfering with a marriage.

Brayden got back on the phone and said tenderly, "Julie... I feel like my life hasn't begun yet...because it hasn't begun with you."

"Oh...that is so sweet of you to say..."

"Yeah, so is it going to get me laid?" he replied with mischief in his voice.

"It's going to get you laid and a blow job too!" I replied with half seriousness.

I thought he might choke, he was coughing and laughing so hard. "Hey Hilary!" he called into the distance. "How much do you think the gas would cost to fly to Oregon right now? I miss you Julie…and I can't wait to see you."

"I miss you too…"

Brayden called me the night before I was leaving for Wichita and he was in a bar drinking. He told me that he met a guy that worked for a sports TV station in Kansas City, and with pride in voice, he said that he had been explaining to him what I was going through in order to come see him. Somehow I ended up on the phone with the guy and he was telling me all of the wonderful things that Brayden should be doing in preparation for my arrival. We had a nice time chatting and then Brayden got back on the phone.

In a voice filled with love and tenderness, he said, "You can talk to anyone, can't you?"

We said good-bye and then about an hour later, I got another call from him and he was now obviously drunk.

In an emotional and commanding voice, he demanded, "Are you on the pill? Because you know that I want kids!" he shouted.

"I'm not on the pill." I reassured." You know that I want them too."

Brayden went on to say that he really wanted to have children but that his soon-to-be-ex-wife, who was 18 years older than he, was still at childbearing age when they married. However, he later discovered that she had been taking the pill without telling him.

He sounded determined as he said, "Well, when you get here we're going to start trying to have a baby!"

OK. I thought. *That was kind of cute.*

He was pretty smashed and then the next thing I heard him say in a loud, emotional cry was, "I just want to be loved!"

The way he said it was as if it was coming from the depths of his soul. It scared me and I thought that I may have made a mistake. *Should I run in the other direction? I barely know this guy anyways.* But then the

Then I looked at her and asked as nicely as I possibly could, "I was just curious, do you have a problem with fat people?"

Brayden's jaw dropped again and this time the table went silent.

She made some excuse, to which I replied, "Well... I was just curious after that fat cow comment that you made in the car."

More silence.

Her date piped up with, "Well, fat chicks need love too." His tone was sincere, which kind of saved me.

Back in the room, Brayden didn't know whether to scold me or back me up.

Then as if a light went on in his head he asked, "Did she offend you with what she said?"

"Yes, she did." I replied. "I don't like the way that she talks about people."

In the morning I made coffee, and brought a cup to Brayden who was still in bed. He seemed almost perplexed by the gesture, but I didn't understand why. So I went in to take a bath. The water was hot and relaxing, as I lay there with wet hair smoothed back from my face. I looked up to see Brayden standing over me and I smiled. He had a slight expression as if he may have caught me in an intimate moment, and he wasn't sure if he should be there. He asked me what I wanted for breakfast and I invited him to join me for a bath first. He looked like he felt a little awkward, as he took off his robe and stepped into the water. He was on the faucet side of the tub, complaining about how hot the water was as he slowly lowered himself in.

"You wimp!" I laughed.

He lowered himself the rest of the way and then, "Ouch !" He leaned back too quickly hitting the faucet.

I offered him my side of the tub but he refused and moved his back into the rounded corner. Steam rose off of the water between us as we lay there talking. For me, it just felt so natural, like I was sharing a bath with my best friend. But I saw slight conflict in Brayden's eyes and small flashes of uncertainty. Before I was ready to get out, he said that he was going to go order breakfast and asked me what I would like to eat. He stood up and dried himself off with a towel, before quickly disappearing into the bedroom.

When I walked into the area where the sink and vanity were, I began brushing my hair and noticed Brayden sitting on the bed waiting for me. He seemed to watch me with fascination, like he had never seen a woman brush her hair before.

Suddenly he hopped up off of the bed and said, "Let me do that for you!" Gently taking the brush from my hand, he hit a snag after a few strokes, and I sensed that he was embarrassed. "You better do it!" he said, quickly handing the brush back to me.

I smiled to myself as I thought about what an incredibly sweet gesture it was for him to try to show me such tenderness and intimacy.

Breakfast came and he had specifically requested flowers come on the tray but they didn't. On top of it, my Eggs Benedict was wrong. He called room service like a man on a mission and insisted that it be corrected. They brought a new tray for me and it came with a vase of small, pink roses. *I still have those roses to this day.* They didn't bring a new plate for him so we could eat a hot meal together, so he sent that food back as well. Both of our breakfasts finally arrived to the room at the same time, and I thought that it was wonderful how he made sure that everything was perfect for me.

Brayden needed to sort through some things with his bank account before we went into Wichita for the day. He made a call and held his finger against his lips to let me know to be quiet. I didn't know it at the time, but he was calling his wife. And when I realized who it was that he was talking to, I was upset.

In my mind I thought to myself, *Did he tell me the truth about the separation? Or did he lie to me and now he doesn't want her to hear me in the background?*

I justified it to myself by reasoning that even if the marriage was on the rocks, it wouldn't be good to cause waves with her. There was no "I love you" at the end of the conversation—so maybe I was right about the call. He had told me that the separation papers were filed, but I had no way to know for sure either way. He had only given me his cell phone number, but then he was on the road most of the time and so there was no reason for a home number. Besides, I only gave people my cell number, too. It concerned me, but I didn't say anything. I was already there—if what we were doing was wrong, then it was already too late. I would just have to give him the benefit of the doubt until I could be sure. *But that would need to happen soon.*

We decided to explore Wichita for the day, but it wasn't until we were in the lobby that Brayden told me Hilary would be going with us. He said we were just waiting for her to come down because she had the car keys.

She's what? I thought to myself. *I didn't spend two days flying to see him just to spend it with her!* I looked at him with total disbelief and said, "If she's joining us for dinner, then I'm getting my own room tonight."

That's when I saw it for the first time: behavior like that of a ten year old.

He was upset at what I said, so he stomped his foot on the ground and in a whiney, mocking tone he said, "Oh...someone just dropped their ice cream cone!"

I had never heard that one before. Maybe it was a Scottish thing— *but I knew that I didn't like it.* I had no idea what to think because this was a grown man and his reaction was so childish. I walked through the lobby to sit in a chair and he yelled something sarcastically over his shoulder at me.

Did he just do that? I thought to myself. *I can't believe what I'm witnessing.*

A couple of minutes later, Brayden walked over to me like nothing had happened, and said Hilary was going to drop us off in town so she could have the car. His mood was completely different now. As if he suddenly realized that I was justified in not wanting her to come with us. *And he had just made a complete ass of himself!*

Hilary dropped us off in Wichita but the incident in the lobby still hung over us like a cloud. Now it was time to really get to know each other as people, in real life, and not over the phone or in a hotel room.

I told myself, *Just get through this—you'll be back on a plane the day after tomorrow.*

I'm not sure who chose the location where we were dropped off, but the area of Wichita that we were in seemed more like a ghost town. Everywhere I turned, all I could see were nondescript buildings of beige and brick. There weren't even people milling about. Everything in Oregon was so green, and it was strange to my senses.

With nothing to distract us, the uncomfortable silences were taking their toll on me and I wished for the day to be over. Then we stumbled upon a little gift shop that was full of funny little bits and pieces. Comic relief—finally! I picked up a book called Bad Cats that had wacky pictures of cats with different facial expressions and humorous captions. Brayden and I laughed so hard that we had tears rolling down our cheeks. We were making such a spectacle of ourselves, he decided that it was better to just buy the book and leave the store. It was a much needed icebreaker and a sense of relief to both of us.

As we passed a brew pub, we decided it might be a good time to have lunch. Brayden slipped into the booth beside me.

"That's good," I said.

"Was it a test?"

"Sort of." I replied with a shrug. It showed me that he wanted to be near me and not separate.

We saw a few cute little kids at the table across from us and we got into a playful conversation about naming our future children.

"James," Brayden said.

"No," I replied.

"But that's my middle name..."

"Oh, well—it's just very formal for a first name, and I thought it would be nice to have a name that sounded more Scottish."

He went on to say that he was born James Morgan Wallace. When he was little, his biological father abandoned his mother and later when she remarried, they changed his name to Brayden James Morgan Loch, adding that in Scotland, you can add to a name but not change it.

He added he grew up in the worst neighborhood in Glasgow. It was so bad after his father left that his mother would walk he and his brother about two miles in the middle of the night to steal vegetables from a farm so she could make soup. It sounded like a made-up story to me, but I could tell by the look in his eyes that it wasn't.

The information started flowing out of him now, and he confessed that he had been married twice. He had been a professional football player in Scotland and when he got married for the first time, he felt that he had just been too young. He had a baby with his first wife, and when the marriage ended he left Scotland to take a job as a flight attendant with British Airways. He lost contact with his son when she remarried. His son would be about nine-years-old by now.

I thought to myself, *How could you possibly leave your own son?* So I questioned him. He said that at the time, a father's parental rights in Scotland were virtually non-existent after a divorce. And it was further complicated when he left to take his job. He didn't know where they were anymore, or if he could even find them.

"Brayden, if we stay together, I want to find your son."

"That would be nice..." he said with a tone of sadness and introspection.

I later looked into a man's parental rights in the UK and confirmed what he said was true, although many fathers were trying desperately to change it.

I excused myself to go to the restroom and when I returned, Brayden told me that instead of calling Hilary to pick us up, he called the hotel shuttle. I threw my arms around him with joy, and told him how happy I was about that! I didn't harbor any anger toward her—I just felt like this was supposed to be *our time* together and I didn't want to spend it with her. I also felt that he was finally paying attention to my feelings without me having to bring it up.

While we waited for the shuttle, we got into a conversation about the game "Rock, Paper, Scissors." I had never played it as a child, which surprised Brayden, so he decided that we should play. We threw the same sign seven times in a row, and each time he would shake his head in disbelief.

"OK, once more." he said.

I was going to throw one sign and then in a split second, I knew that he was going to throw scissors and so that's what I did.

Brayden threw scissors too and with a raised voice he said, "That's freaking me out!"

The shuttle arrived and as we piled in, Eddy Grant's song Electric Avenue was blaring on the radio. Brayden pulled my legs up onto his lap and he held me close as we rode to the hotel. There was a true feeling of love and intimacy growing between us and I remember thinking that I just couldn't believe this was all real—and really happening. We walked into the hotel lobby and while we waited for the elevator, Brayden suggested that we play the game one last time. *Yep*, we threw the same sign again.

"OK…that's really freaking me out! *We are not doing that again!*" he shouted.

I had already begun to realize that there was some sort of unique connection between us. I just didn't know what it meant or how to express it in words—it was something that neither of us had ever experienced before.

Up in the room he asked, "What do you want to do next?"

"Let's go to the pool!" I replied.

We changed into our suits and Brayden lay in the sun while I swam. He seemed withdrawn, and nothing I said could coax him into the water with me. I tried to figure out what was going on with him, as he appeared to be sleeping in the pool chair. But I was fairly certain that he wasn't.

Back in the room, it was time to shower and get ready for dinner. But he said that he was feeling sick to his stomach and so he wanted to lie down.

"Would you go to the lounge and get me some milk?" he asked.

"Of course I will."

I returned to the room with two small cartons of white milk and in a pouty little boy voice he said, "I wanted chocolate."

OK, you big freaking 32-year-old baby! I'll get you your chocolate milk. I thought to myself. But said instead, "It's no problem! I'll go back and get you chocolate."

He was feeling too bad to go out to dinner and didn't feel like eating.

"If I order room service, will the smell make you more nauseous?" I asked.

"No, it won't." he replied, "Please go ahead and order something for yourself."

While I waited for dinner to be delivered, we lay in bed and I read the rest of the Bad Cat book to him. We laughed and wiped tears from our eyes as I flipped through the pages. Dinner arrived and Brayden asked for a bite of the mushrooms and some bread. It was that same pouty little boy voice.

"Thank you... that's nice." he said.

The tone irritated me after the ice cream cone and chocolate milk incidents. But then I thought that maybe in some ways, he just needed the nurturing that he didn't get as a kid. Maybe he was testing me to see if I was capable of giving it to him. It sounds childish, but we all need certain things from our relationships, and maybe that's what he needed from me. It was the whiney, pouty voice that I wasn't sure I could live with. But if that was the worst of it, then I might be able to.

The next day I made coffee and brought him a cup before straightening the bed, just as I had the morning before. There was a look in his eyes as if it meant something to him—like it was special and a big deal. It was our last day together, and we lay back down on the bed with him propped up against the headboard. I was laying on my front facing him when he said that he just wanted to lay there and look into each other's eyes. It seemed strange to me and I felt uncomfortable, but he just gazed at me deep in thought.

"Ask me to marry you..." he said.

"I'm too old fashioned—you have to ask me."

But he didn't.

"Where would we live?" he asked.

"I was upfront with you the first night that we met. I don't want to leave Oregon."

"What about California?"

Brayden had grown up in the cold and rain of Scotland and he wanted to live somewhere warm and dry. "I told you that I didn't want to leave Oregon."

"OK," he conceded, "I'll sell my house and move to Oregon because you're perfect except that one of your nostrils is bigger than the other!" he laughed.

"One of yours is bigger too!" I countered.

He pulled out his camera phone, put it under his nose, and took a picture of his nostrils.

"You're right, it is!" he agreed, laughing.

Brayden went into the bathroom to take a shower and returned several minutes later.

"Room service called while you were in the shower and they referred to me as "Mrs. Loch. Little do they know that I'm only the mistress." I mused with a slight sense of delight and discomfort.

"Mrs. Loch, would you please pour me another cup of coffee?" he replied.

Later that morning Brayden played some songs on his computer while we got dressed. An Eric Clapton song came on and he said that we couldn't be together if I didn't like Clapton.

"Actually, this CD is in my car and I love his music."

The next morning, it was still dark outside when we got ready to leave for his flight. The early morning sky was still sprinkled with stars, and just beginning to change from midnight to dark electric blue. When we arrived at the small, private airport, Brayden still had a few flight checks to run through, so I went into the lobby to get a cup of coffee. He finished his paperwork and then the ground crew began to fuel the jet. The air was warm, but with a faint bite of cold from the early morning. The metallic hum of jet engines started up in the background and the horizon began to glow in shades of pink and yellow. As Brayden walked me back to the car, he was feeling playful—more playful than I wanted to be in an airport parking lot that must be monitored by security cameras. But he was hard to resist and I wasn't sure how long it would be before we would see each other again. Before he turned to leave he wanted me to take a picture of him with my camera phone as a keepsake.

Is this all really happening to me? I thought to myself. *Have I finally met the right man at the right time? It's all beginning to look that way, although I'm still afraid to believe it.*

A couple of days later I was on my way to work when I got a call from him.

"Hello!" I answered cheerfully.

"Julie—are you sure you want this?" he asked, his voice determined with an edge of urgency,

"Because I'm afraid that I'm going to wake up and it's all going to be a dream."

The way that he said it was so poetic and loving, that I almost expected it to be another one of his jokes. But this time he wasn't laughing.

"Yes, I'm sure that I want this. What we have is real and I know that I want this with you."

"Julie, I don't mind selling my house to move to Oregon, but I can't take a loss on it."

"Brayden...I want you to know that I really appreciate the sacrifices that you're willing to make so we can be together. We'll figure it out. I love you."

"I love you too Julie."

"Do you realize that I almost went to Mexico instead of Florida? And then we would have never met."

"If you had gone to Mexico, somehow I would have ended up there—I'm certain of it."

*"I don't have walls to keep other people out. . .
I have walls to find out who will climb over them."*

~Unknown

7

My 40th birthday was approaching, and I asked Brayden if he would fly up for the big celebration. He apologized, explaining that he had a cruise to Mexico booked that same week. I was disappointed and in some ways felt that he should cancel it to be with me—even though I knew it was unreasonable to expect. He suggested that I join him on the cruise, and as much as I wanted to, the party had been planned for months and there would be several others celebrating birthdays as well.

But as the time drew nearer, people began to dictate to me who I could invite and I had had enough of it. I called Brayden to tell him that I would join him on the cruise. I was confused when he back peddled and tried to talk me out of it. It had been only days earlier that he was insistent that I come with him. I knew there was something more to it than he was telling me, and wondered if he was taking his wife, or some other woman.

"Are you taking your wife?" I asked.

"No, of course not!" he insisted. "How could you even suggest that? I'm going with some buddies and what am I supposed to tell them? That I just met "the one" so I'm bringing her with me on our guy's trip?"

I thought it was a reasonable excuse, *but I didn't buy it.*

Timing can be a pretty interesting thing. When I first met Brayden and he told me he was separated, he added that the relationship had been bad for a year and a half. I just assumed that they weren't living together. In a recent conversation though, he went on to explain a few reasons why he had to stay in the marriage a little while longer. His reasons were completely understandable and valid.

He said that he didn't want to complicate things by getting a divorce yet, because he and Janis were still friendly.

On September 5, ten days before my birthday, I got a call from a restricted number.

"Hi this is Julie," I answered cheerfully.

"Hi, this is Brayden Loch's wife."

A wave of shock washed over me. My face went flush and I wasn't sure how I was going to handle this. But I knew if she was calling me, it couldn't be good. There was no time to gather my thoughts.

"I saw your number on *my* phone bill. How do you know Brayden?" she asked calmly.

In a split second, I had to decide if I was going to cover for him, or tell the truth. Maybe he hadn't been truthful to me. My heart was pounding and I didn't know to respond.

"I met him in Key West." I replied, adding nothing more.

"What did he tell you about our marriage?" she asked.

"He told me that you were separated and that things had been bad for about a year and a half."

Long silence.

"Hey—I'm really sorry! I thought that your marriage was on the rocks and you were separated. My father was a pilot and he cheated on my mother through their entire marriage. If I had any idea..."

"Well, in all fairness to Brayden, our marriage *has* been on the rocks for the last year and a half. Boy, I sure am going to hear it from him when he gets home!" "You know, you're not the only one that he's been calling though. There are a couple of others and one of them, he's been talking to for over a year. He tried to convince me they were just friends, and I was stupid enough to believe him."

She left a long silent pause for me to react harshly, but I didn't.

"You know, Brayden's a player and a serial cheater. He cheated on his first wife, too, and that's why that marriage ended. I don't know what you're going to do with him, but he can do whatever he wants to in about three months when I divorce him."

She paused again to give me time to say that I was done with him, but I said nothing.

I began to relax as I processed her calm tone, and what she was saying to me. I thought it was strange that she would say "In all fairness to Brayden" and that she was really going to hear it from him for calling me. That was definitely not what I would have said to the woman who I was confronting about having a relationship with my husband. *Why is this woman calling me anyways if her marriage is over?* It was a brief exchange, but I suddenly got angry that I must not have gotten the whole story from him. He was talking to other women, but we had only just met— so I understood that. But to be put in a position to get a call from his wife upset me. *Her phone bill? They must still be living together.* I allowed myself to get wound up by the call.

After watching my parents' marriage, fidelity was very important to me, and now I was the other woman. Still in shock, I called and left a message for Brayden.

My voice cracking and angry, I said, "I just got a call—*from your wife!* Maybe you're not the honorable person I thought you were! How could you do this to me? How many other women are you seeing, Brayden?"

An hour after I hung up, I realized that I overreacted. I called again but he didn't answer, so I left him a message explaining that I felt that I had overreacted, for which I apologized. Over the next couple of days I called several more times, but still no answer. I knew he would be afraid to speak to me, and now my relief that he had told me the truth about their marriage was mixed with frustration.

As much as I didn't like the idea of him seeing other people, I also knew it wasn't realistic to be in a long distance relationship and expect that he wouldn't. He was a young, good-looking guy and we lived on opposite ends of the country. Besides that, we had only physically spent five or six days together and it was far too early in our relationship to expect it of him. I found it curious that I didn't feel threatened by the thought of other women. Instead, I became aware of a calm, confidence I had in our connection. If our relationship was so vulnerable that it couldn't withstand the distance and other people, then maybe it wasn't what I believed it to be.

I decided that it may be a good time to pay a visit to my psychic friend Margie. I wanted my eyes to be wide open, and not delusional about my relationship with Brayden. I didn't get specific with her about what Janis had told me, but her messages were reassuring.

Then suddenly, out of nowhere when she said, "Brayden's not a player and he's not a serial cheater."

I was dumbstruck! They were the exact words that Janis had used to try to turn me against him. Margie also clearly answered a question that I had tossed around in my mind. Although I didn't believe it, I did still worried that Brayden might be playing me. But I believed her and it was validation that no matter how it may appear on the surface, he wasn't the man that Janis told me he was.

The night before he was to leave for his cruise, he sent me an e-mail.

To: Julie Hopper   September 8, 2006
From: Brayden Loch
Subject: Hey!

Hi there, sorry I havn't called or written to you before now, I guess I've just had a lot to think about recently. I would like to adrss a couple of things frist...

As far as me seeing other women, You know I had seen one other woman there are no others, This was Janis's way of getting to hurt you and me. The "get out of Jail free card" lol..I didn't think I would have need for it, but if you think I do I would love to use it...If I still can?

I do miss you, and I would love to talk and get this all cleared up..I will call you either when i get back from Vacation or during...If you wan't to work through this please reply to this e-mail as Janis has the password for my phone (family plan). Sorry about the trouble and hurt I and this may have caused you...Please let me know what you would like to do..

Love,
Brayden.

To: Brayden Loch   *September 8, 2006*
From: *Julie Hopper*
RE: *Hey!*

   Of course I want to talk to you and work this out. The sooner the better! I have a party tonight, but you can still call me. (tied up with clients right now) I hope that we can talk before your trip.
   I have news for you, I'm sure that she has access to your e-mail too, so set up a free yahoo, will you? I miss you and you better plan on making this up to me BIG TIME.

I love you!

Julie

Later, I began to realize that Janis's call and our near break-up had changed things. Brayden called less frequently. When we did talk, it seemed like meaningless banter. He kept the conversations light, but they always seemed to revolve around me complaining that we didn't talk to each other enough, and that we needed to see each other. Janis had gotten into his e-mail and that was another problem.

   I don't know how he convinced me that it was OK, but he said that he had smoothed things over with her, and needed to keep her happy until he got things settled so he could get a divorce. The dynamics of their relationship were strange to me, and it didn't make sense. With the 18-year age difference between them, it was almost that of a mother figure who knew all along that the relationship would never last. Maybe I shouldn't have been so understanding, but the reasons he gave me for staying in the marriage a little longer did make sense to me. He had numerous opportunities to lie to me, but it turned out that he was always telling me the truth. *Although often leaving out very significant details.*

Brayden often dropped off the radar suddenly and without warning. No calls, no reply to my e-mails, and then he would suddenly re-surface and act as though nothing was unusual. It frustrated me to no end. But I believed that among other things, the synchronicities with our cars and the other pilot were signs that I shouldn't give up on him, that there were unseen forces at work in our meeting. I was convinced that we were supposed to be together, even though red flags were going up everywhere.

The idea popped into my mind one day to see if Brayden was on Myspace. Although I didn't realize it at the time, my spirit guides had begun to give me clear guidance that would help me to understand the mystery of him. I entered his e-mail address in the search for people section, and there he was! My heart sank at the thought of what I might find, but I needed to know who I was dealing with. He had five friends and they were all women. His profile said that his relationship status was a swinger and his religion was Scientology. OK—it sounded like a joke. But as I read the "About Me" section I was shocked. The description was unbelievably vulgar and I wasn't sure what to think. Again, I was faced with: *Who am I really dealing with here? Maybe I just need to run in the other direction.*

I asked him about it the next time that we spoke.

"Oh…I set up that account with another guy who I had a falling out with. He had the password and must have written that to get back at me." he replied.

I thought that it was a pretty lame excuse and I didn't buy it whatsoever. He added that he hadn't been on that website in a long time, and he gave me his password to look at his messages while he booted up his computer. I logged on and it appeared that he was telling me the truth. When he pulled up the website, he reacted as if surprised by what was on it.

"What if Mikala finds you on there and sees that?" I asked with concern.

Brayden deleted the "About Me" description and changed some of his stats. But I was still left wondering what to think of it all.

Our relationship was getting exhausting and it had only been a few months. I was having to defend Brayden to the people around me, which made it even more exhausting. My friend who I had gone to Seattle with told me that I was no longer allowed to say his name around her. And I really hadn't even talked to her much about him. One of my biggest faults is being an open book with my life, and it was a huge mistake. His actions didn't fit the mold of a man who seriously cared about me, and my friends thought he was a player. But as much as I didn't understand his behavior either, intuitively I somehow knew the essence of him at his core. Initially I would react to the things he did because I'm human. But afterward, I would process everything and the pieces would fall together. I seemed to instinctively understand behavior that should make no sense to me.

Knowing Brayden's background and what he had gone through as a child, I came to understand why he had written that vulgar "About Me" story. I believed that he just had a really dark day and decided to let all of his pain pour out of him. I was also certain that I had gotten some significant insight from the story, that there may have been a lot more to his childhood than he shared with me. I now believed that his mother probably had some involvement with drugs when he was growing up, there may have been a lot of men in and out of the house; and it was very likely that Brayden had been the victim of sexual abuse.

I did reality checks on myself constantly with my girlfriend, Kate, to make sure that I wasn't just imagining things, or making excuses for him. Kate was one sharp gal, but she also had it tough growing up. There was sexual abuse in her background as well, so when I explained my theories about his behavior, she agreed that it made sense to her. But I knew if I was going to be in this relationship, then I needed to continue to keep my eyes wide open, and be willing to walk away at any moment.

Brayden had explained his relationship with his Myspace friends: three of them were women who he had worked with, and I could see by their occupations that was true. The fourth was one of the "sex girls," that troll the website for men to chat with for money. And the fifth he claimed that he didn't know. We still had no exclusive agreements about our relationship, but I wanted to know if he was being truthful with me, so I sent her a message, and she replied confirming that she didn't know him. People often "collected" friends they didn't know on Myspace, and I was relieved to learn that he had been truthful with me.

As the weeks slowly passed, I began to gain a greater understanding of him, and why he would disappear, or pull back when we started getting close. I thought the incident with Janis suddenly made him realize that his feelings were getting dangerously strong for me; and if something like that happened again, I might abandon him like his biological father did when he was a kid. My theory began to add up and it would also explain why he was crying that night before I got to Wichita, saying that he just wanted to be loved. Kids are sponges and we carry our fears and issues into adulthood.

His father abandoning the family was hard enough for a little boy. But his mother was struggling to survive, and remarried a man who was physically and mentally abusive. There was far too much stress with the poverty and abuse to have a happy home. And his mother who was the one person in the world who was supposed to love and protect him, stood by while her new husband beat the hell out of him and his brother. I didn't know her, but in some ways I understood that she was a woman without resources trying to keep food on the table and a roof over their heads. It wasn't a decision that I would have made—but I had never been in that position, and had no idea of the struggles she had been through.

I went to see Sophie and Margie periodically to get any additional insight they could share on the situation. Margie cautioned me about his "dark side," but always added that I shouldn't give up on him.

"You and Brayden will have a real marriage, and be very happy together. Unlike so many who may love the person they're with, but are merely co-existing."

Sophie would talk about how strong his feelings were for me, but in the same breath say that he was just "a player." Her readings would be discouraging, but she would also give me clear insight into what he was feeling at the moment.

These were two psychics who frequently told me independently that the very same thing would happen. But now, their opinion of his motive differed slightly. Yes, what Sophie sensed was true. He was being a bit of a player because I knew he was seeing other women. But I had accepted that as a reality until he was divorced, and we were living in the same state. I felt that my intuition about him was growing stronger, as was the guidance from my own spirit guides. So I proceeded cautiously, frequently doing reality checks on myself to make sure that I wasn't in denial about what his motives really were.

Still, Brayden's disappearing had put a constant strain on our relationship. In a phone conversation, I asked him why we weren't talking more often. His reply was that when he talked to me, it made him miss me more. I knew in a sense that may be true, but it was also more about repressing his feelings for me and keeping me at just the right distance so he didn't lose me, or lose control of his feelings. As long as he was distracted by other women, he wouldn't be as focused on me. And he had been a little too active on his Myspace account for my liking. The women that were on there before we met were clearly people that he knew from work with a couple of exceptions. But suddenly he had a few new friends on his site and the women were really attractive. I may not have felt that they were threats to our relationship, but it didn't mean that I had to like it either. We were still long distance and I didn't feel that I had the right to confront him—or that it was realistic to ask him for a commitment. I would rather not have one than to be disappointed that he didn't honor it.

One of the women had a photo of herself behind her laptop, concealing her nude body. She had posted a comment on his site about her missing "her devil." I didn't put it together right away, but she was making reference to one of his tattoos. It was obvious to me that she had slept with him and worst of all, she was the one with all of the slutty photos. Although things like that spun me out, I knew without question that the other women weren't a threat to what we had. I sent him an e-mail telling him that he keeps filling his life with empty people, so that he doesn't risk his heart with someone that he could really love, but he didn't reply.

To: Brayden Loch   *October 28, 2006*
From: Julie Hopper
Subject: This isn't working for me anymore

   No matter how I try to understand and justify this...It's not the way that people that love each other behave. You tell me that you love me, but your actions are telling me that you don't. I can handle your circumstances...but you're keeping me at arm's length and I feel like I'm on an emotional roller coaster. When I told you that not talking to you made me miss you more...Not true. It makes me question us and casts doubt on the relationship.
   Aside from yesterday because you weren't able to call me, I can pretty much count on that if you do tell me that you are going to call (which is rare) that you won't. Hmmm what would you think? E-mail hasn't been reliable and you don't seem to want to correct the phone situation...Where does that leave us?
   I'm not asking you to be in this with me anymore and that's what I feel like I've been doing. If you do want this...let's find a solution, but if you don't, let's just walk away now. I don't want to be checking my e-mail for the next two days to see if you're in or out, so if you want this...I really need to hear from you today OK?

Julie

He left a voice mail for me that same day, and I could hear the panic in his voice.

"Hey Julie it's Brayden. I just got into town and I have to take a quick hop to New York, but I think I'm coming back..." Big sigh. "...tonight. I'll give you a call a little later. OK?"

When he called, I let him have it. I told him not to call me anymore—*I had finally had enough.* He said that he wasn't going to stop calling me but somehow as usual, I got sucked right back in and we started the cycle all over again. I left a voice mail for him and he e-mailed me back saying that he was in New Jersey and that I was acting like a princess. We had an uncanny knack for getting on e-mail at the same time. Either he or I would send an e-mail and the other would immediately respond.

To: Brayden Loch   *November 2, 2006*
From: Julie Hopper
Subject: Phone

The prince better start acting like one and get a freaking phone! Before the princess goes wicked witch on his ass and turns him into a toad! Then they lived happily ever after......

"Are you calling me a freaking toad?!"

"You have a few warts...So what?...You're still pretty cute."

"I'll pop a cap in your frog kissing ass!"

"I double dare you!"

"I physically challenge you!"

"You want a piece of me? Come and get it baby!"

"Do you have messenger?"

Messenger:

"Are we just not going to talk to each other by phone much until your situation changes? I kind of like the idea of a man that can't wait to talk to me..."
"i can't...I miss talking to you"
"So...why do I feel like a broken record asking for something that you want, but don't make an effort to change? I feel like I'm 20 and begging some guy to call me."
"cause cd are in now...not records"
"I have a couple of theories about you Brayden Loch...I'm hoping that it's the one that I like the best, but if you don't keep the plant watered, it won't grow any flowers..."
"ok i'm waiting"
"Serious"
"ok tell me"
"What..My theories? Acknowledge that the plant needs water first....I have to step away again for a minute"
"cactus does'nt...."
"I'm not a cactus....I need LOTS of water...I'm a water lilly"
"Are you up for that?"
"thinking...thinking...thinking..."
"ok"
"OK what?"
"i'm ready"
"Ready for what?"
"the theories"
"No...still need to know if you're a gardener, or prefer cactus"
"gardeners like cactus"
"Then you might need to look to another state....we like it lush and green in Oregon"
"i know that ut gardeners like all foilage....even cactie"
"I'm no cactie...so better to know if you are looking for that now, than later. That was theory number two...that you would be a cactus farmer"

"no i love lilies"

"and you"

"But can you keep them...or do you just like to look at them as long as you can?"

"both of course"

"no point on keeping them if you can't look"

"OK...well let me tell you that you've missed a few waterings... Theory number one (my personal favorite, but don't want to make assumptions) is that you are trying not to let us evolve to a point that the distance is more painful...That you also haven't decided yet whether or not you are ready to let yourself be emotionally vulnerable to me.."

"that;s very very close"

"are you there"

"Well...let's try to work on that because even though it may make it more difficult...you gots to keep your garden green!"

"you gots to...lmal"

"lmao"

"Yeah, wasn't a type O"

"LOI i know"

"you shoud go to www.gizoogle.com"

Brayden always changed the subject and danced around things. The banter was fun—but it was also wearing thin. There was a fine balance for me between working on the relationship and pushing for the fix too quickly. I felt as though things wouldn't change overnight and I needed to be patient. I have tried to explain it to other people by saying that it's like an animal that's been abused. You don't just walk right up and gain its trust no matter how much love you've shown it. It takes time and even then, they will probably never let their guard down entirely. What I needed to decide for myself was how long should I wait for him before making the decision to move on with my life. "Is he damaged or broken?"

Brayden told me the company that he was working for was shutting down and he was having a hard time finding a job that would pay anything. It was November of 2006 and he was thinking about taking a job with Aramco, the oil company in Saudi Arabia. It would pay really well and be virtually be tax free, because he would be working outside of the States. I wasn't happy about it, but what could I say? I went to see Margie and Sophie for their opinion. Margie told me that he wouldn't end up going and if he did, that he wouldn't be there long. Sophie said that he definitely would not go. They were both wrong—and I realized then that they could only tell me what was happening at the time of my reading. We all have free will and anything can change.

Brayden and I hadn't seen each other for three months and I told him if he was going to take the job, then we needed to see each other before he left. He said if he took it, then he wouldn't be able to because he had to leave immediately after training. *That was it!* No matter how strongly I believed he felt for me, if he took the job and left without seeing me, then our relationship couldn't possibly mean anything to him. I sent him an e-mail telling him that if he didn't make the effort, then it was over between us.

To: Julie Hopper   November 10, 2006
From: Brayden Loch
Subject: None

Julie.

   Just to let you know, I'm accepting a job in Saudi Arabia. Nothing left to keep me in the US.
   I miss you.

To: Brayden Loch   *November 11, 2006*
From: Julie Hopper
RE: None

    I really don't know what to say...It sounds like you're implying that you would have stayed here for me and yet you've only stayed in contact with me just enough to keep me hanging on, while seemingly having plenty of time for other people.

    I know the kind of love that I'm capable of giving to someone who is able to give me the same in return...I told you in the e-mail that I sent you on Monday where it needed to begin. If you want this, you will have to overcome your fears and we can talk about where we go from here... if that's not what it is, or you can't...then I really do wish you the best with your new job.

"People are born so that they can learn how to live a good life like loving everybody all the time and being nice. Dogs already know how to do that, so they don't have to stay as long."

~ *Unknown child*

8

I believe that people and animals who are dying, sometimes choose their moment of death, whether they consciously realize it or not. I'm convinced that was true for my Kuvasz, Gypsy. She was the most amazing dog I had ever known—120 lbs with medium length, wavy, white fur and big brown eyes; she was as intelligent as she was polite. Her manners and conscious thinking often surprised me—like the time I was pouring a cement pathway through my garden, and she slowly stepped spread eagle over the cement, carefully missing my plants and flowers. *I adored her.*

It was the morning of November 19, 2006, when I noticed that Gypsy didn't seem to be feeling well. Nothing serious, she just wouldn't take her morning treat. But other than that, she appeared to be fine. My mother was living with me, and we both agreed that sometimes dogs get a little sick, just like people do. We were certain that it would pass, and if she wasn't doing better by the next day, I would take her to the veterinarian.

That evening was unusual. I had an overnight party with some girlfriends scheduled, and my mother was supposed to be home early to check on Gypsy. It was rare that one of us wasn't home by at least 6:00;

so when I got a call from her at 9:00 pm telling me that she came home and Gypsy was dead, I was in a complete state of horror and disbelief. A friend rushed me home and I was certain that my mother must have somehow made a mistake. When I ran through the door, Gypsy was lying on the floor, with nothing out of place. I knelt down beside her and stroked her fir, calling her name and hoping that she would wake up, but she wouldn't. She was only nine years old and now suddenly she was gone—*my baby*. I sobbed uncontrollably through the night until there were no tears left—only silent cries. As the empty weeks passed, I couldn't think about Gypsy without breaking into tears.

I've always believed that animals have souls, even before I read about people having near death experiences and seeing their pets in heaven. I remembered watching an animal psychic on TV, and thought I had nothing to lose. I would see if I could find someone who could connect to Gypsy on the other side. I Googled animal psychics and came across Lisa Green. I read some of her testimonials and was sure that she sounded like the real thing. One of them recounted the story of their dog who came through. The woman's husband was a real skeptic. But as Lisa was telling them about their dog, she started to sing a song that the husband had made up, and sang to the dog when he was in the shower. He was a believer after that, because no one could have possibly known about it.

I called Lisa to set an appointment and she asked only for my pet's name. Then she told me to talk to Gypsy in the days leading up to the reading and encourage her to talk to her, which I did. During the reading, Lisa kept saying that she could feel Gypsy's vibration, but she wouldn't come close enough for her to be able to pick her up clearly. I wasn't surprised because Gypsy was very wary of strangers, and I thought she may have even carried that into the spirit world.

"You've got another dog over there," Lisa said.

"Yeah, I have a few," I replied.

"No, this one has quite the personality! Almost like a princess and she's very cocky."

"Oh, I know who that is!" I giggled.

"It's almost like she's as the complete opposite of Gypsy. This dog is small and black, with a, I want to say bitchy attitude," Lisa laughed.

"That's really funny Lisa, because Gypsy was big and white with a very sweet temperament, and Jamaica was small and black with a terrible attitude. My old roommates gave her the nickname '*the princess bitch.*'"

"Do you have a space in your kitchen, or a breakfast nook that your other dog and Gypsy stayed in when she was alive?"

How could she have possibly known that? I thought to myself in amazement. Now I was convinced that she was the real thing. My house in the country sold before I could find a replacement property with an apartment for my mother. We moved into a rental home temporarily, but as much as I loved my dogs, they weren't allowed to roam the house because of the dog hair. At my last place, they could stay in the entry-way on the linoleum. But as it worked out, the breakfast nook worked better in the rental.

Although Lisa had given me very convincing details, she told me that she wasn't going to charge me for the appointment, because she wasn't able to bring Gypsy through. I was disappointed that she didn't have more information to share with me, but she added that I would have contact with Gypsy at some point in the future.

Before we got off of the phone, I asked her a few questions about what she did. She said that she started out as a medium for people but then she gravitated into readings with animals. I asked if she had ever been told what it was like on the other side and she laughed. She said that one woman on the other side, told her "It's not at all like the Catholics believe it to be." As our conversation was ending, Lisa asked me if I had a shed in my back yard with green trim.

"I have a shed, but it doesn't have green trim," I replied.

"Do me a favor," she asked. "Go out there and see what's in there when we get off of the phone."

I went out to the shed knowing exactly what I would find—just some containers of my mother's from when we had moved. I opened the door and saw nothing unusual, and then noticed that Gypsy's bed was on the floor getting wet. I picked it up and underneath it was a book from the 70's or 80's titled *All you can do, is all you can do, and all you can do is enough.*

Wow, that's a long title! It was strange because I had recently told Brayden that I had done all I could do for our relationship. I wasn't sure if it was a message about him, but later I would worry if I was a good enough mom to Gypsy. I didn't have a lot of money—did she get enough treats? Did I show her enough love? I began to wonder if the message could have been about both of them. *But why had God chosen this timing? Why did I have to lose them both at the same time?*

To: Julie Hopper   December 31, 2006
From Brayden Loch
Subject: Mising you!

Merry christmas! I miss you even all the way from Saudi Arabia.....I wish we could talk.I hope you had a great christmas and you have a drunk new year.....lol. would you like me to stop communicating with you?
I can't stop thinking about you hun...I hope we get to talk soon...

Brayden.

To: Brayden Loch   *December 31, 2006*
From: Julie Hopper
RE: Mising you!

I can't stop thinking about you either...I miss you Brayden. I don't want to think about what could have been I want to think about what could be. There are so many things that I wish that I would have said to you...good things. I just felt that we needed to see each other again to share them with you.

I hope that everything is going well for you there. I would like to talk if you want to.

Love,
Julie

⌖

To: Brayden Loch   *January 13, 2007*
From: Julie Hopper
Subject: None

Brayden,
I can't imagine that you could have read anything negative into the reply I sent to your e-mail, so I can only be left to believe that you didn't mean what you said.
Just for the record...what Kayla wrote in that profile was all in jest. You made quite an impression on her and she thinks that you're cool and has referred to you as her "favorite uncle."
Wishing you much happiness in the New Year!

Love,

Julie

⌖

My niece Mikala had decided to set me up with a Myspace account. She filled in all the details adding the phrase, *"No pilots."* I hadn't gotten a reply from Brayden, so as usual, I was grasping at straws trying to understand why he had disappeared again. Even though I knew it was ridiculous to think he would be that sensitive. It was all just so confusing to me—the way he would pop in and then disappear again. I remembered a term that my Uncle used. He would have told me that Brayden was "bouncing the ball." Meaning that Brayden would check in to make sure that I was still receptive to him; then once satisfied, he could safely disappear until it was time to "bounce the ball" again. It made me angry, but I didn't know how to balance drawing the line with him, with losing him.

A couple of nights later, I got my first "message dream" right before I woke up in the morning.

There was no visual, and I wouldn't call the voice or volume clear, but I heard a woman's voice say:

"Brayden wants to take you on a real date."

We hadn't really had an "official" date before and I wanted one.

The next night she said, *"Brayden has been sexually abused."*

The third and last night she said, *"You will hear from him in three days."*

I couldn't remember ever having three dreams in a row that were so much alike, and I believed it was a message. I had also suspected Brayden had been sexually abused as a child, and thought it might somehow be connected to his behavior.

Just as she said, three days later I got a brief call from him, and we agreed to talk on Instant Messaging the coming Friday. I was so anxious to work everything out, that I sent him a few e-mails ahead of time. I knew the messages must have upset him, because he didn't log on to talk to me.

On January 20, he sent me a friend request through Myspace with no message. It was his way of twisting the knife by inviting me to be one of "his girls." He knew that his activity on the site upset me, so months earlier he began using it as a way to lash out at me when he was angry.

"I have no intention of being another one of your play things on Myspace. I value myself far too much to lower myself to that level."

But as angry as I was, I still had this rock solid belief in what we had.

I was becoming both mentally and physically exhausted by our relationship. One day, I laid down on my couch to take a nap. I woke up feeling hungry, so I went into the kitchen to get something to eat. As I rounded the corner, I was shocked to see two dogs identical to Gypsy sitting there looking at me from the breakfast nook. It was her—both of them! But one had sapphire blue eyes and seemed younger, while the other had brown eyes and seemed more of the age that Gypsy was when she passed. But I knew that both of them were her and a rush of emotions swept over me. *How could this be?* I didn't know which one to hug because they both appeared to be her, even though my Gypsy didn't have blue eyes. Overjoyed, I threw my arms around both of their necks. Then the younger one with blue eyes laid her head lovingly on my lap as I continued to hug the other Gypsy. In my mind, I began to wonder why she wasn't hugging me back. At that moment, she put a paw over my left shoulder and I thought, *What happens next?*

I woke up suddenly, realizing that I hadn't moved from the couch. But that was real—*I knew it!* I was more surprised to find myself on the couch than I was to see her.

Months later, I had another visitation dream of a person in spirit form with the same blue eyes. It was then that I realized that the younger of the two was her spirit body. If she had come only in that form, I would have questioned if it was really her. But years later, the two of them would provide significant validation for a friend of mine, having her own experience.

"Follow your heart and not your fears. . . .
because your heart is most often right."

~Julie Hopper

9

Weeks had passed since my last contact with Brayden; and my logic was in a constant battle with my intuition over his behavior and frequent disappearing. Aside from his Christmas e-mail from Saudi Arabia, I was the one who always opened the door to communication. Yet I still believed that the Universe intended me to be with this man and it was only his deep fear of love that kept us apart.

He said that he would only work in Saudi for a year, but the economy was tanking and if he did well, I knew that he might stay. I had to ask myself if I would risk the real estate career that I had established for someone whose behavior was so erratic. Not to mention the idea of living in a country where I had no rights as a woman and wasn't even allowed to drive a car. It was late February when I felt a strong push to call Brayden.

He answered, "Hello?"

" Helloooo…"

"Julie?" I could hear happiness and relief in his voice. "It's so good to hear from you, hun! I can't believe you called! I'm in the shuttle on my way to the airport, so I can't talk long. I miss you terribly—and it's so good to hear your voice!"

"It's good to hear your voice too…I miss you."

"I miss you too, Julie. I miss you so much!" he added. "I'm going to Paris on Monday for ten days of training. Will you come with me?"

"I would love to, but money is tight right now and I really can't afford it."

His voice still filled with excitement, he replied, "I'll split the cost of the ticket with you and pay for everything else. The company gives me a few thousand to spend while I'm there, so you don't even need spending money."

"Well, that's pretty tempting! OK, I'll price tickets and call you back later. I love you, Brayden…."

"I love you too, hun…."

Although he was willing to share the cost of the ticket, I knew a last-minute airfare to Paris had to be spendy. The timing was bad, but if I didn't go—it was a decision that I might regret it the rest of my life.

Once I had the ticket lined up, I called Brayden to verify the number of days I should book, but he didn't answer. I kept calling every hour—but still no answer and there was no time to wait for e-mail. I was supposed to get on a plane in just a few days, and suddenly he had disappeared again. *What should I do? I haven't firmed things up with him, but I know what hotel he's staying at. Do I still go blindly without talking to him first? This is crazy! Has he changed his mind and was afraid to tell me? I'm going!*

To: Brayden Loch   *March 3, 2007*
From: Julie Hopper
Subject: I'm booked!

I get into Paris at 9:50 am on the 6th. I've been trying to call you, but your cell has been down and although I left a message at your house, I wasn't sure if you had long distance there to call me back. I'll try you again tonight.

I'm so excited! I can't wait to see you!

Julie

On the flight to Paris I met Heather White, a bubbly thirty-something from Portland, Oregon, with big hazel eyes and a wide smile. We connected with each other instantly. She was on her way to Cincinnati for business, and we got into a long conversation about life and how the universe works. I told her that I was on my way to see Brayden in Paris, as well as some background on us and how we met. As she departed from the plane, I said good-bye and handed her my business card.

I arrived at Charles De Gaulle Airport at 10:00am, and kept telling myself over and over again, *He better be here.* I caught the shuttle to the Airport Hilton, remembering that I reminded Brayden in an e-mail to be sure to register me so they would give me a key to his room. I was exhausted from the trip and walked in to find the bed had been made. I knew that it was too early for maid service, and thought about how considerate it was of him to make the bed for me. There was a note on the table that said:

"Julie, there's a VIP lounge upstairs, and a pool and steam room on the lower level. I'll be back around 5:00 pm. Brayden"

That was pretty short and to the point." I thought to myself. *Oh well, we'll see how he is when he gets to the room.*

I fell asleep for the next several hours, waking up just in time to take a shower and get ready for his arrival. My excitement and anticipation quickly grew into impatience and annoyance, as the time passed from 6:00 to 7:00 pm. I still wasn't sure what to think about Brayden inviting me to Paris, and not speaking to me before I left or bought my ticket. Now he was two hours late, and hadn't given me the courtesy to call and let me know that he was going to be late.

Aggravated, I was getting ready to go to the lounge for a drink when I heard a knock at the door. When I opened it, I saw those big, beautiful green eyes standing in front of me with an armful of books and a couple of beers. It had been six months since I had seen him, and I felt caught off guard.

My previous thoughts spilled out of my mouth without thinking and I said, "I thought you were going to be here two hours ago"

"It's 5:00, just like I told you." he replied.

When I glanced back to the clock with military time, I was embarrassed that I miscalculated the time. But even more embarrassed that my first words to him were so sharp. I threw my arms around his shoulders, kissing him as I pulled him into the room, hoping to distract him from my mistake.

As we made love, he became vocal in an exaggerated way, saying several times he was about to come.

"Just kidding! I'm too tired!" he laughed.

Did he just say that? I thought to myself. *We're making love for the first time in months and you're making a joke in the middle of it?* I didn't know what to think, but suddenly I found myself repulsed, and emotionally detaching from him.

We ordered room service and sat side by side on the bed with the dinner tray in front of us. I still didn't know what to think about what he had done, but I didn't want to question him our first night together. I remained quiet in my own thoughts, replying to his light conversation only when necessary.

When dinner was finished, Brayden went into the bathroom and called back to me, "You've already got your razor in the shower!"

As though I was invading his space, but there was no malice in his tone. He reappeared from around the corner with a large and small bottle of Oil of Olay and held them up to show me.

"Look, we have the same lotion," he said with a grin.

I wondered if he had noticed the synchronicities between us all along, and was pointing yet another one out. His demeanor seemed to fluctuate between casual and meaningful; as though he didn't know which direction to go.

The next morning, I opened my eyes to see Brayden standing between the bed and the bathroom, brushing his teeth. He had been watching me while I slept and when he realized that I was awake, he quickly ducked back around the corner. I knew he must have been watching me for quite some time, because he had done that before in Wichita and Houston. He called to me from the bathroom and asked if I would get dressed and come to breakfast with him. Although I still had jet lag and wanted to stay in bed, I reluctantly agreed. I made coffee and I brought him a cup before getting into the shower. I always sensed that small gesture was so meaningful to him—just as it was when we were last together.

Downstairs in the dining room, the hotel restaurant had a huge buffet with all of the foods that I loved about Europe. Fresh untoasted bread, cheese, cured meats and just about everything else that people from around the world might want for breakfast. After we filled our plates and sat down, I noticed him scrutinizing what I had on my plate. As if he was trying to figure me out by what was there. Scrambled eggs, potatoes, sautéed mushrooms, grilled tomatoes, a little brie, prosciutto and fresh mango. I did wonder why he was so curious about it, but these are the little things that tell you about another person.

When we got back into our room, Brayden told me in a *"I have to do my job woman"* tone of voice not to be upset that he couldn't be with me the whole time because he was there to train.

I almost giggled as I asked, "Where's the train station Brayden?"

His expression went blank, as though he suddenly didn't know how to respond and I had just ruined his big moment. So I softened my tone and explained to him that I knew the city because I had been there when I was younger. I had traveled for two months through Europe and I would have a great time on my own. He gave me spending money and I was off!

Before I left for Paris, I told my friends who hadn't been there before that it was overrated. But after a day of wandering around the streets of that beautiful city, I realized it wasn't overrated at all. What I hadn't experienced previously though, were all of the Gypsies. As I rode the train into Paris from the airport, I saw graffiti written all over the buildings that line the tracks, and muddy Gypsy camps with travel trailers everywhere. But they also frequented the passenger trains as strolling musicians; playing the violin and accordion, or singing for loose change—that part I liked.

After an amazing day of walking around and absorbing the sights and sounds of Paris, I went back to meet Brayden in our room. He asked me how my day was and I replied that I had a wonderful time! His expression turned to that of disappointment, as if I was supposed to be dependant and lost without him. Inside though, it made me smile a bit. Although he didn't ask for it, I gave him the change left over from the spending money he had given to me earlier that morning. I could have kept it, but I felt that he was being generous in the first place, and keeping it wouldn't be right. He would give me another $100 the next day—more than enough for lunch and tickets.

We ate dinner that night in the VIP lounge, which was much like the one in Wichita when I met Brayden there: a generous, gourmet appetizer selection, with complementary cocktails. But I was growing tired of having eaten there or room service every time I met him. *Where was my real dinner date that we hadn't had yet?*

The next morning I made coffee and straightened the bed as usual, and as he watched me, he had the same look of appreciation on his face. When we walked into the dining room for breakfast, a very handsome man around 60 with white hair and mustache looked up with a wide grin, as though he knew Brayden. It was Jess—another pilot for the oil company who was also there training and his wife. In Saudi Arabia, unless you're hired full time, your wife can't go with you, so she met him in Paris while he trained. Brayden introduced us and we sat down at the table next to them. There was just something about Jess that I connected with, and I could sense that he felt it, too.

After another day of absorbing the sites of Paris, I returned to the room expecting another evening in with hotel food. The city was a 20 to 30 minute train ride away, and Brayden had to study in the evenings. I was pleasantly surprised when he walked into the room and said that someone recommended a little village to him that was close by with two good restaurants. One was Chinese, and the other French. I hadn't been to a nice, French restaurant before and after all, we were in Paris and it was our first "real date."

We began to get ready for dinner and I pulled out my dress slacks.

"Oh please don't wear those! I don't want to get dressed up!" he protested.

So I slipped on my expensive pair of jeans, with a low cut black dress shirt and a pair of heels. I saw him glancing at me from the corner of his eye. His body appeared ridged—as though he didn't want me to know that he was watching me. I turned to him and asked if he thought that my blouse showed too much cleavage, but he wouldn't look at me directly. He just mumbled and didn't answer. I was annoyed that he couldn't answer a simple question. But when I thought about his strange reaction, I realized that I may have been sparking an emotion that he didn't want to surface.

This would be the first time out of the hotel together since I arrived. It was March and the nights were cold. We each pulled our black leather jackets from the closet and he looked at mine as if intrigued by it.

He stroked the leather of my coat slowly and said, "The leather feels the same as mine."

I thought what he said was strange, but then I remembered earlier when he pulled out our matching bottles of Oil of Olay. He not only recognized the similarities between us, but was also pointing them out in a quiet introspective way. We had what seemed to be a psychic connection, and although these were small things, they all added up.

We were just getting ready to walk out the door, when I slipped my Tanzanite and Diamond ring onto the middle finger of my left hand. He looked down at it and then back up at me.

"Is that a fuck you Brayden?" he sneered.

It caught me off guard, so I looked down at the ring and then back up at him. I didn't know how to respond and so I said nothing. I knew in a split second what he meant by it and although his comment and tone was harsh, it made me happy. Brayden was telling me that he wanted to put a ring on my left ring finger, but he knew that he wasn't in a position to because he was still married. To him, it was as if I was rubbing it in. What he didn't know, was that I used to joke to people that I wore my ring on my middle finger as an eff you to the guys who loved me, but weren't ready to marry me. Brayden had never heard that story though.

We slid into the hotel shuttle and drove to a small French village in the countryside. As we stepped out of the van, the air was crisp and we could faintly see our breath. Brayden asked if I wanted to take a walk before dinner and I agreed. He held my hand as we walked through the dark, cobblestone streets. That was one of the things that I noticed about him—he always held my hand or touched me in some way, even when we were just walking through the hotel.

We walked past old stone houses with windows lit up and people settling in for the night. The air was moist and we could smell the scent of burning leaves.

"I miss that," he said.

Brayden had grown up in Scotland where it's much cooler and had been living in warm weather climates. The smell combined with the cold was wonderful and I agreed that I loved it, too. As we walked, we talked quietly about how he grew up. I asked him about the scar on his lip and he explained that he had gotten it when his stepfather had beaten him. That he wasn't allowed to play marbles because it would put holes in his shoes. And that his brother was sent to live with their uncle when he was big enough to defend himself, but he was left behind.

As we continued to walk, we talked about everything but nothing in particular. He said that he may finish training early and if he did, then they would want him to leave on Tuesday. It was now Wednesday and my heart just sank. It would mean that I would have to change my ticket, and we would have less time together.

We arrived at the quaint little restaurant, which appeared to have been a private home at one time. It was obviously a family-owned business, and I believed that the chef and hostess were husband and wife. The dining room was dimly lit and cozy—not much bigger than a large living room, with ornate early French style furniture and white tablecloths. The hostess seated us in the far back corner where it was private and handed us menus. I was relieved to find that they were in both French and English. We decided to order a bottle of wine and

Brayden quickly handed the list to me. I was going to be no better at choosing than him, but he didn't want the responsibility of selecting the wrong wine.

For me it was easier—we wanted red, so I looked for the more affordable bottles that were marked with little red hearts because they were house favorites. I held my hand up slightly to ask that the chef come to our table and pointed to three bottles on the menu, looking back up at him with a question mark on my face. He chuckled and smiled before pointing to one of them. I nodded my head in agreement and the wine came. As the chef decanted it into a glass pitcher, he strained the wine to remove sediment as he poured.

Pretty fancy! I thought to myself. *You don't see that very often—or at least I don't.*

Brayden appeared intrigued by the way I ordered the wine, and seemed to watch my actions very closely. We decided to choose an appetizer, but he didn't like scallops and I didn't like oysters. Anything with wine, garlic and cream couldn't be bad, so we ordered the oysters. When the appetizer came, Brayden insisted that I try them first. As much as he seemed to struggle not to show his feelings for me, he always put me first when we were together, and did all of the gentlemanly things that a man should do for a woman.

The oysters were served with a special tulip shaped spoon, but they gave us only one. He handed it to me and said, "You first."

I scooped the first oyster into my mouth.

"How are they?" he asked with anticipation.

I looked up at him wide eyed, with a closed smile because my mouth was still full, before replying, "Oh my God—these are amazing!"

The next oyster was his, so I passed the spoon to him. It wasn't appropriate that we share a utensil in such a nice restaurant—but I loved it and the way that we passed the spoon back and forth felt intimate. The hostess realized that we were one spoon short and dashed over to the table with a second one. *I was a little disappointed that she brought us another.*

Next came a small lemon sorbet as a palate cleanser, followed by an interesting three item assortment as a starter for each of us. On a small, rectangular, wooden tray, we were each served a half dollar size Quiche Lorraine, a ham and potato croquette, and a tablespoon with the handle bent into a loop, which was filled with some kind of minced meat. It was delicious—but I was fairly certain that I wouldn't have wanted to know what was in it.

This was the first time that Brayden and I had dinner out together, and it couldn't be more perfect. The restaurant was dimly lit and intimate. We were in Paris together for our first real date. As Brayden and I talked over dinner, he frequently reached over the table to touch my hand lovingly. Everything was relaxed, and we were just two people who were falling in love.

Dinner arrived and I had ordered steak medallions with Foie Gras and wine sauce. Brayden's was similar, but without the Foie Gras and with different potatoes. He seemed to be disappointed in his meal, so once he was finished, I offered him the rest of mine. His eyes darted around the room like he wasn't sure we should do that and he didn't want to be caught. So I lifted up both of our plates and quickly exchanged them. What I began to notice about Brayden was that he was overly cautious about his manners and correctness. I knew that it must be self-taught, because I was certain that he didn't learn it growing up in the worst neighborhood in Glasgow. I loved these little things about him and, I had such a high degree of respect for him knowing where he came from, and what he had made of himself.

Behind our table in the area they used to pour drinks, we noticed a little dog with long, white hair and big brown eyes peeking out from a closet. It belonged to the owner and Brayden turned in his chair to try and coax the little dog to our table. The dog looked up at the hostess/owner as if to say "Can I?" She patted her leg in approval and he trotted over to our table to say hello. It was absolutely adorable and something that would never be allowed in the States. I loved that about Europe—*and I loved him.*

The shuttle picked us up and we held each other close as we rode back to the hotel—whispering softly and stealing kisses. In the room, we talked about what an amazing dinner we just had as we began to undress. Brayden took out his contact lenses and put his dark framed reading glasses on, before pulling me close to him. As we began to kiss, his expression changed suddenly. He pushed me to the bed, pinning me down in a playful but forceful way. His grip began to hurt and I asked him to stop, but he wouldn't let me go. My demands grew louder, but he insisted that I kiss him first. I was growing angrier by the moment, and wouldn't kiss him. The situation was becoming borderline serious to me—he must have realized it too because he finally released me from his grip.

He began pacing around the room in his all white underclothes, socks and dark framed glasses. Tapping quickly on his chest with his index finger saying, "I'm the man in this relationship!"

Although just moments ago things had started to get questionable, seeing a grown man march around in his under clothes was almost childlike and cute. I found it humorous and difficult to stay angry with him. He was in the wrong and now he was ranting. I want a man who's "the man" in the relationship. And he was telling me that he was in charge—*even though he wasn't in charge of me.*

More pacing and now he seemed to be reasoning and talking more inwardly to himself saying, "I should have known better than to try to be with someone that I had no business trying to be with!"

OK, I'm starting to get this. I thought to myself. But it didn't change the fact that I was still pissed at him. We had just had this amazing, romantic dinner and it was feeling too good to him, so he decided to sabotage the evening. Somewhere inside, he didn't think that he deserved me—so now he was stomping around the room telling me that he was right about it all along.

Something in him shifted and I began to freak out a little inside; as I watched his personality change to that of the ten year old I saw in Wichita just briefly. A child-like glow comes over his face when it happens, and his big green eyes flash with excitement. He was standing near the bathroom facing me in his white underclothes as he started demanding that I tell him that I was sorry.

He was smiling and he wasn't angry, but then he playfully started jumping up and down like a kid having a tantrum saying, "Say you're sorry! Say you're sorry!"

But I wouldn't.

What I later came to understand is that adult survivors of child abuse can experience Post Traumatic Stress Disorder. You don't know what will trigger it, but they have a self-defense mechanism that kicks in, and I don't think that they themselves even realize it. It just triggers and takes them into a protective place. I had just watched him go through what I believe were four phases of it: first, there was the self-sabotaging of his happiness, then, trying to regain control, followed by justification and blaming someone else for what he himself created. When he had gone through all of the phases, he retreated into a zone where he has complete control and protection over himself. I further recognized that Brayden had the ability to turn off his feelings for me at least temporarily. Although I had always suspected it, the next morning I would fully witness it for the first time.

His mood shifted and he was now angry again that I wouldn't apologize. I may have understood him—but I'm human and reacted to the moment. I went into the bathroom and just sat there on the cold marble floor for a half hour, trying to cry so that I could get my emotions out. I couldn't stay in there any longer, so I changed into a bathrobe and climbed into bed. He was calm now and studying. I was sure that he understood he had been wrong.

"Why are you wearing a robe to bed?" he asked softly with concern.

"Because I'm not ready to take it off yet." I replied quietly.

I began to read a book, but was too distracted by my own thoughts to pay attention. I took off the robe and climbed under the covers with my back to him. A few minutes later he climbed into bed without saying a word, and turned out the lights. I lay there thinking that I didn't want to have hard feelings for the rest of the trip. We were in Paris—the most romantic city in the world. And most of all, I loved him, no matter how crazy he appeared at times. I knew that he self-sabotaged, but he had been doing that since Janis first called me. It was as if he was testing me to see how hard he could push me, and if I would stick around, no matter how difficult it got. It was too dark to see him, so without saying a word I rolled over and straddled him. As I leaned down to kiss him, he grasped my arms with a firm, gentle grip, lifting and pulling me towards him as if I weighed nothing. As he kissed me, it was as though every ounce of passion that he had in his body came through his lips. The intensity of his emotion was unexplainable, and I had never experienced anything like it before.

But the next morning was different; the edge was back and he was turning off those feelings that he had such control over. As he was getting dressed, he walked around the room with a smug look on his face as if I was beneath him. I was lying on the bed watching him and telling myself that he's still just in his protective zone, when he came over and tossed my daily walking around money on the bed in front of me. The way that he did it was as if I was a prostitute, and he was paying me for the night before. I didn't like it, but it really didn't bother me much because I understood what was happening. And I didn't want to ruin the trip by saying anything to provoke him any further. I just hoped that it would pass.

For the first time since we had been in Paris, Brayden didn't hold my hand or touch me as we went down to the restaurant for breakfast. But when we walked into the dining room and sat down next to Jess and his wife, the tension eased because Brayden would never allow that edge to show in front of anyone else. As we ate breakfast, Jess's wife began to complain that she had been redecorating the house and Jess wouldn't help her or give her an opinion. I looked at him and then at her.

With an out stretched hand towards Jess, as though to comfort and defend, I replied, "It's because it's just not important to him."

I could see acknowledgement in Jess's eyes that I was right, and he appreciated it. I think that Brayden did, too, because he was starting to realize that I understood a man's behavior in ways that other women may

not. I had to—because I needed to learn how to think like him in order
to save our relationship.

We went on to talk about the Middle East and how things were
there. I shared some little-known facts about Kurdistan, and they
seemed to be impressed that I would have such insight.

Jess said, "So, Brayden tells me that you're dad was a pilot."

"Yes he was." I replied.

I explained that he was the youngest Captain to date when he
achieved that title, and he did it with a ninth grade education. I added
that my dad used to say he had difficulty hearing the frequency of the
female voice. That brought roaring laughter to the men at the table!
Pilots learn to tune certain things out because of the noise in the
cockpit—my father's reason for tuning out the female voice was obvious.

As we talked, Brayden said something about me being from Seattle.
I looked at him with an expression of disbelief and cocked my head to
the side.

"I can't believe that you just said that!" Pointing my knife in his
direction, I added, "You know that I'm from Portland."

"Portland/Seattle—it's all the same." he said casually.

I was sitting there trying to understand why he would say such a
thing, besides the fact that he was still upset with me. He clearly knew
that I was from Portland.

I thought to myself, *OK... now I get it. You told your friend that I was
just a little piece of something casual that flew in to keep you entertained, and now
he's impressed by me and sees that I have substance. You have to justify what you said
to him before I got here. You're a Jackass!*

It was Jess' wife's last day in Paris and she wasn't comfortable getting
around the city on her own. She had planned to stay at the hotel for
the day, so Brayden decided to volunteer me to show her Paris. I wasn't
too happy about it because Jess' wife was a short, small-framed woman
in her 60s. I liked to move quickly around the city and explore, and
I was pretty sure that she wouldn't be able to keep up with me. But
what could I say? Brayden and Jess left to go to class and Donna and I
hopped the train into the city. We actually had a really nice time together

and she kept up just fine. When we arrived back to the hotel, we decided to have a beer and take a swim.

It was now Friday and while I waited for Brayden to get back to the room, the phone rang. I wasn't sure if I should answer it or not, because he was still several months from being able to file for a divorce. We didn't discuss it much, but I knew that the marriage was more of a roommate situation due to finances, so I answered the phone. It was the pilot whose position Brayden was training to take over, and he seemed anxious to talk to him. Brayden had already told me that the guy was nitpicking everything.

As I spoke with the pilot, he was asking me a lot of questions that I couldn't answer. Had Brayden taken his final? etc. I explained that he would have to talk to Brayden himself. I knew that he was taking his final that day and when he arrived back at the room, he was glowing with excitement. The Chief Pilot was impressed with his flying and he had aced his check flight. He couldn't have been happier as he told me that the approach to the Eiffel Tower was amazing!

I gave him a big hug and kiss as I proudly told him, "I always knew you were a great pilot!"

"Thanks! That means a lot to me knowing that your father was a pilot."

"That pilot whose position you're training for called and was anxious to talk to you."

"What did you say to him?"

"Nothing except that he would need to talk to you, and you would be back soon. He asked if you had taken your final."

"What did you tell him? You didn't tell him that I was taking it did you?"

"No, I didn't say anything."

Hmmm. . ., I thought to myself. *If they want him back on Tuesday if he passes, then why doesn't he want him to know that he did?* My antenna went up.

Dinner was in the lounge again, but Brayden was happy and so I was too. He always catered to me and took great care to make sure that I had everything I wanted. We came back to the room and started flipping through TV channels. Watching South Park in French when you've had a few drinks is pretty hilarious. He flipped onto a nature channel and a shark was just about to eat a seal.

"Turn it! Turn it! I can't watch that!" I pleaded.

Forgetting to turn the channel, Brayden thoughts seemed to shift inward as he replied softly, "I can't either...sometimes I cry."

God I love him! I thought to myself. *Most men would never share something like that.*

Later on, something else about Brayden and animals would stick in my head. He was a big dog lover, but when my dogs would bark in the background he would say, *"Cut that dog's tail off!"* I always thought that it was a really odd thing to say, but never questioned him about it. I began to wonder if something had happened when he was a kid, and if one of his pets was hurt as punishment for him.

Saturday would be our first full day together. I knew that we would probably be having dinner in Paris, so I wanted to wear something that would be appropriate for a nice restaurant. I pulled out my black slacks that were casual enough for day time.

"Ohhh, please don't wear those!" he said. "I don't want to get dressed up. Please wear your jeans."

So I slipped on my nice ones, dress shoes with thicker heels, and a tailored white dress shirt that showed my curves.

He looked at me quickly and then away. He looked back at me and said, "You look beautiful."

It was the first time that he had said that this trip, and it took me by surprise.

The day was sunny and it was borderline as to whether we needed our jackets, so I decided to take mine just in case. As we approached the hotel restaurant for breakfast, he said that he realized that he had forgotten his watch in the room, and would I go up to get it for him? My intuition instantly told me that there was a reason behind it—that he needed the time to call someone while I was away. But what could I do? Our relationship still wasn't on a solid foundation and as much as I didn't like it, at that point I didn't feel that I had the right to question him or make demands. The only question in my mind was if he was still under a pretense of a marriage, or if it was someone else. The only relief that I had was that whoever it was, wasn't calling the room and he didn't ask me not to answer the phone—*that would have been the end for us.*

As we rode the train into Paris, we sat in a booth by the window facing each other, and got into a conversation about the people who stand by the freeway exits holding signs for money. We both agreed that we felt guilty that we may not be giving money to someone who was truly in need, but that a lot of them just needed to get a job.

"There's one woman that I always give money to." I said.

He looked at me with wide eyes, "A woman?" he asked with surprise, because you normally only see men. "Why do you give her money?"

"Because she's old and she looks like she's had a really hard life."

He looked at me with an expression of deep love and affection, and without saying a word, he leaned forward to brush his finger across my cheek. His thoughts seemed to turn inward, as he looked down and lowered his hand to his lap. Turning to gaze out of the window, he was lost in his own thoughts. I wondered if he might have been recalling how hard his mother had it when he was growing up. Maybe he appreciated my compassion.

We got off of the train and our first stop would be the Eiffel Tower. Brayden was in Paris for the first time, and he had promised me that he wouldn't go to the top without me. When I had been in Paris previously, I hadn't gone up and it was a first real "moment in Paris" that we could share together. On one of my earlier excursions, I had stumbled upon a wonderful farmers market near the subway station on the Ave D'Iena, between the Arch De Triumph and the tower. I had seen it featured on the Food Network and was really excited to have found it. So we agreed to walk through on our way to the Eiffel Tower.

There were all sorts of interesting things that you wouldn't normally find at a market in the States, like unusual seafood and every kind of pate you could possibly imagine. We bought some foie gras that we would make part of a picnic the following day, and decided that we would find another market in the morning so we weren't carrying too much while we were site seeing.

As we started back toward the tower, Brayden mentioned that he had been running long distance with an organized group and that he was doing really well. He went on to say that one of his regular running partners was female.

"Is she your girlfriend?" I asked, with the trip to the room to retrieve his watch fresh in my mind.

"No! Why would you ask that?"

"I was just curious."

"We'll, she did just break up with her boyfriend."

Now why the heck did he need to add that? I wondered.

Gypsies in ragged clothes pan handled everywhere. We saw one walking with her foot slid sideways into her shoe as if she was crippled and her ankle bent. But she just wore her shoe that way to make herself look pitiful. I had already figured them out, so I explained to Brayden that if they came up to us and asked if we spoke French or English, to just shrug his shoulders as if he didn't understand them. Minutes later one of them approached us and it worked perfectly.

While we stood in line to buy tickets at the tower, Brayden confessed to me that he and Jess had gone up the day before I arrived. I was disappointed, but reassured myself that it shouldn't be a big deal to me. We watched the people around us as we stood in line, glancing up occasionally at the tower shadowing over us. A couple of gay guys in front of us were making a spectacle of themselves, but things were playful between Brayden and I, so we ended up getting a little cozy in line ourselves.

I reached into his pocket and whispered in his ear, "I wish we weren't so far from the hotel."

"We could find a quiet place close by." he whispered.

I considered it for a moment, but getting arrested for public indecency in a foreign country, didn't sound like a risk I wanted to take.

We spent some time at the top of the tower, scanning the city for different landmarks, and following The Seine River as it wound its way through the city. Maybe I just hadn't been at such a high vantage point in a European city before, but I found it interesting that because Paris was so old and they used the same stone throughout the city, all of the buildings were the same color. The only definition was that coming from the shadows cast from the streets and alleyways.

Brayden made plans for us to have dinner at the restaurant in the tower, but it was still early so we went to the lounge for a beer. He made a quick call to his mother in Scotland and I hoped that he would make a reference to me, but he didn't. After the call, we went into the gift shop where he insisted on buying all of the souvenirs that I wanted for my niece and nephew.

Still too early for dinner, we wandered around the city window shopping and exploring the different neighborhoods of Paris. We had a small bag that held the foie gras, souvenirs and other items that I brought from our room. I always carried a hairbrush because my hair was very fine and looked stringy after a day outside. We traded off responsibility for the bag and then suddenly realized that it was gone. The last time that we saw it was on the subway when Brayden had it. He was angry with himself that he lost the bag, and couldn't seem to get over it. To me it was no big deal because the cameras weren't in the bag and everything else was replaceable.

As I stood there trying to console him, we decided that maybe someone who needed those things more than we did would find the bag.

Still upset but joking he said, "Yeah, it's probably going to be some bald vegetarian from Paris."

Between the look on his face and his comment, I could hardly contain my laughter because the bag contained duck liver, a hair brush, a tourist book, and souvenirs. None of which a bald vegetarian from Paris would ever want or need.

Next we decided to tour Notre Dame Cathedral and although I had been there before, I waited to go inside until I was with Brayden. I loved the stone gargoyles with animated expressions that were perched around the exterior. The interior was just as stunning as I had remembered it to be, with soaring, carved limestone ceilings, and magnificent stained-glass windows. We walked around the cathedral, whispering softly, hearing only the shuffle and quiet echo of footsteps against the stone floors. The Cathedral was dimly lit, except for shafts of white light beaming from the windows, piercing through the veil of incense that hung in the air. The feeling of hundreds of years of history was absorbed into the thick, limestone walls and the atmosphere was other worldly.

As we walked outside, we squinted from the glare of the sun as our eyes adjusted to the light. We were hungry, and in Paris there's a crepe stand on every other block. Earlier in the day we passed one up that didn't have the ingredients that I wanted. I had assured Brayden that the stand next to Notre Dame had absolutely everything. Well—they had absolutely everything except for mushrooms, which was what he specifically wanted. I suddenly felt selfish, but I wouldn't have guessed it because they had everything else imaginable.

In a little boy pout he said, "I wanted mushrooms!"

I apologized to him again because I really did feel bad.

I ordered my crepe and Brayden ordered a hot dog. When he quickly finished eating, I asked him to help me finish mine. It needed to be cut with a knife, so after he made the cuts, he lifted the knife to his mouth, running each side of the blade down his tongue to clean it.

"Did you just lick your knife?" I asked with amusement.

A blush of anger and disappointment with himself washed over his face and he said, "I can't believe that I just did that!"

"It's OK!" I laughed. "If it would be alright to do that anywhere, it would be here."

"No it's not!" he responded harshly, frustrated with himself.

Waiting underground on the train platform, a young guy dressed all in black with dark hair and eyes started pacing around quickly and mumbling to himself. Suddenly he kicked a vending machine hard. He spun around, paused and kicked and punched it as hard as he could for about 30 seconds. He was talking to himself as he looked up and started walking in our direction.

Brayden put his arm across the front of me and pushed me back hard against the wall, whispering firmly, "Don't look him in the eye."

The guy walked past without incident, but it would have only taken a glance in his direction to cause a problem. Being with someone who can protect me was important. Brayden may not have had the physical size, but he had the speed and street smarts. I had no doubt that I was safe with him.

It was dark outside and growing colder as we walked around the city. Brayden didn't bring a coat with him, so as we made our way to the next train station, I wrapped my arms around him and rubbed his arms to keep him warm as we walked. He felt ridged to me, but it wasn't from the cold. I could sense that it wasn't the kind of intimacy and act of love that he was used to. It was strange how I could sense what was going on in his head, although it was also clearly reflected in his body language.

The next morning we got an early start and he was lying across the bed watching me get ready.

"Do you love me?" he asked in a light tone.

I looked at him and said, "I love you, but I'm not *in love* with you."

To me there was a difference, and as much as I knew that he was "the one," he hadn't given enough back to me in order to take my feelings to the next level. He didn't seem surprised by my answer because he had to know that we hadn't gotten to that point yet.

I reminded him to bring his coat this time and we were off for our last full day together. I still sensed his walls, but I was getting used to them. We had been lying in bed the night before reading when I made the comment that I would be glad when his walls finally came down, so we could just start having fun together.

"Walls?... I don't have any walls."

"Oh yes you do. But eventually they'll come down."

He didn't reply.

On the train I noticed a group of young American women in their 20s and I asked them where they were from. They said they were from the States, but their husbands were in the military and they were living in

Germany. They had decided to take a girls trip to Paris and were having a great time. We had a nice conversation and then they asked us how we met.

Not wanting to dominate the conversation, I turned to Brayden and said, "You tell them."

He gave them a quick recap about meeting in Florida when I was on vacation, and then ended it by saying that I left my young niece alone overnight in the hotel room, while I spent the night with him. I was embarrassed and the girls looked shocked. I told Brayden that he didn't need to share that part! I laughed and assured them that my niece was perfectly safe, and added that it all worked out because I knew that Brayden was "the one" the first night that we met.

One of the young women went on to talk about the Gypsies. She said that a female had accosted her on the train because she wouldn't give her any money, and then spit on her. Fortunately when the woman threatened to get physical, a big guy who was watching the situation unfold, pulled the woman off and sent her on her way. She went on to talk about the Arch De Triumph and how they were shocked to see that one of the carvings was of a man with a huge, erect penis.

"Oh, I hadn't noticed it," I said. "We'll have to go back and take a look at it."

Brayden made a joke about not needing to go see the penis to which I replied, "Well… if you've seen one penis you've seen them all."

Now it was my turn to stick my foot in my mouth. Brayden brought that statement up months later and we both laughed about it. Once a remark has flown out of your mouth though, you can't just put it back in. The girls told us that we had to see the Eiffel Tower when they lit it up at 7:00pm and we agreed that we would definitely make a point of seeing it.

At the next stop when they got off the train, we said our good-byes. Brayden and I continued on as I watched an inward look of contemplation appear on his face.

After a few moments, he looked up at me and asked, "If a woman ever harassed me would you defend me?"

I thought it was a strange question for a man to ask a woman.

"You know that I would." I replied. "Would you defend me if someone was harassing me?"

With a penetrating look of conviction on his face and his tone now very serious, he replied, "That would never happen."

Brayden wasn't a big man, but if the situation ever arose, I had no doubt that he would defend me with everything that he humanly had. The more that I thought about the unusual question though, the more I wondered if it may have come out of a remembrance; possibly that of his mother standing by while he was abused by his step father. It made sense—if he was going to trust another person with his heart, he needed to know that I would protect him under any circumstance.

We really didn't have a plan for the day but it was sunny and we knew that we didn't want to spend it in a museum. I wasn't getting much input from him and so I led the way. He had been picking on me and was being mildly argumentative. Earlier in the trip, I e-mailed my girlfriend, Kate, and told her he was acting a lot like an adolescent boy who liked a girl a lot, and so he picked on her. Kate was my rock and through everything, she always listened, never judged, and tried to help me understand what was happening below the surface with him.

I had met her when we were in the manufactured home business together. We weren't close at the time, and then we reconnected when I got into real estate and she became a loan officer. She had integrity and cared about people, but was very smart and strong enough that you wouldn't want to cross her. In many ways we were a lot alike, but she was tall and slender with beautiful, sparkling brown eyes and long dark hair—just a naturally beautiful woman, both inside and out. On the surface, she was a real girly girl with her long porcelain nails. But like Brayden, she didn't have it easy growing up and I think that's why in many ways, she understood him as well as I did.

As we wandered through the streets of Paris, I tried to break the tension by asking Brayden what he wanted out of life and what would make him happy.

"I don't plan my life!" he replied sharply.

I had a choice of how to react, so very calmly I said, "Well...our lives hardly ever turn out the way that we plan them to be." He said nothing as we continued to walk. "You know….you're pushing me away."

"Why would I want to do that?" he asked, defensively with an edge of concern.

I shrugged my shoulders as if to say "I don't know," before replying, "But you are." I knew that he wouldn't behave this way if he surrendered to his love for me but I was helpless to bring down his walls unless or until that happened.

We found ourselves at a shop that had old French photography displayed on the sidewalk. I had been looking for two specific Robert Doisneau prints for quite some time, and hoped to find them. As we separated to look through the different photographs, I was approached by the shop keeper.

He looked over his shoulder at Brayden and asked, "Is he your husband or your boyfriend?

"He's my boyfriend." I replied.

"Well he's very lucky," he said. And he swept his hand from my face, then down towards my feet and told me how beautiful I was.

I smiled at him politely and said, "Thank you. You should tell him that," as I looked in Brayden's direction.

He turned to look at Brayden and then back at me as if to say, "I can't tell another man that."

They say that there are no chance meetings and somehow the right people are put in your path. I believe in that completely although it may not always be obvious at the time. Or, the meeting may be for the other person's benefit. On my outing with Jess' wife Donna, a shop keeper spontaneously gave me a rose. When I got back to the room with it, Brayden asked why he gave it to me. But I said that I didn't know.

I walked over to where Brayden was standing as he was thumbing through the photos. Apparently he had noticed my exchange with the shop keeper.

"What did he say to you?" he asked.

"If you were my boyfriend or my husband." I replied.

"What did you say?"

"That you were my boyfriend."

With a look of surprise on his face, he asked, "Why did you tell him that?"

His question and response confused me. *What am I to him if not a girlfriend?* I thought. But in some strange way I knew that it felt more safe for him to look at me as a close acquaintance than someone he could have serious feelings for. When the man reappeared next to us, Brayden started to struggle as he began to ask him something in French.

"He speaks English." I said, mildly irritated by his last question.

Brayden asked him about the prints and he replied that he didn't have them. Then the shopkeeper leaned in to Brayden's ear and said something in French. Brayden's eyebrows raised but he didn't tell me what was said. I didn't ask—but I had an idea.

We sat down at an outdoor café to have a drink. Brayden ordered a coffee while I had a glass of wine. I could have drank the whole bottle with the way things were going. I could still feel that his walls were up, but I managed to have someone take a photo of us together.

As we continued on, we found ourselves on a long, narrow cobblestone alley. I saw a store with various North African and Middle Eastern items and wanted to go in. Years ago, I dated a Moroccan and I've always been drawn to things that were exotic. The previous shop keeper had also been from North Africa or the Middle East. So with Brayden trailing behind, I walked toward the back of the store. As I passed several men behind the shop's counter, I could feel their eyes follow me while they whispered quietly to each other.

I was examining a small round painted pot when I heard voices raised in unison reacting in an odd way.

As I turned to see what was happening, Brayden walked up to me looking very sheepish and said, "Kiss me."

"Why?"

"Just kiss me now!"

"Why?"

"Because they asked me if you were my wife, or my girlfriend."

"What did you say?"

"I said neither."

I looked at him with an expression of mild anger and confusion at his reply to them. So I playfully shook the pot at him as if he might just find it up the side of his head. He asked me again to kiss him and I figured that based on my reaction, the men behind the counter weren't going to believe that I was nothing to him. So I kissed him. A small roar of approval rose up from behind the counter. I wasn't sure what it was all about, but I let it roll off of me as I frequently did. My later guess was that he was proving to them that he could seduce a stranger. But that guess wasn't my first.

I knew that I wasn't a casual relationship to him—that was obvious to me. So the only reason he could have for these strange interactions with shop keepers was an attempt to know how I truly felt for him without asking. He was testing me and my reactions. Regardless, he was going about it the wrong way, as usual, and I didn't feel like playing his game. I was testing him, too.

Earlier, when I started seeing his activity on Myspace and then all of his appearing and disappearing, I looked something up on the internet about how to spot a player. I had met one or two in my life, and I just wanted to make sure that I wasn't in denial about him. The thing that struck me was that it said a player would be very confident and comfortable in the relationship. That certainly didn't describe Brayden because you could cut the tension with a knife—and yet I still felt this amazing connectedness to him. We often communicated without having to speak and we really didn't even have to make much of a facial expression to know what the other was saying. Even though we had only spent a maybe ten or eleven days together in person.

I wanted to take him to rue Montorgueil, a street that I had been to earlier that I felt was quintessential of what you would expect Paris to be. The narrow cobblestone street was lined with colorful shops that sold everything you might want to put a romantic picnic together—flowers, wine, pastry and cheese. We had lost our Foie Gras, but we were headed to the lighting of the Eiffel Tower later in the day and I wanted to pick a few things up to make it special. It was only 4:30, but most of the shops were already closing down. Brayden sensed my disappointment and in the most tender and loving way, he said that he was sorry that the shops were closed. That would soon change though, as we found the one wine shop that was still open.

He was suddenly disagreeable and wouldn't help me choose a bottle of wine. I struggled as I tried to ask the opinion of the shop keeper, while he stood there with arms folded and the ability to speak some French. Next we needed a little bread and cheese to go with the wine, so I tried to include him in the decision. As we began tasting the different cheeses, I said no to one of them because it was hard like Parmesan. It wasn't one that you would normally eat on its own and so because I didn't want it—*he did.* But as I started to argue, I caught myself and let it go. The shopkeeper uncorked the bottle of wine and gave us two little clear, plastic dessert cups that would work just fine as wine glasses.

"What do you want to do now?" he asked.

"Well—I thought that we would head to the Eiffel Tower and have a picnic if that's not too romantic for you," I replied with mild sarcasm.

"I'm not hungry!" he protested.

"Then don't eat!"

The day was warm and there wasn't much conversation between us as we followed the Seine River towards the Eiffel Tower. I began to complain about my feet hurting and Brayden offered to carry me on his back. He always mixed this combative behavior with the core of who he really was, which was very thoughtful and kind. I told him that I would manage because I was thinking to myself that I probably didn't weigh a whole lot less than him—if any. Finally, I just had to stop and give my feet a rest.

"Are you thirsty, too?" I asked. "Would you mind getting some water while I sit down for a bit?"

Without a word or hesitation, he turned and dashed across the street.

When he returned, he said, "They must have seen me coming." It was 4 Euros (about $6) for the water.

Apparently Brayden had a habit of getting the short end of the deal on things.

We rested a bit and then continued up the Seine towards the Tower. By the time we arrived, it was dusk and the sky was deepening into a dark, electric blue. The grass had become dewy and moist, as the warmth from the day condensed against the cold night air. Without a blanket, Brayden spread his leather jacket out on the ground for us to sit on before excusing himself to find a bathroom.

I didn't want his jacket to get damaged so while he was gone, I moved everything to a bench that was closer to the river. As I sat there and watched the lights of Paris reflect off the water, Brayden jumped toward me playfully from behind to try to scare me, but I caught him first. He slid onto the bench next to me and I suggested that we pour a glass of wine. The tower had just been lit up to a warm, burnt orange glow, and the contrast was striking against the deepening blue sky. We weren't expecting any more than that as we gazed in awe at the beauty of it.

He poured the wine and then set about spreading the cheese and bread out on the bench between us. We each took a little piece and then I realized how cold and breezy it was becoming. I started to ask if we could sit closer but before I finished my sentence, he moved everything to the end of the bench so we sat beside each other. Pulling me close to keep me warm, he began to kiss me softly as a scruffy Gypsy woman suddenly approached us. She was in her early 20s and asked for money. We shook our heads no and then in French she asked for some of our food. I didn't know what she was saying, but I shook my head no and then nodded to the side as if to say move on. She sneered and said something in a nasty tone before skulking away. I asked Brayden what she said and he replied, "She wanted our food and when you said no, she called you a cunt." I looked at him with an expression of shock, and we both burst out laughing.

We sat there talking quietly, stealing kisses and sipping wine as we watched the lights of Paris in the distance. Suddenly the Eiffel Tower began to sparkle and I had never seen anything so beautiful before in my life! We were right at the base of it looking up at this glowing tower of burnt orange against a brilliant dark blue sky, and it looked as though thousands of little diamonds were sparkling all over it. A woman walked by and we quickly asked her to take a photo of us. She only took one and as luck would have it, the photo turned out beautifully.

The cold was becoming unbearable, so we decided to find a place to have dinner. I explained that I had stumbled across a restaurant and shopping district near Notre Dame Cathedral, which was made up of windy, narrow, cobblestone streets, and had just about every type of cuisine that you could possibly imagine. We rode the train to Notre Dame, finishing our wine and acting like a couple of playful, school kids in love. Brayden suggested that we spend some private time in the bathroom and although it was tempting, it was filthy so I shrugged off the idea.

We arrived at the Latin Quarter and explored the lively, narrow streets while looking for the perfect place to have dinner. Brayden asked me what I wanted to eat, and I replied anything but a sandwich or Chinese. I felt like I had been living on sandwiches since I arrived there.

"Hey!" I heard with a loud shout. "Where are you from?"

The voice came from across the alley, but seemed to be directed at us. I looked over and it was one of the doorman who stand outside of the restaurants trying to usher customers in. We were quite a distance away and the alley was crowded with people. So I was surprised that he would be talking to us.

I pointed at myself and he said, "Yeah, you!"

I called back, "I'm from Oregon!"

As we paused for just a moment we heard, "I'm from New Jersey!"

Why did this person suddenly decide to share this with complete strangers? I thought to myself. *And why us? When there were so many other people milling around much closer to him?*

I called back to him again and said, "You're from New Jersey and hawking food in Paris?"

"Yes!" he replied with a shrug, shaking his head in agreement.

I waved to him with a smile and we continued on. Brayden was quiet and the exchange seemed to puzzle him. I was getting a lot of attention while in Paris, but I don't think that was what it was about. He had been fascinated that I could have a conversation with a complete stranger. Like the guy from the sports station in Wichita that he put on the phone. And now I was talking to more complete strangers, including the girls on the train. I think that he loved my self-confidence because as I would later come to realize, his self-esteem had been pretty much destroyed by his upbringing, although to meet him, you would never guess it.

I'm a big foodie, so I wanted to read all of the restaurant menus posted at the doorways before we made our decision, and we seemed to have difficulty in agreeing.

With annoyance in his voice he said, "Just pick one and let's eat!"

"OK, let's eat here at this Greek restaurant."

We were led to the lower eating area in the cellar, which was dimly lit and had great atmosphere. I could see the pouty little boy face coming and excused myself to go to the restroom. When I returned to the table he was even more unhappy. The waiter brought over our two complementary glasses of cheap wine and we began to look at the menu.

"It's late and I should be studying!" he said sharply.

The energy rolling off of him was so bad that tears began to stream down my cheeks. It seemed like every time things started to flow between us, he would create a conflict. We were only going to have one more night together, and it would be at the hotel because he had to study. Since we had been in Paris, we had only sat down to one real dinner together and we weren't going to have this one either.

The waiter was tall and dark, probably not Greek, but definitely from North Africa or the surrounding area. As he approached our table I could tell that he had been dealing with far too many tourists. I looked up at him trying to compose myself but knowing that my eyes were filled with tears.

"I didn't realize it, but it's later than we thought and my friend has to get back to the hotel. So we're not going to be staying for dinner."

His eyes narrowed and he pointed to the wine that we had been served.

"You'll have to pay for that!" he demanded.

I looked at him incredulously and said, "Well you don't have to be so rude about it! We'll pay for the wine. Just bring us the bill."

As we walked out of the restaurant, I told the owner and the guy that ushered us in how rude the waiter had been, and we would never be back.

We rode the train to the hotel in silence and as hard as I tried, I couldn't stop crying. Brayden was sitting across from me, and I sucked in short quick breaths while I kept apologizing for not being able to get control of my emotions. He looked at me with pain and compassion in his eyes and asked me why I was crying. I didn't answer him, I just kept apologizing for crying.

We walked from the train station through a dark parking lot on our way back to the hotel. He was 20 feet in front of me, and now it was my turn to be passive aggressive. I hung back so he would realize what a jerk he was for letting me walk by myself at night. When we passed through the lobby, I hoped that no one had seen my tears. He and I always had such a strong presence of togetherness—even with the walls.

In the days before, we always touched in some way as we walked together. I remember him having his back to me as he was turning to leave a counter. His hand in his left jacket pocket, he slightly extended his elbow and I knew that it was my cue to take his arm. He would do that frequently without looking at me and it was extremely subtle. Brayden knew that there was something almost telepathic between us and he seemed to enjoy it. But at the same time, it was a connection that scared him.

Once in the room, he picked up his books and I scavenged what was left of the bread and cheese. I offered him some but he wasn't interested. I finished eating before climbing into bed with my clothes still on. As I turned onto my side facing the wall, I began to think about everything that had happened on the trip. As much as I loved him—I just didn't think that I could put myself through this any longer.

"Why are you wearing your clothes to bed?" he asked with concern.

"Because I don't feel like taking them off yet."

He started sighing frequently as he flipped hard through the pages of his training manual, making as much noise as he possibly could, but I ignored all of the commotion.

"Are you still pissed at me?" he asked softly.

Turning to look up at him I replied quietly, "I'm not pissed...*I'm hurt.*"

A few minutes later I decided to change into a robe, and as I came out of the bathroom, he was standing there waiting for me. He took a step closer and put his hands around my shoulders.

Looking deeply into my eyes, he said softly, "I'm sorry."

I scanned his expression and studied his eyes—they seemed watery and red around the edges like he was holding back emotion. He went on to say the waiter had been rude and tossed the menus on the table in front of him. I studied his eyes again to see if he was sincere.

Hugging him, I whispered in his ear "It was a small thing."

Both of us relieved but still distant, we climbed into bed and fell asleep.

It was now Monday and I was leaving the next morning. Brayden still had some things to finish up at training, so I went back into the city alone to see Jim Morrison's grave at Cimitiere du Pere-Lachaise. The cemetery is world famous because it's not only beautiful, but it's the resting place for many famous literary and musical figures. Oscar Wilde, Chopin, and, of course Jim Morrison, to name a few. The cemetery is also known as The City of the Dead and it was like a maze of above ground tombs. I found Morrison's grave and in many ways, I suppose that I expected it to be grander. The sarcophagus was black and white granite with a simple name marker. Flowers and a couple of half smoked cigarettes had been placed on it as offerings, and someone had scribbled on the stone with a Sharpie *"The Soul Of An Indian Will Come Back To Dance On Fire."*

I didn't have a lot to do that day aside from visiting the museums. I had walked most of the city, so I felt as though I was just killing time until Brayden got back to the hotel. I wasn't into the usual tourist souvenirs, but I usually tried to bring back a little memento from my trips that reflected where I had been. In New York, it was a toy checkered cab, Key West was a few seashells and Wichita? Well...what could you bring back from Wichita? I went into a shop and found a little five-inch silver replica of the Eiffel Tower that had rhinestones on it. It reminded me of the night that we had been there and the tower sparkled. I bought two of them, one for each of us.

It was still early when I returned to the hotel, so I decided to go to the lounge to use the internet. I wrote Brayden a quick note letting him know where I would be, and then put a lipstick kiss at the end of the message. I propped the pad up with the little tower that I had just bought for him, and as I headed to the door, he walked came into the room.

"Oh! I was just on my way to the lounge." I said.

"Give me a minute and I'll join you." he replied.

He noticed my note and the little tower, and walked over to the desk, picking up the pad to read the message. He didn't say anything and almost had an aloof expression on his face. But I knew that he really liked those little expressions of love—although he pretended not to notice them.

In the VIP lounge, we poured a beer and sat down to talk about our day.

"What time did you change your flight to?" he asked with disappointment in his voice.

"It's at 10:00 am."

He looked within himself for a few moments before saying, "That's too bad. Mine isn't until the evening."

He continued as if the walls were finally coming down on our last night together.

In a quiet, vulnerable voice he said, "You asked me what it was that I wanted out of life and what would make me happy. I want someone who will love and take care of me as much as I will them. What do you want? What would make you happy?"

This was a question that Brayden had sharply refused to answer the previous day—and now it was as though he was talking about what we wanted from each other in our relationship. He was suddenly beautiful to me once again because he was showing me his true self and not the walls. *The man I loved, and was so incredibly drawn to.*

"I want my life to be an adventure. I want to be with my best friend, someone who will love and take care of me as much as I will them. I want to be comfortable financially and I want to have babies."

He looked at me with love and anticipation in his eyes and voice, "Do you want to have a boy or a girl?"

"Healthy." I replied.

"Do you think that you would want that with me?" he asked.

"You have best friend potential." I replied with a grin.

Brayden had just been so difficult the last several days that I wasn't absolutely sure that I could tell him that I wanted it with him, even though I knew that I did. I just wasn't sure if I was right and these walls of his would eventually come down, or if he was just this difficult by nature.

We went on to talk about some of the things that bothered me. "I don't like your Myspace activity Brayden. I'm not jealous because I know that you don't have with them what we have together—but it bothers me."

He explained that several of the women he had known through work. One he didn't know at all. And the other one he had seen briefly before he left. "You can verify that with any of them and you can see my account."

We pulled up his Myspace page and my 15-year-old niece was listed as a friend. I shot him a sharp look of disapproval, as he shrugged his shoulders innocently and said that she sent him a friend request.

"I think that it's entirely inappropriate for Mikala to be listed as one of your friends when you're talking to other women!"

"I'm not!" he pleaded.

There were no recent messages so I relaxed a little. And like a couple united, we looked at each profile and he explained the relationship, or lack thereof. I pulled up the profile of the brunette with the slutty picture of herself naked behind her lap top.

"Look at this!" I exclaimed.

He shushed me because he didn't want anyone else in the lounge to see or hear.

"I hadn't seen that picture before," he replied.

I shot him a look as if to say, "Do you seriously think that I believe that?" "Is that the one that you dated?" I asked with disgust.

"Yes."

"We'll my niece is on here with you and that's what she sees when she looks at your friends!" I replied in a disapproving tone.

There was nothing more that needed to be said. We changed the subject and now it was just about the two of us, and how much we loved each other. Brayden held his arm around my waist tightly as we walked to the downstairs lounge to get something to eat. Whispering private jokes into each other's ear, we made quiet observations about the other people in the room.

He made a joke directed at me so I said, "*OK...* just for that I'm ordering a Margarita!" I knew that a Margarita at the Paris Hilton, had to be a $20 drink if they even knew how to make one.

When we got the tab, he said, "Your Margarita was 17 Euros!"

"Yep! Serves you right!" I laughed. "$6 more than I thought it would be!"

It was all play with us that night and Brayden decided that we needed one more drink from the VIP lounge to take to our room. With no bartender in sight, he playfully grabbed a full bottle of Baileys Irish Cream and tucked it under his arm. Grabbing my hand with the other he said, "Let's get out of here!" And we ran for the elevator.

Back in the room, it was as if none of the tension from the past week ever existed. His walls were down and he was finally allowing himself to show his true feelings for me. After we made love, I felt a sudden and profound sense of love for him as he rested on top of me.

Without realizing it, I whispered, "I love you."

"I love you, too." he replied softly.

We hadn't spoken those words with heartfelt meaning the entire trip. Now it was like a release and dissolving of the final barrier between us.

I felt myself drift into sleep finally secure in his love and in his arms. But my peace was abruptly broken when I woke in a panic.

"I haven't even packed and we have to get up early!"

I threw my suitcase on the bed and began quickly pulling everything out so I could re-pack it neatly. Brayden lay back against the headboard, watching me in amusement. With everything in its place and ready to go, we no sooner fell asleep when the phone rang with the wake-up call.

We jumped out of bed and as I rushed to the shower, I called back to him, "Will you make coffee this morning?"

He gave me look as if to say, "But you always do that."

Then without a word, he made coffee and brought a cup to the counter where I would be getting ready. Through the glass shower door, I could see him half watching me while he shaved. I drew a big heart in the condensation on the shower door and started to write a message.

"You're writing it backwards!" he called to me.

Embarrassed, I quickly wiped it away, but I could sense his disappointment that I didn't finish.

I had to go down to the business center to print my ticket, so we agreed that Brayden would meet me there with my bags. I was having trouble with the printer and just as I looked up, time stopped for me and my eyes and heart locked on this gorgeous man in a suit jacket walking into the room. I was mesmerized by him. After a couple of seconds, I realized that I knew him—it was Brayden. He came to where I was sitting and still in a bit of a daze, I explained my dilemma.

"May I?" he asked gently, as he leaned over me to take control of the mouse.

I was so incredibly drawn to him at that moment—I physically felt as though the very essence of my being was pulled into his body. It was a surreal experience, and almost painful as I resisted my intense desire to reach out and touch him.

Brayden printed the ticket and we walked to the dining room for breakfast. He stared at me blankly from across the table, and I looked down to notice that I was holding a small slice of bread with an inch of jam piled on top. I could sense his amusement both in making fun at me, and knowing that he could speak to me without words.

"What? It's more like sweetened fruit than jelly." I defended. I had found some of that French jam to bring home with me because I loved it so much.

As we left the dining room the waitress called out," Good- bye!"

"See you tomorrow!" Brayden called back to her.

Tomorrow? I thought to myself. *You're supposed to be leaving and you're not. That's why you didn't want the other pilot to know that you had passed your exam.*

"Brayden? Why did you say that you would see her tomorrow?" I asked casually.

"Oh, just habit," he replied.

You're lying to me. I thought to myself.

We piled into the airport shuttle and waited for the driver—and then we waited some more. I leaned over to Brayden and said that I thought that we could have walked to the airport by now. He laughed quietly hoping that the driver didn't hear me.

At the airport, he didn't pull my suitcase for me, which I thought was strange—*did he suddenly lose his manners?* I wondered. But he seemed to be lost in his thoughts. We made a plan that he would stand in line to exchange my left over Euros, and I would check my bag.

When I returned, he was waiting patiently for me. We stood searching each other's eyes, not knowing when we might see each other again. He didn't seem to want me to leave, and he was struggling to find his words.

His gaze showed concern, as he asked, "Will you wait for me?"

We both knew what that meant. He still needed to get a divorce and I couldn't go to Saudi Arabia if we weren't married. I don't know what I was thinking—maybe I was just nervous, or wanting to put pressure on him to make it happen sooner.

"Do you want me to just wait for you and put my life on hold?" I asked.

His face went flush. "No." he replied. "Not just put your life on hold— but wait for me." he said in a soft, vulnerable tone.

I didn't know what to say because I felt as though agreeing to wait, simply meant less pressure on him, and more waiting for me. So I wrapped my arms around his neck and we kissed until I had no choice but to leave him and go through security.

As I walked through the turnstile, my heart was pulled between love and confusion, as I turned back and he was still standing there watching me. I wanted so much to believe that he would follow through and we would be together, but I felt like he was continually pulling that hope out from under me. He waited there watching—he didn't leave until I was out of site.

I returned home from Paris and kept thinking about the reasons why Brayden might have sent me home early. I wondered if it was because he needed an excuse for me to leave, in order to make time for someone else. But he was a complicated person, so I wondered if there was more to it than that.

I realized that I was missing the blouse my sister lent me for the trip, so I called the hotel. As I suspected, he was still registered but there was no answer in his room. He had stayed in Paris for two days after I left. When I finally reached him on his cell phone in Saudi, I asked if he had found the blouse and he said that he hadn't. His tone with me was indifferent, and I knew that I had caused damage with my answers to him at the airport.

"Brayden, I'll wait for you, but where do we go from here?"

The tone of his voice turned angry and sarcastic, "You'll wait for me? Now?" he replied with his voice now raised.

"Yes, I will—but where do we go from here?"

"I invited you to fucking Paris! It is what it is!" he sneered.

I was silent, not knowing how to respond. He abruptly said goodbye and hung up. I didn't know what to think. I later reflected that he was being vulnerable to me by telling me that he wanted us to be together as soon as it was possible. But the statement that I made concerning waiting around for him, could be interpreted by him as rejection—which couldn't have been farther from the truth.

Weeks passed without a call from him, so I went to see Margie.

"Don't give up on Brayden," she said. "You haven't heard from him, but his life would be haunted without you. He sent you home early because he was losing control of his feelings for you and he needed to get away in order to regain control of them."

It did make sense to me when she put it that way—he didn't have the ability to avoid me and distance his feelings while we were sharing the same hotel room. And although he seemed to go through waves of letting his guard down, he also created conflict to keep a distance between us. Maybe it was too hard to maintain the balance, so he sent me home early.

*"The deepest bonds of love are often forged silently
below a tempestuous surface."*

~ *Julie Hopper*

10

Before leaving for Paris, the only client I was working with at the time had the last name of Loch, Brayden's last name. When I returned from my trip, I found that an associate of mine had written an offer for them on a house, listed with an agent whose last name was Glasgow, Brayden's home town in Scotland. A few days later, I got an e-mail from Heather White, the woman that I met on the plane when I was on my way to Paris. She wanted me to write an offer on a house for her that she found on McLaren Court. That was the last name of the first Scottish/ Italian pilot that I was in love with. They were all last names and what were the chances? I thought that it was my guide's way of letting me know to hang in there—I was still on the right path with him.

I called my friend Kate and asked her if I was imagining things. Was I making more of it than I should be? She knew the whole story about the llamas, the Jeeps, and the Lear jet ties.

"No you're not!" she replied. "And that is just too weird to be a coincidence! Julie, these things only happen to you. You have to write a book!"

Kate had been telling me from the beginning that I should write these things down as a special remembrance of my relationship with Brayden, but now she was suggesting a book.

"Yeah right Kate, like someone wants to read about my life?"

"Yes, but these things don't happen to everyone Julie."

"But they do!" I protested. "You just have to pay attention to the patterns."

I had to agree with her though—maybe I was getting a little extra encouragement from above, to help me hang in there with Brayden when at that moment, I was feeling very discouraged.

Later I would find that it was just one of the many other signs to follow. The Brayden/Duff connection, the Jeep etc…was one thing. But I had never even met someone with the last name of Glasgow. Let alone the chances of writing an offer for someone who I met on a flight to see Brayden and wanted to buy a house on McLaren Court. *How many streets are there in Portland anyway? And what are the chances that I would sit next to someone from Portland who would buy a house from me?*

If I wasn't paying close enough attention to my messages, my spirit guides had my full attention now.

There are no chance meetings.

I hadn't talked to Brayden since March when he reminded me that he had invited me to *"fucking Paris."* That was the first time that he had used that kind of language with me, and it was so out of character for him that I didn't know what to do anymore. I didn't feel like my patience was getting us anywhere, and no matter the signs—I had to ask myself if I was in denial.

From: Julie Hopper   *April 8, 2007*
To: Brayden Loch
Subject: None

I tried to call you yesterday morning. I was sitting by the ocean having coffee… It was so beautiful and then I started missing you. I had to think twice as to whether or not I should call you. After all this time, I shouldn't feel that way.

I've struggled to make sense of the lack of contact between us over the last several months but I can't. I've made all of the excuses...It's your situtuation, etc...but no one is too busy to call someone that they really want to talk to and nothing appears to have changed. Every day I hope that I'll get a call or an e-mail from you and it doesn't come. I just don't have it in me anymore to ask for something that should come naturally.

Still, I've felt like maybe there is something going on in your head that you're not telling me. If so, now is the time to get everything out in the open because I was crying on and off all day yesterday because of what I have to do.

Brayden I love you...I like who you are, your opinions on life and just being with you, but as hard as this is for me, I'm just not a priority to you and I haven't been for a long time. I still have hope of having a family, but there's a chance that I may not be able to have one...would you still want me if I couldn't? What I want most is companionship and someone to share a life with. I won't be open to someone else as long as I'm holding on to the hope that you'll wake up one morning and decide to make me a bigger part of your life. This hurts so much, but this has to be good bye for me.

Love and best wishes,

Julie

From: Julie Hopper   May 2, 2007
To: Brayden Loch
Subject: I wanted you to know this

Hello,

After my last e-mail, this one might seem a little out of place. But this didn't occur to me until later and I needed to put it out there and get it off of my mind.

We didn't talk about when or if you were getting the things that you need resolve with Janis taken care of, but I know that even if you did, it would be difficult to change your situation in Florida while you're still in Saudi. Although I don't know what is going on with you, I could sense that your loose ends did seem to be frustrating you in relation to us. I could be wrong.

I just wanted you to know that when (I hope not if) you become ready to allow things to develop between us, I would help you take care of things here if you needed it. That includes taking care of your dog while you're gone if you wanted me to. Actually, that would help me out because otherwise, I'm going to have to get some company for Ku'a.

I'm sorry that I had to say good bye like I did. I just didn't know what to do anymore and you weren't talking to me. I can't imagine that I was wrong about you, because I can still feel you with me. It was just too hard to want someone that didn't seem to want me back.

I hope that all is well with you!

Julie

⋙✕⋘

From: Brayden Loch   May 7, 2007
To: Julie Hopper
RE: I wanted you to know this

Hello there,

I sure was glad to hear from you afer all this time. After your last e-mail i wasn't sure wether I should contact you. You just seemed so angry and upset about my lack of conact with you due to my schedule. I am so glad that you have decided to get in touch. I am looking at alternative employment right now, due to the fact that being away from the States, Ronan and not talking to you is taking more of a toll on me that I originally imagined.... I enjoyed our time in Paris together and wish it could have been more, or wish we could have really discussed some pertiment issues. I know I'm not being toatally fair on your feelings and emotions thats why I didn't contact you after your last e-mail. I wish life wasn't so hard either. I guess if life was easy we wouldn't appreciate the good times as much.

I just want to say the spark and fire we initially had together I feel is stil there deep down, it just needs to be woke up. I do think of

you frequently and miss you. I wish I could say more or something a little more convincing to make you beleive me..... just seem to have dificulty finding the right words.
I miss you teribbly and hope all is well with you.

Yours,

B.

From: Julie Hopper   *May 7, 2007*
To: Brayden Loch
RE: I wanted you to know this

Hello,

I'm glad to hear from you too... I was beginning to think that the tattoo of your name I got on my ass was premature ;-)

I can understand why you would think that I was angry in my other e-mail, but I left the door open, so you shouldn't have worried about contacting me. You're right though, you haven't been very fair to my feelings...if you just needed time to think, that's all you had to say and I would have understood it.

The e-mail was more a result of frustration and I was at a point where after all of these months of not having regular communication, I had to make a decision between waiting to see if things would change, or being more open to other people, which wasn't what I really wanted to do.

The distance is a terrible disadvantage...just my luck that I finally meet someone that I can really see having something with and we're not even in the same country...It's hard enough to really get to know someone when you're in the same city. That's really what I want...there is so much that we don't know about each other, I just want the chance for us to have that opportunity and see what develops.

I can only imagine being in your situation and how hard it must be. You're right, there were a lot of things we should have talked about and I really regretted not having those conversations, but the time just went by so fast. I would still like to have them if you would...please let me know. I miss you too!

Love,

Julie

Brayden and I continued the usual pattern—he wouldn't respond to a message or I would get mad about the lack of contact. Then, suddenly he would reply and we still wouldn't address the issues.

To: Brayden Loch   *May 26, 2007*
From: Julie Hopper
Subject: Knock Knock

Who's there?
Olive
Olive who?
Olive you!
    I am sooooo beginning to get you Brayden Loch...(I think) You climbed into that freaking cave of yours didn't you? Well, go towards the light young man.........
    We didn't talk about one pertinent issue. I need some good swimmmers cause my eggs are getting dusty. Can we talk about that? I'd really like to, but if you don't I understand. I'll probably take this web camera back if I don't hear from you before you leave Jedda, but I would love to be able to see you.

Julie

He asked me to wait for him until he got his divorce but the communication wasn't improving and I wanted to have children. Although his reasons for staying in the marriage were entirely valid, it was getting to the point that I may have to make the decision to move on with my life without him—something that I didn't want to have to consider.

To: Julie Hopper   June 25, 2007
From: Brayden Loch
RE: Knock Knock

Guess what I do have his password now, but it no longer matters because Brayden and I now only have a business arrangement. While he has been fucking you he was still fucking me and telling me that he loved me, always wanted me in his life (I'm sure he was telling you the same thing) and wanted our marriage to work out. Yes for the whole year you have know him. During his visit home I have learned by getting into his email that you are not the only cunt he has been fucking during this last year.

Good luck to you.

And legally I am STILL his wife.

The stab of her words quickly turned to pity, as I imagined what kind of person she must be to speak that way. Janis went on to send me e-mails from his account of sexual messages and naked photos from other women. Some were long before he and I knew each other, and others were around the time we first met. Although she said that he was making promises to her—I also knew that she was fully aware that the marriage was over long before I met Brayden. I absorbed it all while still trying to look at the big picture.

The synchronicities between Brayden and I were undeniable. There was something mystical at work in our meeting regardless of his current circumstances. The Loch, Glasgow, McLaren connection when I came back from Paris, reinforced my belief that the Universe was trying to tell me not to give up on him. I just didn't know if I could endure it much longer. I needed resolution, or closure.

To: *Brayden Loch*   *August 8, 2007*
From: *Julie Hopper*
RE: *I left out the most important thing*

I would like to know what you want, even if the answer is that you don't know.

Julie

To: Julie Hopper   August 8, 2007
From: Brayden Loch
RE: I left out the most important thing

Julie,

I know what I want..... I want it all , Kids, House, Cars, Success and a happy relationship. I just find it hard to think or even believe I'm entitled to that, especially being all the way over here. When I was back in the States I truly believed it could have been possible with you despite all Janis has told you.

I wish I new that I could have all I wanted, but that would be a perfect world and I know thats not what we live in. I also know that it's unfair to keep hurting you the way I seem to be doing and that's inexcusable of me, for that I am deeply sorry. I wish I had all the answers, or at least a couple of them.

I still think of you often and miss you, I just don't want to keep hurting you. I wish I knew what to do.

Brayden.

I noticed how he capitalized everything but a "happy relationship" He went on to say that he doesn't deserve it. From the time he was a child, love was an emotion that had only betrayed him—the thought of believing in something that he's never had before and then losing it tormented him. So he manifested his fear in ways that sabotaged the possibility of love and happiness because he didn't know how to deal with it. I thought that I was beginning to truly understand him, but it didn't change the fact that nothing was changing.

To: Brayden Loch   *August 9, 2007*
From: Julie Hopper
RE: I left out the most important thing

    It's good to hear from you..
    First of all, you aren't going to be there much longer are you? And of course you're entitled to everything that you want and it's all obtainable...you just have to decide if you're ready for it and quit telling yourself that it's too much to ask for and isn't possible. And. . if you want those things with me or, if you aren't ready now and will go on to have them with someone else in the future.
    I could be completely wrong, but I think that I understand you in many ways that others might not. So forgivness was easy and although there are changes and decisions that would have to be made for us to be together, I can look forward and not back if you want to see what we could have....I know what I want, so it's really up to you now.

Julie

To: Brayden Loch   *August 20, 2007*
From: Julie Hopper
Subject: PS..

 I know that you have another leave in September. I happen to have enough air miles for a round trip from Tampa to Portland.
 There are open flights available. Please let me know if you'll let me book one of them for you.
 I miss you so much!

To: Julie Hopper   August 28, 2007
From: Brayden Loch
RE: PS..

 I'm sorry hun. I want desperaly to be back in September, however my work has asked me to work until December 1st. I'm givin it a little thought, just so I can earn a little extra cash for now... I know how that looks to you but please don;t read anything other than me just trying to pay off some debt. I would really love to come visit you In Portland... (Oregon...Seattle...lol) I will see what my schedule is for December..so far they tel me I'm off the first to the 22nd...How's about a visit then?
P.S I miss you too.

To: Brayden Loch   *August 29, 2007*
From: Julie Hopper
RE: PS...

 I'm sorry, but I have nothing left to say.

Julie

"How's about?" Joking or not, that tone was a little to casual for me and the pattern remained the same. I want to see him, but he makes excuses as to why we can't. I get upset—and he disappears or does something to try to get a reaction from me. I still kept an eye on his Myspace page, and he suddenly had 20 new women on there. Far too many for him to just be making "new friends." Because they were all from the States and he was half-way around the world. I knew he was trying to get a reaction from me and he wasn't going to get one. *I had had enough!* He must have Googled me, because my business website has an online information request that can be sent to me.

10/5/07

What is your name: Brayden Loch (the ass)

Phone number: you know it

E-mail address: THAT TOO

What information are you interested in? YOU, YOU, YOU, YOU I SHOULD HAVE KNOWN BETTER. I LOVE YOU.

To: *Brayden Loch*   *October 7, 2007*
From: *Julie Hopper*
Subject: *None*

I got your e-mail from my website...I also saw all of your new friends. Brayden...I've gotten nothing but games from you since Janis first found my number and called me. It was like the switch on us was set to dim. For the last 14 months, I haven't been able to get back what we first felt for each other...as hard as I've tried.

When we saw each other in Paris, it had been 7 months since we had seen each other. It would be 9 more months from that time if we saw each other in December like you proposed. You've had many opportunities to see me in the last 14 months and it hasn't been a priority...I'm just another play thing in your toy box that you take out when you feel like it.

I will not compromise on what I have to have in a relationship and among other things, they are...

TRUST, COMMUNICATION, HONOR, RESPECT, FIDELITY, HONESTY, LOVE, FRIENDSHIP AND INTEGRITY.

None of which you've shown me since the very beginning. I Love you and I hoped that with time together and when the walls came down, that we might have all of that....at this point though, you haven't shown me that you are ready for that kind of a relationship.

If or when you are ready to have a relationship minus the games...then call me.

Julie

The next day, suddenly all of the women were deleted from his Myspace page except for the original friends and three of the new ones. One of them appeared to be an older woman, who he knew I wouldn't be threatened by. Another I wasn't sure about and the last, was a very attractive woman around my age who had photos of herself on private planes. I suspected that it was someone he may have worked with before, and it might not be inappropriate for him to delete her. But she was far too attractive for me to believe that she was simply a friend. Her name was Claire.

There was a picture of Brayden in her album with the caption "My favorite pilot." And another of her laying on a bed, with her lap top in front of her, legs apart and ass hanging out from her shorts. Why would these women think that pictures like that would get them anything other than sexual interest? Unless sex was all they wanted. *Another one of his "Hos to go,"* I thought.

Brayden didn't post the little comments on other people's Myspace sites like the women did. Probably so as not to incriminate himself I suspected. But he had a new one from Claire—a little cartoon joke about phone sex. Brayden liked his phone sex because he was away in hotels so often. I knew exactly what that comment meant—she was more than just an acquaintance.

He had been popping in and out of my life for months now, but I still believed that we were meant to be together. He never threatened our relationship with words, although his playing around on line should have been sufficient. But what was still new to me in my experience with him was that I didn't feel jealous in the normal way—or fear losing him to another woman. I would have never felt that way with another man. It would have torn my heart to pieces. Phone sex wasn't my thing, so there was nothing for him to gain by maintaining a relationship with me except *me*. I just had to get through the weeds with him.

I was so drawn to him that my evenings were spent drinking too much wine on my back porch and trying to put the pieces together. After Claire's comment and knowing that she was involved with private planes, I connected the dots. I found the website for the company he had flown for in Florida. It was a long shot, but I looked up the employees and there was a Claire Rousseau who was an account manager. I did a people search for that name in the area that the company was based in. Up popped a Claire Rousseau whose birth date matched the website address for the Claire on his page.

Eventually Brayden called and I asked him who she was. He said she was a client and I didn't say anything more. I knew that he had another leave coming up in December, so I asked if he would fly to Portland to see me.

"I've already committed myself to work through my leave because I need the money," he replied.

"That's it, I've had it Brayden! I don't want you to call me again and I don't want any more of your fucking e-mails! I'm done!"

His voice rose up in a desperate cry and as it broke he pleaded, "I made a mistake!"

"I'm sorry Brayden. I can't do this anymore."

To: Brayden Loch   *November 17, 2007*
From: Julie Hopper
Subject: December

Brayden,
    I want you to know that if you call to tell me what day and time to pick you up at the airport, that would be a call that I would be happy to take. Beyond that... there is no reason for you to ever call me again.
    You run from what you need the most without giving yourself a chance to find out if there was ever anything to fear at all. Telling work that you had a family emergency and that you have to take the time off would be a good idea...because this is one.
    I don't know if you can change things, but I can't be pulled back into this beyond December because I love you too much and I want a family...not just children, but a man that loves me and wants to be with me.
    I never imagined us ending, but I can't help you overcome whatever is holding you back any longer.
    I will never stop loving you.

Julie

To: Julie Hopper   December 18, 2007
From: Brayden Loch

    If I could be there in December I would. How dare you call me a womaniser..... If I was, which I am not, I wouldn't be so hung up on you. I want a family too, not just you. I also want to be loved. I can see that you made your decision.

To Brayden Loch   *November 27, 2007*
From: Julie Hopper
RE: December

There have been three times this year that you had an opportunity to see me and haven't. Two of them I asked you to and the third I left open for you to decide. All with plenty of time to schedule it....I know what that means.

If you truly loved me and wanted a life and family with me... nothing would stop you from seeing me. Do you see that it is you that is making the decision?

Julie

To: Julie Hopper   November 27, 2007
From: Brayden Loch
RE: December

The decision I am making is getting Janis and my debt paid of by next year so as that when I get the things that I need to taken care of, we can go our seperate ways with nothing left to finish. I am on track to do that, In the mean time I want to make my current employer happy, and as I didn't know where things stood with us, I agreed to work my leave and make more money.

I know how you are and feel, you made it perfectly clear, and it's something that I'll have to live with. I guess I should just stop telling myself I can have what I want. I've dug myself a huge hole and now I can't seem to get out. Sorry you feel the way you do about me. You deserve to be happy and I don't seem to be the guy giving you what you want or even deserve.

I do think about us and how it could have been. I hope you have that one day, just as much as I do.

Always,

B

P.S. I would have liked to at least have thought we could have been freinds if nothing else!........

To: *Brayden Loch*   *January 16, 2008*
From: *Julie Hopper*
Subject: *None*

    Sorry for breaking my no e-mail request.
    Maybe the connection that I felt to you was one sided. In any case I would have liked to have seen each other one more time before letting go of it.
    I figured that you have another leave due in February or March. If you still want to see each other, book a flight to Portland for three weeks and call me to let me know...If what we had is still there, we'll want all of the time. If it's not, then you can always change your ticket.
    You said that you dug yourself a huge hole...so I'm throwing both of us one last rope if you want to use it. You can have everything that you want in life Brayden....you just have to believe in it and believe in yourself. If you don't want to come or you can't, please don't respond to this and I wish you only the best.

    I didn't hear from him and it was agonizing.

To: *Julie Hopper*   *January 30, 2008*
From: *Sophie Douglas*
Subject: *Thinking about you*

HI,

   Kind of weird, but when I woke up this morning my first thought was something really good is happening for Julie this week. I am sure my guides were giving me a message I need to pass on to you, so look for something happy and exciting to happen in the next few days.

Love,
Sophie

To: Sophie Douglas   *January 30, 2008*
From: Julie Hopper
RE: Thinking about you

Hi Sophie,

   I was going to wait to see if something bigger happened before I sent this, but it wasn't an hour after I got your e-mail that I found out that Brayden sent a message to my niece asking her to tell me that he missed me. He's obviously trying to open the door, but the only reason that I can imagine that he didn't contact me directly is that he's not coming back to the States in March. I told him not to contact me if he wasn't.

   He usually does something to contact me about the 1st of the month. That seems to be the pattern. I would imagine if you received a message about something good happening, that it would be more than just a message telling me that he missed me. I'll let you know if anything else happens, but would you ask if he is returning to the States in February or March? If not, maybe he'll want me to meet him somewhere. Let me know if you get any impressions on it and I'll keep you posted!

Julie

She replied saying no, that she didn't think that the something really good was Brayden. The tone in her e-mail was disapproving like, *"Give up on him already!"* That disappointed me but I still had hope!

It always confused me why Margie seemed to have positive messages about Brayden and Sophie didn't. Sophie would talk about he and I having had past lives together and that he wasn't learning his lesson of commitment. So she just kept calling him a player. Although I hoped that Margie was right about him, I didn't feel like I was in denial when my own intuition told me that he and I were destined to be together. I waited a couple of days and then I couldn't take it longer. He hadn't replied to my last e-mail, so I decided that he probably wouldn't. As I grew to realize, my own spirit guides would give me little pushes of inspiration to take action at just the right moment.

To: Brayden Loch   *February 2, 2008*
From: Julie Hopper
RE: Sorry for the e-mail...

I wanted to call you but couldn't find your home number and couldn't get through on your cell. I didn't know how long before the connection would be back.

Do you not want to see each other? When we said good bye at the airport...I didn't think that it would be the last time that I would ever see you again.

I miss you more than you know.

The next day I was at my office and realized that I had missed a call. I planned to check my messages later, but something told me to check in now. I pushed the buttons for voicemail.

"Please enter your password.... First new message sent February 4, 2008 at 3:57 pm."

In a melodic Scottish voice trying to sound more confident than it was, I heard:

"Are you screening your phone calls? It's Brayden. I just got your message, uhhh, I guess you don't want to speak to me! If you change your mind, I'm in the States for a week... almost. 813-045-8679. I hope you're doing well. I did think to call you but after our last conversation, well...I just wanted to respect your wishes. But I did get your e-mail and it made me feel good! Sooo I guess if you want to talk, 813-045-8679. Take care."

Without hesitation I called him back and we talked about how much we missed each other. I explained to him how my friends and family didn't understand why he wouldn't come to see me.

"Do I have to come to Oregon to show them how in love with you I am?" he replied.

Did he just say that? I thought to myself. Brayden has never told me that he was *"In love with me."*

Later in the conversation he would say it again. And as we talked, my voice started to break as tears rolled down my face.

"Are you crying?" he asked.

"Yes…"

"Why?"

"Because I miss you so much."

"I miss you too Julie. I miss you terribly"

He went on to explain that he had brought a plane to Wichita, Kansas, for repairs, and while the plane was there, he would be training in Dallas.

"Oh, I use to live in Irving as a kid. It's just outside of Dallas. I have air miles! I'll come see you!"

We were both excited—and I felt as though he was truly letting me in for the first time in months. I booked the flight for the following day and called him that evening. As we spoke, he was telling me how much he missed me and then suddenly in the background, I heard a glass tip over and a woman react.

I paused. "Where are you?" I asked.

"In my room."

I didn't say anything—I didn't know what to say. But I had a flash back to the time in Wichita, when he held his finger to his lips—a call that was to a wife who I believed he was separated from, and although he was, it still bothered me. He told me how much he missed me and couldn't wait to see me. And I acted as though nothing had happened. If I confronted him now, he would just say that it was the TV. But I was upset with myself later when I realized that I could have asked him what he was watching.

"What do I do? My ticket is booked, but I suddenly feel that I need to hate him. Maybe I've been wrong in thinking that our love could somehow heal his emotional scars—this could just be who he is. I'll go! If nothing else, we'll hash it out for good when I see him.

On the plane, I started thinking about all of the patterns that I had seen with him.

Am I understanding his walls? Am I getting encouragement from my guides not to give up on him? Or am I just fooling myself and this guy is a total player?

It made no sense, but there was something inside of me telling me that other women were like a numbing agent to him—if he had a distraction, then he wouldn't feel as much for me. Once on the plane it just left my mind. I still can't believe it—but it did.

*"Life is not measured by the number of breaths we take,
but by the moments that take our breath away"*

~ Unknown

II

I searched the crowded concourse for him, looking forward and occasionally back, scanning the room. Suddenly I realized that I had just seen a pair of eyes focused on me. I looked back quickly and our eyes locked. It felt like a scene in an old movie—just as it had in Wichita. Brayden stood frozen in his steps as I walked toward him. Our eyes never left each other's. The crowd of people faded into the background, and I saw only him in front of me. As I grew closer, I asked myself, *Am I still attracted to him?* It had been a year since we had seen each other, and our contact had been inconsistent. My question was answered instantly, when I saw those amazing green eyes up close again. We politely said hello, and as we reached for each other, our bodies pulled together like magnets; kissing deeply and embracing as if it would be impossible for us to part.

After several minutes, Brayden pulled away and said, "Let's get out of here!" as he guided me toward the exit with his arm wrapped firmly around my waist.

A physical sensation came to my throat, as if I would suffocate without his lips on mine. It was a strange and intense experience, similar to that in Paris when I felt my energy being pulled into his body.

He leaned into the car to put my bags in the back seat. *Why is he taking so long?* The suffocating sensation returned to my throat, and it felt like an eternity waiting until I could feel his lips again. He seemed to be adjusting the two bags far longer than it should have possibly taken. I wondered if he was using the time to regain his own composure. I was relieved when he finally stood back up and I could kiss him again.

"We should get out of here," he said softly. A wave of disappointment washed over me, before realizing he was right.

I had already made the decision that I didn't want to be sexual with him as quickly as we had in Wichita and Paris. We hadn't had one of those dates that create sexual tension—not that we needed one now. But with all of my flight delays, I didn't have a chance to have dinner and I asked if we could find a restaurant. We were both in a state of euphoria and had excitement in our voices.

"What are you hungry for?" he asked.

"Steak and seafood!" I replied cheerfully.

Brayden loved his Cajun food, so he wasn't excited by my choice. Reluctantly he agreed and typed the request into the GPS.

As we drove he asked, "So, what do you think?"

I stroked his hair and said, with amusement in my voice, "You look like a baby." He appeared so much younger than I had remembered. But his dark hair was now flecked with grey, and I mentioned it.

"Yeah, I've pulled a couple of grey hairs out of my chest. If I find a grey pube, I'm going to be really pissed!" we laughed.

"It's the stress you know," I replied, twisting my fingers through his hair. He knew I was right, and he didn't reply. His flying in Saudi had more take offs and landings than a pilot would normally make in a day. But I also knew that he wasn't happy there.

Brayden drove fast and recklessly, as though he wanted to get dinner over so we could be alone. He pulled into the parking lot like a maniac.

"I guess they didn't get the memo that this was your parking lot!" I laughed.

We had chosen Mac's Steak & Seafood and as fate would have it, the place was a Cajun restaurant. We screeched to a halt and Brayden jumped out of the car, opening my door and pulling me toward the restaurant so quickly that I almost lost my footing.

The restaurant was empty except for the bar where they were celebrating Mardi Gras. As we sat in the booth beside each other looking over the menu, the love exuding from both of us was impossible to contain.

Brayden turned to me with excitement and inward pride in his eyes as he said, "You're glowing!" *But so was he.*

"That's because of you," I replied with a big smile.

Our waitress returned with our drinks and began to tell us about the dinner specials. "We have a delicious *etouffee* with an assortment of seafood including crawfish, scallops and..."

"He doesn't like scallops," I interrupted proudly, remembering our dinner in Paris. Brayden's eyes lit up surprise, impressed that I had remembered.

Over dinner he lovingly fed me little bites of food. We couldn't keep our hands off of each other and were kissing so often that he said in amusement, "They're going to kick us out of the restaurant!"

We both laughed. Neither of us could control it, nor did we care. The love between us was almost overwhelming.

The waitress returned to our table to offer us dessert. She herself had made the King Cake for the Mardi Gras celebration."But not in the usual way," she added. "Because King Cake is typically so bland."

"Is there a baby in it?" I asked.

"No," she replied.

Brayden shot me an excited and questioning look, "*A baby?*"

"Yes," they usually bake a toy baby into the cake," I replied.

That wasn't what he was thinking though. He thought that I was suggesting the cake might bring us some luck, because we had talked so often about wanting to have a baby together.

After the waitress left the table, Brayden made a comment, joking about her weight. It was so out of character for him, that I knew he was testing me. It was a reflection of the stand that I had taken against his co-pilot in Wichita; when she made fat jokes. Not long afterward, he had sent me another joke by text message that he knew would offend me. It was as if he was testing to see if I would compromise my morals

to be agreeable with him in order to win his favor. On both counts
I didn't, and I stood by what I believed in by not allowing myself to
indulge in a joke at the expense of others. He was attracted to my
compassion and integrity, and he wanted to make sure that I was really
the person that I presented myself to be.

After wrapping up the leftovers, we started the drive back to the
hotel. I like my wine—you don't spend 40 years alone looking at the
same four walls without a man or children to fulfill your life and expect
that you might not tend to drink a lot. Brayden had been living in Saudi
Arabia where alcohol was forbidden, and told me that three out of four
house fires were from homemade stills exploding. I had a couple of
drinks on the plane and then a recommended Hurricane and wine at
dinner to his one beer. But I wanted to stop at a convenience store on our
way back to the hotel and pick up a bottle of wine.

The store clerk informed us that it was a dry county but I wasn't
used to that. "Where's the closest county that sells alcohol?" I asked. It
was several miles away.

Brayden looked at me with disappointment in his eyes and said
softly, "You don't have to drink to be with me."

I suddenly felt ashamed and embarrassed with myself and although I
wanted my wine, "You're right," I replied.

As we passed through the lobby of the hotel, the front desk man
made a joke to Brayden, asking where he had found his new guest.

"Oh, by the side of the road," I joked.

But as we continued up the elevator, I suddenly wondered if that
same desk man had seen Brayden's visitor the night before. I was now the
second woman in his room in two nights, but I couldn't think about it.
My love for him was overflowing and nothing would change that.

I had carefully planned what I wore to meet him. Although Dallas
would be warm, Portland still had freezing temperatures when I left,
so I wore a bright, lime green turtle neck with black slacks. The color
looked electric against my blonde hair and the turtleneck showed my
curves. Underneath, I wore the same black, lace teddy that I had worn
in Wichita. Brayden was slower and more gentle this time than he had

ever been before, and we were lost in each other's eyes as we carefully undressed each other.

Finally content and with our bodies entwined in a close embrace, we lay in bed talking about everything, but nothing in particular.

Brayden got up to go to the bathroom and as he came back I said, "You're so handsome! But you'd look even more handsome with a cold glass of ice water in your hand," I giggled.

Without saying a word, he went to the kitchen, reappearing with water for me. Our mood was now light and playful. We hadn't seen each other in a year and yet it felt as though we had never been apart. Like we *really were* with our best friend, just as I told him that I wanted when we were in Paris.

Playfully fighting over the microwave, we re-heated the leftovers from dinner. Brayden had a habit of always having the TV on, one that he had picked up from spending too much time alone in hotel rooms. But tonight there was no TV. We just lay in bed together, eating and laughing over private jokes that no one else would understand.

He also had a strange habit of watching the same movies over and over again. I think that it may have been an escape from reality when he was a kid. He was from Scotland and although he had lived in the States for the last several years, I never had to explain anything to him. He knew every US Pop culture reference, even those that should have been long before his time. His mind was sharp and he retained everything. I was surprised at times by the little details he remembered.

Shortly after we first met, we got into a conversation about what we loved about each other. I had only seen him for a few days in Wichita and yet he said, "I love your confidence, your compassion and kindness, the way that you sweep your hair behind your ear, the way that you point your toes when you're lying in bed, and the way you call my name when we make love."

I loved his intelligence, his sense of humor and compassion. And although I didn't share it with him at the time, most of all I loved him for the part of himself that he kept concealed from everyone else. The part of him that I knew instinctively, as only someone who truly understood him could appreciate—I loved his complex vulnerability. At times when he surrendered to it as he had this night, without trying he transformed me into the person that I knew I had buried deep inside of me—He brought out my joy.

When we woke up the next morning, Brayden said that he slept better than he had the entire trip. I knew it was his way of letting me know that it was because we were together. But as we began to talk about what we wanted to do that day, I asked him to kiss me.

"*Noooo!*" he said playfully, as his eyes flashed with excitement. "I have morning breath!"

I asked again, "Please kiss me…"

"*NO!*"

He had that excited, playful, little boy look on his face, just like he did when he was jumping up and down in his underwear in Paris. I recognized it so clearly. These were his walls or defense mechanism kicking in. To kiss me in the morning without sex would be intimacy and that would create vulnerability. I had begun to see the pattern with him: an amazing first day or two together and then friction. Then the last night together would be amazing again. I hoped that wouldn't happen this time.

We decided to go to Cracker Barrel for breakfast because I had never been there before. As I put my make-up on to get ready, he sat on the edge of the bed watching me with fascination.

I turned to him and asked calmly, "Why did you send me home early from Paris?"

"What are you talking about?"

"You stayed for two days after I left," I replied casually.

"Why do you say that?" he asked.

"Because you didn't want the other pilot to know that you had passed your exam, and when we were leaving breakfast to go to the airport, you told the waitress that you would see her tomorrow."

"Oh, I just said that out of habit,"

"I called the hotel to check on the blouse that I lost and you were still checked in."

He sat there with a poker face as if he wasn't going to show his hand no matter what I said.

"Who is Claire Rousseau?" I asked.

"I used to work with her."

"Oh, that's funny—you told me that she was a client." He sat there without expression because he had just been caught in a lie. "You really shouldn't lie to me Brayden. I always find out," I replied, my voice tinged with disappointment and saying nothing more.

Our table at the restaurant had a peg board game and the goal was to remove all of the pegs and play like checkers until you only have one left. Brayden said he had mastered the game and set about playing. He had obviously forgotten his system because it took him several tries to get it right. I was becoming annoyed after the fourth time because he was giving me a play by play, *Yawwwn.* He finally got it right, *Thank God!* I realized that he could be very determined and a little obsessive over things. I suspected that it was because he had to be hard on himself in order to become successful and get out of Glasgow. It annoyed me, but at the same time I understood and admired it about him.

After breakfast we walked to the car and as he opened the door for me, he asked, "So, what do you want to do now? I have a couple of hours before I have to be at training."

"It might be fun to drive by my old house." I replied.

"What's the address? I'll put it into GPS."

"1728 Sunnybrook Drive." My parents made me memorize the address as soon as I was old enough, and now here I am 35 years later and I still remember it.

As we drove, I thought that I recognized some shopping malls and street names, but it wasn't nearly as nice as I remembered it to be. Now it was just plain, boring strip malls and not very green. As we turned into my old neighborhood, things began to look familiar again. It was an average middle class neighborhood with a mixture of wood and brick houses. The streets were lined with big oak trees and the cracks in the pale grey cement roads had been filled in with black tar, making squiggly lines in the streets.

My childhood home looked exactly the same as we pulled up to the curb.

"This was your house growing up?" Brayden asked.

"Yes."

"It's not at all like my house growing up."

"Apartments?" I asked.

"Yes."

I knew they weren't just apartments. He grew up in Glasgow's equivalent of the projects. This must have seemed like a mansion to him compared to where he grew up, and this home was fairly modest for Irving.

"That's the master bedroom," I pointed out. "My father added that bay window. I remember trying to dig to China by that patch of ivy."

"You tried to dig to China?"

"Yes," I laughed. "I used to put on my rain coat and goulashes with nothing on underneath and play in the rain water at the curbs. Texas is so dry but when it rains, it rains buckets and it was like a little river flowing past my house. I was hit by a car here. Our friends the Zarates owned a snow cone truck and after I got one, I was crossing the street and a woman who was driving too fast hit me. The snow cone was red and my father thought it was blood. He pulled her out of her car, threw me in and rushed me to the hospital. I was OK, but I was on crutches for a long time."

I continued to tell Brayden stories from my child hood. "Call your mom!" he said with excitement. "Tell her where we are!"

I called my mother and told her we were at our old house, as I described everything including the round brick wall that my father had built. Then I put Brayden on the phone with her. She had only talked with him once before when I was getting ready to go to Wichita. He had been drinking and referred to himself as Shrek. Funny because Shrek had a Scottish accent and I have no other idea of why he would say that. Brayden was beautiful in a manly kind of way and he had to know it.

My mother proceeded to tell him how unpleasant I was when I wasn't talking to him, and that I thought about him 24/7.

He didn't know how to respond. "I'm going to put Julie back on the phone," he replied quickly, as he tossed the phone at me like it was going to burn him.

Brayden offered to knock on the door and ask the current owners if we could take a look inside but as thoughtful as it was of him, I didn't want to bother anyone. We turned the car in the other direction and headed down the street.

"That's where Patti Price lived, her father was a Pan Am pilot."

We continued to the end to a cul de sac. That's where the Zarates lived." The house was still Spanish style and hadn't changed a bit in the last 35 years.

"I used to play in those flood water ravines that run behind the houses. You couldn't let a kid play somewhere so concealed anymore." He sadly agreed. It was nearing time for Brayden to go to training so we headed back to the airport.

My plan was to make some sort of romantic picnic in our room that evening, so I set about looking for stores to find the gourmet items that I wanted. It wasn't coming together like I planned and it was almost time to pick him up, so I gave up for the day. When I arrived back to the room, he had gotten out of training early and had already been for a run and a shower.

I wrapped my arms around his waist and pulled him close to me, whispering softly and tasting the salt from his perspiration as I kissed him behind his ear.

"I like that," he said tenderly.

"You taste salty," I whispered again. "All I need is a shot of tequila and a lime," I giggled, as I moved towards his lips.

He tasted the saltiness on my tongue as I moved to his other ear. "I guess I should have taken a better shower," he said softly with mild amusement.

As we lay in bed talking, he said that he had been offered another job in Saudi Arabia and he asked me what I thought he should do. Brayden had promised me that he would only be there for one year and this would be his second. It paid really well but he still didn't like it there.

"You're asking the wrong person, because money just isn't that important to me," I replied.

"It isn't to me either."

"Then you need to follow your heart and not your fears, because your heart is most often right. But if you take it, I can't even come to see you."

"You could if we were married," he replied timidly.

I was so focused on not wanting him to stay in Saudi that I didn't realize he was asking me to marry him—but he was. I rolled over, staring at the ceiling as I began to cry. Brayden came closer to try to comfort and reason with me.

"When most women cry, their mascara runs down, yours runs up!" he laughed, as he wiped away my tears. "Go wash your face!"

I washed the black smear from my eyes, not knowing what to think. The distance between us had already made our relationship so difficult, that I didn't think it could withstand anything more.

As Brayden got dressed, I noticed the clothes he wore were trendier and very different from what I had previously seen him in. The TV was on and he had the channel set to one of those people's court shows. He made an off-handed remark that he had learned to watch the show Desperate Housewives. The way he said it was like he had accomplished something that might gain my favor. I disliked the moral values and relationship drama that programs like that and the one we were watching promoted. But I also knew that he must have learned to like it because he was spending time with someone who watched it.

"Do you watch Jerry Springer too?" I asked with mild disdain. His proud achievement didn't get the reaction that he expected and he went silent.

Later that evening as we lay in bed, he held me close. "Tell me that you belong to me," he asked tenderly.

Looking up at him I asked, "Do you belong to me?"

"Yes," he replied with love in his voice.

"Brayden... I can't share you anymore. I can't!"

"You don't have to, Julie."

Although I wanted to believe him, I wasn't sure if I could trust that he was finally serious and we truly belonged to each other now. A look must have come over my face because with gentle concern he asked, "What are you thinking right now? I can always tell when there's something on your mind."

"Can I tell you tomorrow?" I asked.

"Alright," he replied and we continued to lay there facing each other, enjoying the moment and holding each other close.

As we settled in to sleep, he pulled my leg over his hips, and adjusted me into my favorite sleeping position. I was surprised by it. *Had I done that with him before without realizing it?* We had been tangled up in each other in a beautiful and intimate way. Now, my position had grown to be uncomfortable and as much as I didn't want to, I had to adjust myself out of his arms, sensing his disappointment as I turned over.

The next morning, the first thing he asked was what I was thinking about the night before. It was a question that I hoped he wouldn't remember, but I felt that it was important I be honest with him.

My tone wasn't accusing, it was more that of reflection as I said, "I was thinking about how much I love you... About all of the women in your life and the e-mails that Janis sent to me last summer. I don't want to share you anymore, Brayden. I only read the e-mails once, but I saved them in case I ever needed help letting you go. And if I did, then I would read them again."

I watched as tears welled up in the corner of his eye. "I know that it's hard for you to talk about, but it was even harder for me to see them."

We hadn't discussed the matter much before. We both knew that it was an unpleasant incident that should never happen again, and I didn't feel the need to remind or berate him unless it did.

Brayden tried to dismiss the e-mails as something that Janis had fabricated. "Is she really that awful?" I asked.

He didn't reply, and I knew that he was only trying to pretend they weren't real. Somehow we ended up at the computer and I opened my e-mail. He went through each of them and understandably, he was left speechless. There was his dirt—right there in front of both of us to see.

One of the e-mails was from a Molly McDermott with the obligatory boob shot, "How about some fun with no strings attached, unless you want to attach them."

She bothered me most of all because although I knew that it was only a sexual relationship, they seemed to have known each other for a long time and those relationships aren't typically easy to give up. He was quiet now, but I hadn't brought it up to punish him. He asked me a question that I didn't want to answer, but I felt that it was important to be honest about what was on my mind the night before.

Later while we were talking he said, "Maybe we should be careful, because what if you get pregnant?"

Brayden and I had always talked of wanting children together. *Why would he say that?* "Do you want me to go to the pharmacy?" I asked, pausing for an answer that didn't come. "If you want me to go then I will."

He was silent. Acting as though nothing had happened, we went to breakfast before I dropped him off at training.

I was now a woman on a mission! Our time together was always spent in a hotel room and I wanted to do something special for him. I found the City Market in Dallas, a huge gourmet food store that had everything I could possibly want. I bought grapes and mangos; fresh bread; meats and cheeses; marinated mushrooms and Cipolini onions; German beer and Prossecco, an Italian version of champagne; and two small chocolate truffle cakes. I didn't forget the strawberry milk, because I knew how much he liked it. On the way back to the hotel I got a sudden inspiration for chilled shrimp, so I stopped at another store for that. I had already bought some pre-cooked flat iron steak with cilantro chimmichuri sauce, but thought that when in Texas, you should have beef brisket.

The plan was to have everything ready when he got back to the hotel room, but that wasn't going to happen because it was already getting late. I didn't want to do this the next day, so I stopped quickly at a place that was famous for its BBQ. Already discouraged because of the time, I was waiting in the car at a stop light when I felt a sudden jolt forward. *Oh great!* A young girl had hit me and we pulled over to call the police. The damage wasn't bad, just black marks across the bumper, but I wasn't a registered driver for the rental car. I called Brayden and left a message on his voicemail but he didn't call me back. As it turned out, the girl didn't have a license or insurance either.

Struggling with the groceries, I managed to make it to the elevator in one trip. The accident had only felt like a tap, and although I didn't feel anything earlier, I now began feeling tightness in my lower back. *Maybe I'm just stressed*, I reasoned with myself. Barely making it through the door of our hotel room, I was relieved when I dropped everything in the kitchen.

Turning the corner into the bedroom, Brayden was laying against the head board reading with ankles crossed and an empty beer glass on the table next to him. The expression on his face was that of indifference, as he looked up and asked if I was OK. But it was clearly obligatory and he didn't express any real concern for me. I told him that I was fine, but that I could feel my back tightening.

"Would you like another?" I asked.

"What?" he said defensively.

I nodded to his empty glass on the nightstand and said, "Another beer?"

He nodded yes, with indifference.

Attempting to give him an excuse for his bad manners I asked, "Did you have a bad day in the simulator?"

Again, he just nodded, as I walked toward him opening the bottle. I couldn't imagine that he would be mad at me. I had done nothing wrong and yet his mood was being directed at me like I was the one at fault. *His mood and my accident are not going to ruin my plans!* I set the beer down next to him and decided that I could throw this together quickly.

Except for the shrimp and veggies, everything else just had to go onto a plate. I arranged everything beautifully: white wedges of cheese with clusters of red grapes; meat evenly overlapped in slices, shrimp fanned out with cocktail sauce in the center; asparagus and purple fingerling potatoes with remoulade sauce. I dumped out the little basket filled with things to make coffee and lined it with a napkin for bread.

As I moved, I knew that I was going to be in trouble: my back was growing increasingly worse. Brayden laid there watching me, doing nothing to help, but that was just fine with me. I was struggling enough as it was and didn't need any more disapproval from him. I held my lower back as I bent down to place the plates on the coffee table in front of the couch. It was a beautiful display—certainly the best that I could accomplish in a hotel kitchen. I lit a Glade candle that I picked up at the grocery store and put it on the table. I just had to plate the mushrooms and onions and we could sit down together.

I called to him from the kitchen and asked if he would open the wine. Expressionless, he walked toward me and I saw him glance at the table with indifference. *He's not going to ruin this, he's not going to ruin this, my back is killing me!* While Brayden opened the wine, I put the last plate on the table and walked over to turn off the TV. It was Dr. Phil and he didn't need to join us for dinner. I meant for this to be special and even in Brayden's mood, it had to be obvious to him that I had put a lot of thought effort into it.

"Why'd you do that?" he shouted.

"What?"

"Why did you turn off the TV?"

"Are you serious...?"

"Yes!" he shouted.

"OK! I'll turn it back on because it's SO important to you! But I thought that we *might* be able to have dinner without Dr. Phil! I can't figure the TV out! You can turn it back on yourself, Brayden!"

He walked past me and plopped on the bed laying back against the head board. I began to have an entire conversation in my own head: *I just went through all of this work to do something really special while in obvious pain. He decided that he was going to be mad at me the moment that I walked through the door, and if it wasn't the TV, then it would have been something else. You just go ahead and pout you big freaking baby! I'm going to enjoy the food that I worked so hard to put together.* I poured myself a glass of wine and sat down on the couch to make myself a plate.

"This is really delicious, Brayden. Would you like some?" I asked.

"I'm not hungry!"

That was it! I decided to myself. *I'm not going to sit here in front of him while he occasionally looks up at me with disdain. I need some distance.* Picking up my plate and wine, I moved out of his view to the kitchen table. *Noooo... I think that I should have a little candlelight too!* So I went back to the coffee table and retrieved my ambiance.

While I wrapped up my romantic, picnic dinner for the refrigerator, I began to wonder if this was about the photos and e-mails discussed earlier. I had seen him do this before when he experienced a potential threat to our relationship, and he would withdraw or create a reason to be mad at me. His asking about being careful not to get pregnant, further convinced me it may be true. He had a way of turning things around on me, even when he was in the wrong. Margie had told me once that it was his way of playing offense. If he found a way to be angry back at me, then he gambled that I would be the one to try to make up, taking the light off him. It worked beautifully and I almost always fell for it. Later I made a conscious effort to try to recognize it as it happened. *But he was a master.*

Brayden walked into the kitchen and started making a packet of instant oatmeal.

"Are you sure that you don't want some of this?" I asked, as if nothing had happened.

"No, I want oatmeal."

OK, I thought to myself, *You have your oatmeal you big freaking baby!* He grabbed a strawberry milk from the fridge and lay down to watch TV.

"I don't understand why you're so mad at me, Brayden. I tried to make a nice dinner, I bought you beer and strawberry milk, and all I did was turn off the TV while we ate."

"You didn't buy that beer for me! I don't drink German Beer!" he replied harshly.

"Well—I'm really sorry about that! I was in a gourmet store and they didn't have Miller!" The tone of my voice was raised. "I suppose that I didn't buy the strawberry milk for you either!"

"You don't like strawberry milk!"

"Yes I do!" I protested.

It's pointless and this is a stupid conversation.

My back was becoming increasingly painful so I called my sister who had had a lot of health problems.

"Get some Excedrin," she said. "It's good to relax the muscles."

Brayden asked if I wanted him to go to the front desk and get some, but I replied, no. "If by chance I did get pregnant, I don't want to take any."

"You're being ridiculous!" he said. "Do you want to go to the hospital?"

"I don't know if it's bad enough, maybe I'll feel better in the morning."

He picked up the phone and called the front desk. "Hello, my girlfriend was in a car accident and I wanted to know if there's a hospital nearby."

Girlfriend? That's the first time I've ever heard him refer to me as that.

He got off of the phone and told me where the nearest hospital was. "Are you sure that you don't want to go?"

"No, maybe I'll just take some Excedrin."

He went down to the front desk and brought it back for me. By the time he returned to the room, I was really in pain.

Brayden called back to the desk to get the address of the hospital, saying, "My gir...*my friend* needs to go to the hospital. Can you give me the address?"

OK, now I'm not the girlfriend any longer. "No, I don't want to go," I responded. "I can't afford it. I'll just see how I feel in the morning."

When it was time to go to bed, he was still upset with me and said, "I'll sleep on the couch."

"If you sleep on the couch then I'm getting another room!"

We started to argue about everything. I picked up the phone and asked the front desk if they had any other rooms, and how much they were. $200. *I can't afford that right now,* I thought.

I hung up the phone and in a very calm and commanding voice he said, "You DO realize the consequences if you do that don't you?"

He was telling me that if I walked away from him like he had been afraid of all along, that it would be over and he would never forgive me for it. I had to be able to be there with him even when it got rough. It was understandable and I shrunk at the thought of losing him and the dramatics that I had just displayed. We went on to argue and he picked up the phone to mock me, by asking the front desk if they had another room he could stay in. But his tone was serious.

In silence, we each climbed into bed and as I lay there for a few moments, I thought about my old destructive patterns of fleeing a situation. I knew what I had done was wrong, and I could no longer behave that way—especially with him.

"Brayden?" I said quietly, "My mother use to run away like that when I was a kid and maybe that's where it came from. I want you to know that I'm sorry."

Without looking at me, he listened in silence, only giving me a slight nod of acknowledgement. But he wasn't going to let me off the hook that easy.

With the lights now off, he moved as far to the edge of his side of the bed as he possibly could. Reaching my arm around him to break the ice, he pushed it away with force, the moment that I touched him. I had apologized to him, and it was one thing not to respond to my touch, but to push me away like that was inexcusable. I jumped out of bed and started pulling the extra pillows and blankets from the closet.

"Quit making so much noise!" he shouted.

You're such an asshole, I thought to myself, as I made a bed on the couch, exactly what I told him not to do.

We were both silent as we got dressed for breakfast the next morning. He started to walk toward the door and I called to him, "Hold on! I just want to get my jacket." But he left without me.

OK, so this is how it's going to be? He had never shown me such disrespect and I didn't know how much more I could take. The last thing that I wanted was to have breakfast with him. So, I went to the hotel business center to send a few e-mails. Finishing quickly, I thought to myself, *Now what do I do?* I had seen him as I passed the breakfast room, and I either had to go back to the room, or sit at a table with him. If I sat at another table, that would make another dramatic statement. I would rather skip breakfast than to feel more of his rejection.

As I started toward the elevator, I physically felt as though I hit a wall of energy, and an outside force was pushing me back towards him. *No! I don't want to go!* I argued. But the energy only seemed to grow stronger and more urgent—It was the strangest experience. Surrendering, I went to the buffet to fill my plate. *I hate this... I hate this...* And again I thought about sitting at another table, but that energy reappeared and seemed to urge me toward Brayden's table. Without saying a word, I sat down beside him so I wouldn't have to look at him directly. He said nothing to me as he continued eating, occasionally glancing up at the news on TV. I ate as quickly as I could, then picked up my plate to put it in the bus tub and returned to the room. Without a doubt, I had been guided very strongly to have breakfast with him and as uncomfortable as it was, I somehow knew that I had done the right thing.

I made some calls to find a chiropractor, but the answer was just as I expected. "There's probably not a lot we can do. Just put some heat and ice on it."

When Brayden returned to the room I asked, "Do you want me to change my flight and go home early?"

He shrugged and gave me a slight shake of his head no, but didn't say anything. I couldn't tell what he wanted from me, but he didn't seem to want me to leave either. I had to ask myself though, *What is the point in staying?* We drove to the training center in silence and he got out of the car without looking back, or saying good-bye. I already knew the drill. He would call for me to pick him up and if I was too far away, he would get a ride from someone else. This trip really wasn't going the way that I had hoped for, but I could see a similar pattern with him from Wichita and Paris. I was willing to bet that our last night together would be wonderful and everything would be OK again.

I drove to Walgreens to buy a heating pad and ice pack. There wasn't much to do in Dallas, so I decided to go to the room and take care of my back.

Brayden called and said, "Wait 20 minutes and then come pick me up."

I waited for 20 minutes on the dot and then just as I started to walk out the door, he called.

"Where are you?" he asked with anger and frustration in his voice. "I told you to pick me up in 20 minutes!"

"I'm sorry—I thought that you said to wait 20 minutes and then leave."

"Please come pick me up NOW!"

When I pulled up in the car, his arms were folded and he was pacing back and forth. I could tell he was pissed at me, and he slid into the car without saying a word. I had a soft rock station on the radio and as we drove back to the hotel, he grabbed the knob with over exaggeration and switched it to a country station. *OK, you made your point,* I thought to myself. *You want to let me know that you're in control, but I'm not going to react because it's not worth it. You just go ahead and have your power, mister!*

Back in the room there was only more silence, before Brayden finally turned to me and quietly asked if I had changed my ticket.

"No," I replied.

A look of relief washed over his face, but he didn't say anything. I lay on the heating pad and watched TV while he sat at his computer. Lost in my own thoughts, I processed everything that had happened on the trip. I began to question if maybe this was just his personality, even though I knew in my heart that it wasn't. But if it was, then I knew that I could never be happy with him, no matter how much I loved him, and no matter how strongly I believed that a higher power intended for us to be together. It was time to lay the cards on the table.

I walked over to where he was sitting and leaned against the desk. "Brayden, there's something that I haven't told you about myself."

He looked up for a moment, but continued to half ignore me.

"I'm a very spiritual person, and I believe that we were meant to be together. But you're always creating reasons to put a wall between us."

He didn't say anything.

"The first man that I was in love with as an adult was a 32 year old Scottish/Italian Learjet pilot that was eight years older than me. The same age as you when we met, but you were eight years younger. You and I both drive the same car from the same year, but you got the color that I wanted. We both bought those cars because we had big white dogs. And we both basically drove the same cars before them. I really think that we met because we have the opportunity to have a love that most people don't ever get the chance to experience."

"Why? Because it's destiny?" he asked sarcastically.

I realized that it was going to be a losing battle to try to reason with him. If his mind was closed, then I wasn't going to be able to open it.

"Just think about it," I replied before walking away.

Although we had never discussed it, Brayden knew that there had to be some sort of fate or destiny involved in our meeting. He himself had pointed out the uncanny similarities between us. And in the beginning of our relationship when I said, "Do you realize that I almost went to Mexico instead of Florida? And then we would have never met." his reply was " If you would have gone to Mexico, I would have ended up there—I'm certain of it." But now the reality of it was a threat to his control over his emotions, and he was either unable or unwilling to process it.

My back hadn't made much improvement so my mom suggested that I take a hot bath. The hotel had a Jacuzzi, so I put on my suit and told Brayden where I was going, but he didn't seem to care. The hot water worked wonders as I sat in front of a strong jet with the water pounding on my lower back. Feeling much better, I headed back to the room and decided to go out for dinner.

"Do you want to join me?" I asked.

"No," he said flatly.

I passed by a Mexican restaurant that was lit up like Las Vegas with big palm trees and water fountains in the tile courtyard. *This place has to have great food!* I sat in the bar watching sports as I continued to process everything. *Maybe as much as I believe in us, we just aren't going to work out. How could I live with his behavior? Maybe it's just the way that he is and I'm making excuses about the walls.* Dinner was mediocre to say the least and I was losing my appetite thinking about the possibility that I may just have to let him go—regardless of how much I loved him.

Brayden said nothing to me when I arrived back at the room. I didn't want to make things worse because I still had hope for us, but he was making it very difficult for me to hold on to that hope. If I slept on the couch again, I would be quitting. If I slept in bed with clothes on, that would be making a point. I remembered something that I heard someone say once, "If you win the argument, then all that you've done is won." I always liked that saying. I went into the bathroom and slipped on a hotel robe, walked to my side of the bed and slipped it back off before I climbed into bed. I tried to go to sleep while he watched TV, but everything kept running through my mind.

The next day would be our last together, and I certainly wasn't going to spend this one in a room with someone who wasn't speaking to me, *Why? Because I had turned off the TV to have a romantic dinner together. Yes, that was definitely worth the wrath of Brayden.* Even though I knew there was more to it than that. When I was a kid, we use to go to Six Flags over Texas. It was a lot like Disneyland with all of the rides and cartoon characters. *"That's what I'll do!"* I thought. *I'll go to Six Flags!*

"Brayden? I was thinking about going to Six Flags. Do you want to come with me?"

"What's the point? You don't like the scary rides. There would be nothing for me to do!" he replied with disdain.

"OK, well I'm going to go," I replied calmly ignoring his remarks. "If you need anything, give me a call." I was half way there and decided to call the room. "Are you sure that you don't want to join me? It should be fun and it's better than sitting in a hotel room."

"Why are you asking me? I told you that I didn't want to go!" he said.

"OK, just checking," I replied cheerfully.

I arrived to the park only to find that it was closed for the season. *Great! Now what do I do? I can't go back to the hotel and I don't want him to know that I didn't have a wonderful time without him.* I started driving aimlessly and stumbled upon Old Town Grapevine. As I wandered through the shops, my mind was in a fog as I continued to think about our relationship ending. I had pretty much had enough of his mistreatment of me, and I was no longer certain if I had the ability to continue to overlook it.

Slowly as the fog began to lift, I began to process the situation more clearly. I knew without question that this wasn't the real him—he had integrity and was kind hearted and compassionate. There are moments when you're able to look into another person's soul and I had looked into his. The bad boy behavior was a blanket of defense that he had wrapped himself in at an early age. I had seen it in a girlfriend of mine who had been emotionally and sexually abused as a child. She tested her relationships beyond reason to see "who stayed and who quit." She understood it about herself, but seemed powerless to control it. The damage that took place resulted in a level of emotional immaturity that could only be healed through time and trust in the person she was with.

Brayden's bad day in the simulator or me turning off the TV had nothing to do with this. He was self-sabotaging. Talking about the e-mails Janis sent and making a decision about his employment put our relationship in jeopardy and it scared him. In my heart I knew that it wouldn't be this way if we were together because he wasn't this irrational by nature. But the way he dealt with real conflict probably wouldn't change, at least for quite some time. Volatile and dramatic relationships were all he had ever known, and that wasn't me. I've always said, "You are who you're around." So although I knew I couldn't change him, I hoped that with more time spent together, I could find out if the behavior would correct itself.

I dreaded returning to the room, and was relieved to find that he wasn't there. I thought he must have been running. Brayden's wallet was laying on the desk beside his computer. I'm the kind of person who wouldn't look in a drawer at somebody else's house, but if I took a quick peek it wouldn't hurt. I was afraid if I did more than that, he might notice something was out of place. When I opened it, I saw his insurance card. "Brayden Loch, policy number xxx, 2000 Jeep Grand Cherokee, Green, 4 door." *Hmmm. . . I guess in some ways I always wondered if he had told me that we drove the same car as part of a pickup line, even though he told me what he drove before I did. Now here's the proof right in front of me.*

I settled onto the couch with a book and my heating pad. When he came back from his run, he said nothing to me as he walked into the room. After showering, he lay down in bed to watch TV.

"You do realize if it's like this when I get on the plane tomorrow, that we'll never see each other again," I said.

He didn't reply, but seemed only to be deep in thought. A little while later, I could see that mischievous expression start to appear on his face.

"Come over here," he said playfully.

"No," I replied, without looking up from my book.

"Pleeeeze?"

I walked over to where he was laying with my book in hand, thumb between the pages so I wouldn't lose my place.

"What are you reading?" he asked, as he snatched the book from my hand.

"It's Michael Crichton's book *Next*. Can I please have my book back?"

"No!" He held it away from me like a little boy taunting me.

"Fine!" I said as I walked back over to the couch and picked up the newspaper.

I heard the sound of paper tearing and I looked up to see a sly grin on his face. "I'm tearing your book," he said tauntingly.

"That's OK," I replied casually, "I'll just buy another."

The tearing sounds continued, but later I would discover that he was only running his fingernail across the page. *If this is his way of breaking the ice, then I don't much care for it,* I thought to myself, as he watched me ignore him.

My friend Kate and I had been texting each other with play-by-play updates.

"Why don't you just call her?" he asked with frustration and annoyance in his voice.

Probably because he wants to know what I was saying to her, I thought to myself. I didn't reply.

"What's he doing now?" Kate texted.

"Acting like a total motherfucker!" I texted back.

Brayden came over to the couch to stand over me. "What are you saying to her?"

Calmly looking up at him from over my paper, I replied, "What a mother fucker you're being."

He kept his game face on but I knew inside that he was amused by my defiance. I silently changed my expression as if to ask, *"Are there anymore questions?"*

Saying nothing, he returned to the bed and watched me with ankles crossed, rocking his feet back and forth. In need of a distraction, I went into the kitchen to make a plate of leftovers from the expensive picnic dinner he had refused to eat. As I sat on the couch reading the paper and plucking grapes from the stem, his face lit up like he just swallowed the canary.

"Aren't you going to offer me some?" he asked playfully.

"Do you want a plate?"

"Well, I want something on it. Not just a plate!" he replied jokingly with slight sarcasm.

Oh! You think you're real freaking funny don't you? I thought to myself. Ignoring him, I lifted up my newspaper.

His tone now soft and polite, he asked, "Would you please make me a plate of food?"

Without a word, I went to the kitchen and put several things together that I thought he would like.

When I brought it to him, he took the plate and set it down on the bed quickly, grabbing both of my wrists hard and held me there, playfully. His eyes lit up and I saw that person who seemed to get triggered now and then.

"Let me go!" I urged.

"No!"

Grinding my teeth but not quite angry I said, "Let me go!"

"No!"

I had been taught by my father how to twist my wrists in this kind of situation to get away. I almost had it, but he was too strong.

"Oh!" he laughed. "You almost got away from me there!" And he let me go, probably remembering what happened in Paris when he had pushed me too far.

Calmly, I turned away and then he was on his feet behind me. I walked over to a basket of crackers and picked several up. As I walked back to his side of the bed, he trailed close behind me, intrigued by what I might do next. I lifted the blankets on his side of the bed and quickly crumbled the crackers onto his sheets. He grabbed me to make me stop and the moment turned light-hearted. Brayden swept the crackers onto the floor as I walked into the area where my suitcase was, and watched me as I changed into my yoga pants and tank top. He rolled his eyes as if to say, "She's putting on granny clothes." But what I put on was cute and sporty. The black teddy wasn't coming out of the suitcase—yet.

I climbed into bed to watch a movie with him, not mentioning the disagreement. The mood was much lighter, but it wasn't going to turn around right away.

He ate the food that I had brought him and asked, "Do we have more shrimp?"

We? I thought. *It sounds like "we" are a couple.* So I went to the kitchen and brought him more shrimp.

"Do we have more asparagus?"

"Yes." There was that *"we"* again. I was so focused on it, that I forgot to get more for him.

Still hungry, Brayden decided to order food to be delivered.

"What do you want?" he asked, as we held our heads together scanning through the menu.

We decided to share a cheese steak sandwich and some wings. The food arrived in a brown paper grocery bag. As I lay a bath towel down as I usually did when we snacked in bed, he had the same look of intrigue and fascination as he had when I had done it before. For some reason, Brayden decided to poke eye holes and a mouth into the bag and put it over his head. I was laughing so hard, that I had to take pictures, as he proceeded to eat his sandwich and wings while wearing this paper bag on his head.

It made me reflect on my many dark days without him when he disappeared without contact. I would douse my pain with too much wine and watch *The Holiday* with Jude Law because he resembled Brayden, and it was my way of feeling closer to him. In the movie, Jude's character put a napkin over his face and was Mr. Napkin Head. Now, it reminded me of Brayden's paper bag head. The pain had been almost unbearable and I tortured myself by watching other movies that reminded me of us: *P.S. I Love You, Atonement* and *P.S.*, a wonderful movie which most people haven't heard of. Sometimes one after the other, until I couldn't stay awake any longer. I was tormented knowing how strong our love was, but that Brayden was constantly fighting it. The movies helped me to feel connected to him while he was gone.

When the bag came off and it was time to watch a movie, Brayden started flipping channels.

"Can we watch School of Rock?" I asked.

"I just watched that!" he protested.

"So what? You just watched this one earlier."

So as one movie had a commercial, he would flip to the next. I was looking at the screen laughing, when in my peripheral vision I could see that Brayden had been watching me for some time. And I could sense that he was thinking about how much he loved me, but when I looked back at him, he quickly turned his head and pretended to be watching TV.

As the movie ended, Brayden leaned over me, silently watching his own fingertips as they moved smoothly across my chest, and up to the back of my neck. Pulling me closer, he kissed me deeply, as his hands moved carefully under the straps of my top, and down from my shoulders.

The next morning, he sat on the corner of the bed and watched me in fascination as I put on my make-up and did my hair. I slid on my jeans, which had become tight from my many months of drinking my pain away.

He said with a smirk, "Do you need a shoe horn to get into those?"

"I know, huh?" I replied in agreement.

But then I realized it was another test to see how I would react. He almost seemed perplexed that I didn't get angry at the comment like many women might.

We both seemed to be in quiet contemplation as we packed our suitcases. His flight was earlier than mine, so he would return the rental car and I would take the airport shuttle. After breakfast, I helped him out to the car with his bags. He was headed to Wichita to pick up the plane he had flown back to be repaired, and I asked if there was any way that he could change his flight so we could have more time together.

With a big, tender sigh he said, "You know that I can't do that." I was disappointed, and wasn't ready to say good bye. "Hop in the car!" he said with excitement.

We drove around to the hotel lobby. "I need some coffee, come with me!" It was his way of delaying our good-bye a little longer, as he pulled me quickly by the hand and into the hotel. As we sat in the car with his coffee, I wrapped my arms around him and tears began rolling down my cheeks.

"I don't want you to take that job," I pleaded. "But I understand that you have to do what's best for you."

"I haven't taken the job yet," he replied softly, with reassurance in his voice. "I'm sorry, hun, I have to go now but I don't want to."

We kissed goodbye and I stepped out of the car. I could see him watching me from the rear view mirror as he drove away—then he was gone.

"I don't love you because I need you...
I need you because I love you"

~ Erich Fromm

12

We all look back at things that we've said and done that make no sense whatsoever—I'm no exception. After our time in Dallas, I began wondering if what Brayden said was true. That we now belonged to each other and I no longer had to share him. I called and got his voicemail.

"Hi, I was just thinking about everything. I just thought that I would call Molly so that I'm comfortable knowing that the relationship isn't going to continue."

When Brayden called me back, he was beyond angry. "I can't believe that I you would consider doing such a thing! That is SO obscure!"

I realized at that moment how ridiculous it was, but I was already in trouble and he wasn't going to let me back track.

"She doesn't even know who you are! You're being ridiculous! I have things to do! I have to get back to work!"

Click.

To: Brayden Loch   *February 16, 2008*
From: Julie Hopper
Subject: The car

Did you verify that the accident wasn't covered under the insurance that you purchased? If the car had been parked and someone hit it, it would have been covered so I don't know why it wouldn't in this case since it wasn't my fault. I need to know because otherwise I need to try to get my deductible covered by the owner of the car which isn't likely to happen. I'm hoping to wrap this up as soon as I get the revised police report back.

So... I guess that I should just assume that our relationship is now over? Is that what you want?

To: Julie Hopper   February 18, 2008
From: Brayden Loch
RE: Car

I'm pissed at the whole contacting Molly thing. You are right a relationship with no trust is no relationship at all. I was and am angry with that issue.....

I sent several e-mails and called him with no reply. Looking back through all of my old messages, I hadn't realized how confused I was myself. I would send one trying to talk him out of taking the job and then the next I would tell him that I would probably go with him— *"Probably."*

Brayden needed to know that if he allowed himself to love, that I wouldn't change my mind and leave him. I had been focused on *his walls*, but my own were becoming clearer to me. I had gone to Sophie and she said something that struck me as odd.

"Does he know what you really want from him? Because I don't think that he does."

How could he not know? I thought. But looking through the e-mails, I really wasn't making myself clear. I was resistant to the idea of giving up my career to go to Saudi Arabia; but I was also trying to leave the door open so he could make his own decision whether to stay in our relationship or not.

I had spent too many years trying to control my past relationships, trying to convince the men I was with that we belonged together. The Empath that I had seen years earlier told me that my lesson to learn in this lifetime was to learn to love without control, and I had to continually remind myself not to try to control it. There was a fine line between working on our relationship and not holding on too tightly. After what Sophie said, I realized that I was going to have to make a decision. *Am I going to choose my career over the love of my life? And is my belief in what we have so strong that I will gamble the career that I've built, and leave it all behind to start a life with him?* His past behavior didn't make me feel secure in that decision, and even though I knew I wanted to be with him, I still felt uneasy.

To: Brayden Loch   *March 6, 2008*
From: Julie Hopper
Subject: Just another thought :)

I know that right now you're just trying to figure out what is best for you and that understandably should be your focus. I of course am thinking about how your decision might affect us. I suppose that it only matters if you want a future with me...I seem to talk more about it, but I hope that you want it too. I talked to a couple of people that know others that have a similar situation and it's working for them. They are going for the money, but she is staying in the States.

I know that we would actually see each other more than the people that I've heard about because I have a job that allows me to be gone and travel. I have a tendency to live and think outside of the box, so I'm open to anything and really like the idea of a short term sacrifice for the long term benefit. I don't need to sell real estate like you need to fly, so if it didn't work being apart, I could go there but that idea depends on how you feel about us. Maybe if you took it, you would want to leave your options open so that you could meet someone that already lives there.

Anyhoo :) I'm in baby! Whatever you decide is fine with me. I know that I want to be with you, but if your plans don't include me, I still want only what is best for you.

Love,

Julie

He didn't reply but a couple of days later, he answered my call.

"Did you make a decision about the job?" I asked.

The tone in his voice was somber as he replied, "No."

"Did you get the e-mail that I sent you?" I said with mild excitement.

"You sent me an e-mail?" he asked with concern.

"Yes."

I heard him breathe in a couple of hard, quick breaths , like someone who's trying to hold back from crying.

"I have to get off the phone. I'll call you tomorrow!"

I was confused. *Why was he getting so emotional?*

The next day Brayden called me.

"Did you read my e-mail?" I asked with excitement.

"Yes."

"So you know that I'll go to Saudi with you, right?"

"Yes," his tone still a little somber.

"Why were you so upset when I talked to you yesterday?" I asked.

As he started to explain, his voice began to crack and he was breathing in those hard, quick breaths that I had heard the day before. I could hear him fighting back his emotions as he began to speak.

"Because you gave me an ultimatum in Dallas: you or the job. Then you didn't call me and then you said that you had sent me an e-mail."

"But you did read my e-mail and you know that I'll go with you, right?"

"Yes," he replied.

I hadn't given him an ultimatum in Dallas, I had only expressed my concerns; adding that I understood that he had to do what he felt was best for him. But he knew my heart wasn't in going to Saudi Arabia, and he felt like he was between a rock and a hard place. We talked a couple of times more before Brayden dropped out of site like he frequently did. I knew that he had a dark side and that he was probably sorting through his life. He was under a tremendous amount of pressure trying to balance his career and our relationship. Things had been so rough in Dallas that I could hardly believe it myself, but I had gone from loving him before the trip to being deeply in love with him now.

To: Brayden Loch   April 4, 2008
From: Julie Hopper
Subject: All that I know is that I'm in love with you...

I read a quote that said...I don't love you because I need you...I need you because I love you. And I do need you Brayden.

I wasn't going to e-mail you again because I don't want to communicate this way and I want to give you space right now if that's what you need. But I crossed the line in Texas from loving you to being in love and now I'm just worried that because I've let my feelings go there, that somehow the bottom is going to drop out.

If it's time that you need then take it. But if your good bye last week was your last one, then it's important that I know.

Always,

Julie

He wouldn't respond to any of my attempts to reach out to him, and I was becoming frustrated as I tried to understand all of his dynamics, even though I knew it stemmed from his childhood. I decided to surf the web for information on adults who had been abused as children. I wanted to know if they followed any behavioral patterns in their adult relationships. I felt lucky to have found the website *adultsurvivors.blogspot. com* because it explained so much of Brayden's behavior.

The article talked about how adult survivors frequently had something similar to Post-Traumatic Stress Disorder. Not only was it beautifully written, but a lot of it sounded very familiar to me. It explained Brayden's personality changing quickly at times, like a defense mechanism kicking in. It didn't scare me anymore, it just helped me to understand him better and recognize when he was in a different zone, so that I could try not to react in a negative way. It was a relief because it confirmed much of what I had already suspected about his behavior.

The article said that when children are being abused, they take on the responsibility for the abuse as if it's their own fault, because they look up to their parents and don't want the parent to be at fault. Even though they clearly are. This goes on to destroy their self-esteem because they take on the responsibility for being a bad person and deserving this punishment from the parent. The child grows up to believe that they don't deserve to be happy. This really struck a chord in me because the previous year when I asked Brayden in an e-mail what he wanted, his reply was "Cars, Career, Kids and a happy relationship. But I don't feel like I deserve it." He had capitalized every word except "happy relationship," ending by saying that he didn't feel that he deserved it.

I was at a loss for what to do. Brayden and I needed some real time together so I could get through to him. But he was half-way around the world in a country that I couldn't go to unless we were married, and he was still keeping me at a safe distance. I figured that he wouldn't read the article if I sent it, but maybe he would read just enough to recognize some of his own feelings and it could possibly help. I sent the link to the article with no message and I got no reply. In some ways I was glad because it could have backfired on me and made him angry. A few days later, I followed it up with an e-mail.

To: Brayden Loch   *May 13, 2008*
From: Julie Hopper
Subject: I left this out

   There is an internal beauty that I see in you that I'm not sure that you see in yourself....I've told other people about it, but I don't think that I've ever told you that I see it in you.
   That's all..I just wanted you to know that I recognize it in you.

To: Julie Hopper   May 17, 2008
From: Brayden Loch
RE: I left this out

   Just thaught I'd let you know that I didn't take the job in Saudi Arabia... I wans't sure if I should even send you this e-mail at all. But I leave here the end if next month. I'm looking for other jobs right now but nothing has come up as yet.
   I hope your doing well.

Brayden

To: Brayden Loch   *May 17, 2008*
From: Julie Hopper
Subject: I left this out

   I'm glad to hear from you because I didn't know if you were OK. I'm also glad that you didn't take it because I had a feeling that it wasn't the right decision for you.

Were you not sure that you should tell me because you don't want to be together? It's important that I know. Please don't wait to answer.

Julie

To: Julie Hopper   May 17, 2008
From: Brayden Loch
RE: I left this out

I didn't tell you because I couln't be honest with you if I don't know what I was doing with myself first. It sounds a little selfish I know but it's the honest answer.

To: Brayden Loch   May 18, 2008
From: Julie Hopper
Subject: I left this out

That really doesn't answer my question if you want to be together...I wish that you would realize that you can be honest with me. It may hurt me, I might get upset...but I need to know where this relationship stands instead of making assumptions.

I really do understand feeling that way and not knowing what you're going to do with yourself. I've been there so many times myself and it's confusing as hell, but if you want to be together, we need to start talking by phone and making decisions together to see if we can figure it out.

I'm worried that it's not going to be possible for us...I told you the night that we met that I was worried about that. I have big roots in Oregon. Not only my family and friends, but I love it here and it's taken me years to build up my work. I love you too, but I know that it would be hard to find a job that would allow you to live here. That is...if you wanted to.

Please let me know if you want to try to work it out.
I love you...and I miss you.

Julie

He didn't reply and several weeks later when he finally answered my call, I felt like I had just won the lottery. It was ridiculous and most women would have just given up, but I was certain that eventually we would have a breakthrough. When Brayden answered, he was happy to hear from me. He had found another job in Saudi Arabia flying as the private pilot for a Saudi prince. It was a good job and it paid really well. I was disappointed, but the economy had tanked in the States and I knew that he wouldn't have been able to find a good job here.

He still had a joint account with his soon to be ex-wife in Florida. They made an agreement that he would pay for all of the bills and she would manage the money. Once they were divorced, she could continue to live in the house rent-free for a year and he would pay all of the expenses.

"And what do you get?" I asked.

His reply sounded ridiculous to me because she was definitely getting the better deal, but I understood his decision. He went on to tell me that she had been skimming an extra $1,000 per month from the account, and I said that he just needed to get the divorce and be done with it. I told him that I had come across a website that had some answers that might resolve his dilemma and that I would send it to him.

To: Brayden Loch
From: Julie Hopper
Subject: Website link

June 30, 2008

I'm really concerned for you that if she is willing to skim 1,000 a month that you will have gone through all of this and something won't go right in the end. You should also have your credit checked to make sure that she hasn't opened any other accounts in your name.

I'm glad that I called today....I wasn't sure if I should. It was so nice to hear your voice, I just wish that you weren't so far away. Have a safe trip and we'll talk more when you get back to Paris.

Love,

Julie

To: Julie Hopper   July 1, 2008
From: Brayden Loch
RE: Website link

Mind your own business bitch and by the way I am now naming you in the divorse. So good luck. It's STUPID bitches like you THAT believe his bullshit that caused us to divorce in the first place.

Oh and by the way he has had a girlfriend in Saudi and has since last year and never has had any intentions of ever really being with you. You were and always be just a piece of ass to him. My marriage and how Brayden and I handle it is none of your business.

Janis was in his e-mail again. I didn't hear from Brayden after that and it was all becoming too much for me. I reflected back to our time in Dallas when I first became suspicious that he was dressing more stylishly than he ever had before, and had stated almost proudly that he had been watching the TV show "Desperate Housewives." It was as if I should be impressed by it, when in fact, shows like that repulsed me. I knew immediately he must be watching that program to make someone else happy. But I also knew that a young man living and working in a Muslim country would have a regular sex partner, so Janis referring to a girlfriend didn't surprise me, even though it hurt to hear the words.

I was the one putting all of the effort into our relationship and it just kept going in circles. I wanted to have a child and I had been planning on having one on my own before I met him. Then I put it off hoping that things would come together for us, and we would have one together. Over a month passed and I realized that I needed to make a decision. I was about to turn 42 and time was running out for me. I ordered a catalog from a sperm bank and looked through it to find the right combination of what I wanted. Most of them were Scottish, of course.

To: Brayden Loch   *August 14, 2008*
From: Julie Hopper
Subject: My doctor's appointment

Brayden,

I'm sorry to send an e-mail because I know that she'll read this. I just couldn't bring myself to call you after not hearing from you. I struggled with whether or not to send this at all, but I don't care anymore. You'll understand why when you read it.

I was in a store a few weeks ago and a boy about 12 came in by himself and it was obvious that he had been crying...my heart just broke for him. I knew then that the pull was too strong to ignore it and wait for a three person family. I can't risk waiting any longer and not being able to have one of my own. I know that I'll make a great mother :)

I'm telling you this because I've chosen a donor and now it's just a matter of setting my first appointment. I plan to do that by the end of the month. There is absolutely no room for regrets once I've started the process and if there is a conversation left to be had between us, now is the time to have it. It's completely up to you. Am I scared?

Absolutely....But I'm more scared of wanting something and dwelling on the "what if's" until I lose the opportunity.

As I said...there is no room for regrets and so I at least need to know that you got this. You don't always get my messages and I have no way of knowing if a reply actually comes from you. If we have nothing left to talk about, then please just leave me a voicemail simply saying that you got this so that I don't keep sending it and I can move on. Having to send it multiple times will only reinforce that she was right and I really didn't know you at all. If that's the case, then I wish for you, or both of you, nothing but the best.

Julie

To: Julie Hopper   August 15, 2008
From: Brayden Loch
RE: My doctor's appointment

Julie,

Greetings from Megeve, (south of France, in the Alps)
Don't ever apologize for sending me an email. I'm glad you have decided to email me. you stopped calling and like I said before I don't want to call you and upset you, when I don't know if you want to hear from me.

So who is the donor? and how do you intend to conceive? I am glad and disappointed at the same time that you have made this decision and wish I could be a part of it.

Why do you say "you wish for me or both of us?" Janis has her life and I have mine. She now has a boyfriend whom "i think" she is content with. please don't loosetouch with me as I think that will be up there as one of the worst days I know. You are truley a beutifull person and I want to have you in my life in any capasity I can.

Brayden.

What I left out of my e-mail was one of the little signs that my spirit guides had given to me. The little boy who came into the store crying had ended up in the check-out line in front of me with a small container of Chinese food. That was no big deal, but as we were standing there, I felt a strong pull to reach down to hug and comfort him. At that moment it was as though someone had tapped him on the shoulder and he turned to the cold drink case behind us. When he came back to the line, he was holding a container of strawberry milk. He could have gotten a soda or anything else. Besides Cajun, Chinese food and strawberry milk were two of Brayden's favorites, and we had just had a conversation about it in Dallas.

After getting his e-mail I called him. He was in Geneva, Switzerland and we talked only briefly because he was on his way to interview a pilot. In my mind though, I wondered if he was meeting a woman. He explained that the Saudi Prince had a house in Megeve and that he spent a lot of time there. We talked about my plan to have children and that I wanted to have this baby with him. He wanted it too, but he was running late and could he call me tomorrow? The following day I didn't hear from him and so I called. He had lost his passport and was frantically trying to find it. I knew that he would be unable to leave Switzerland without it, so as much as we needed to talk, the timing wasn't right.

I got a call from him a week or two later and he was in an airport on his way to Mexico. I didn't ask, but I hoped that he was going there for work. I knew in my heart though that he probably wasn't, which would mean that he wasn't alone either.

We began to talk about our relationship and having a baby, his voice cracking as he said, "What if you change your mind and then it's too late and then we've made a mistake?"

"I won't change my mind, Brayden."

The background noise suddenly became so loud, that I could barely understand him.

"I'll call you when I get back," he promised.

I truly believed that he wanted this with me, but I wasn't certain that he could overcome his fears. I sent him messages to reassure him, but there was no reply. I thought about what Sophie had said. *"Does he know what you really want?"* I realized that I was asking him to have a baby with me but I wasn't bringing up marriage. Maybe he didn't realize that I wanted both. I just wanted him to be the one to ask me.

Everything was swirling around in my head. I knew that Brayden spent a lot of time on the internet and he had an international phone. *Why would we have to wait to talk until he got back?* I would get sudden flashes of inspiration as to how to reassure him how wonderful our life would be together. Then I would call and leave sweet voice messages sharing my thoughts with him. *OK, I'm going to have to stop this,* I thought. *He's going to think that I'm a crazy person and I'm trying to control this too much.* So I decided to just lay it out there in an e-mail.

To: Brayden Loch   *September 3, 2008*
From: Julie Hopper
RE: Would you consider becoming my husband?

That's how I know that I won't change my mind Brayden. I kept hoping that you would ask me but you haven't....Please don't make me ask you through e-mail. I hoped this could happen in person.

Love,

Julie

It was September 10 and I was at an open house for one of my real estate listings.

Brayden called and spoke tenderly as he said, "I just got back from Mexico and listened to your voice messages. All ten of them!" he laughed.

"Ohhhh! I'm so sorry!"

"Don't ever apologize for leaving me a message," he replied.

The rest of the conversation was an emotional blurr. We were just two people telling each other how deeply we loved one another. As we said good-bye, he promised that he would call me the next day.

That night, I looked at his Myspace profile, like I frequently did, and there was a new woman that had been added as a friend. Her name was Kristy and the photo of her was obviously on a cruise ship. Brayden had taken a Mexican cruise shortly after we first met, and now he's just gotten back from Mexico. *That's it! He's just a player and that's all he will ever be! All of this fate and destiny business is just coincidence and I let myself get sucked into it!* I was absolutely furious with him.

I called and got his voicemail. "Hey, it's me…." I said lovingly as my voice trailed off. "I was just thinking about how much I love you… and then I saw your new friend on Myspace!" my tone turned harsh and sarcastic. "I have to tell you Brayden Loch, you're really good! I've met a few players in my life but you're the best that I've ever met. I really believed that you loved me and wanted a life with me. You know all of that emotion and voice cracking when we talk? You ought to use that on Kristy because it's very convincing! I really loved you Brayden… but I guess that I was wrong about us. Take care!"

I relayed the message and situation to my friend Kate and she said, "Why does he insist on poking the bear?" She continued by saying she thought that I had overreacted. It made me second guess myself, but this relationship was exhausting me and he had just pushed me way too far this time. I had absolutely no interest in ever talking to him again. I was finally done! I harbored great anger toward him and disappointment toward myself. And when I would get flashbacks of the true love, tears, and emotion that he had shown me, I disregarded it, even though I knew his feelings for me were real and it wasn't possible for anyone to act so convincing.

For me, that feeling didn't change until the morning of October 10, when I woke up with an overwhelming feeling that I needed to call Brayden and ask him to marry me. *Where the hell did that come from?* But it wasn't going away and the urgency increased as the hours passed. I called Kate and told her how I was feeling.

"Yesterday I despised him and never wanted to speak with him again. And today, I wake up wanting to ask him to marry me? Am I freaking crazy?"

"No, you're not crazy!" she assured me. "If you're feeling it that strongly then maybe you're supposed to do it."

"OK, but I can't believe that I'm about to do this!"

I paced the floor nervously with my phone in hand, as I took a couple of deep breaths. Pressing the button for contacts, I scrolled through and found Brayden's name and held my breath.

He answered, "Hello?"

"Hi, it's me... I have something to talk to you about."

"Are you pregnant?" he laughed, in an uncomfortable way.

"No," I replied, taking another deep breath. "Brayden... I'm in love with you, and 'this thing' that we do has got to stop." He made a sound of agreement. "I have something to ask you and I'm really nervous, so please bear with me."

He was silent.

"A long time ago you wanted me to ask you a question and I told you that I was too old-fashioned and that you would have to ask me. Well—I'm going to ask you now." *Deep breath.* "Will you marry me?"

Without hesitation he replied, "You know that I would at the drop of a hat! But what about the distance?"

My voice became determined as I said, "If it's important then we'll work it out. Is it important?"

"Yes."

"Then we'll work it out, right?"

"Yes."

My tone turned soft as I said, "You didn't officially answer my question—Will you marry me?"

"Yes!"

"Thank you."

"You're welcome." And we giggled.

After talking about how much love we had for each other, he said that he was in Dubai and on his way to have a drink with another pilot when I called.

"I have to go meet this guy, but I'll call you in about an hour or so, OK?"

An hour passed and I was anxious. *Is this real? Did we just get engaged?* I needed to talk to him again so I could be sure. I didn't want to seem too anxious, but I couldn't wait any longer. I called him back and asked what he was doing.

"Still having a beer," he laughed.

"Are you sure that you want this?" I asked with concern.

"Julie... I know that I want it. I just want to make sure that you want it too."

"Oh, I want it!" I said with enthusiasm.

"I'm just tired of making bad decisions in my life." he replied with mild disappointment.

"Well, this is the best decision that you've ever made! I'll let you get back to your beer now," I laughed.

Brayden called me a little later and I asked him, "Can I get excited now?"

"Yes," he said lovingly. "You can get excited now."

"You do realize that I'm already planning our wedding don't you?"

"Don't you think that we should see each other again first?" he replied with a laugh.

"I guess so," I shrugged.

We were happy and excited. It seemed as though after all of this time, the chase was over, and we were finally headed in the direction that we both knew that we wanted all along. Little did I know, our biggest challenges were just ahead of us.

"All the trials and tribulations, the greatest losses, are gifts to you. It is an opportunity that you are given to grow. This is the sole purpose of existence on this planet earth. You will not grow if you sit in a beautiful flower garden and somebody brings you gorgeous food on a silver platter. But you will grow if you are sick, if you are in pain, if you experience losses, and if you do not put your head in the sand but take the pain and learn to accept it not as a curse, or a punishment, but as a gift to you with a very, very specific purpose."

~Elisabeth Kubler-Ross

I3

As the years progressed since my first spiritual experiences, I had learned to sense when my spirit guides were around, and how they would sometimes calm and reassure me in a very subtle way. I also knew they had made the synchronicities between Brayden and me so obvious, that it would help to prevent me from giving up on him through all of the struggle and pain. If there had been fewer, or only minor coincidences and synchronicities, or both his deep love and fear of it wasn't so obvious to me, then, without question, I would have given up on him. But it was clear to me that the universe was not only at work in bringing us together, but in keeping us together—even with all of Brayden's self-sabotaging. Their guidance was about to become more obvious than it ever had been before, and without it, I surely would have walked away from him.

After our engagement over the phone, Brayden and I talked daily via webcam. That much contact on a regular basis hadn't happened since the very beginning of our relationship. We didn't talk much about getting married, or children. We just spent the time growing accustomed to the change in our relationship after so many months of talking infrequently. He had just had time off when he was in Mexico, so he wouldn't be able to take time off again until December or January. I didn't question him about Mexico because it no longer mattered. But he assured me that he would come to Oregon so we could make plans. *Thank you, God!* It was now mid-October and with being able to see and talk to him as if it was in person, I was sure the time would fly by.

Brayden was considering another job that would bring him back to the States and he was just waiting to find out the terms of the contract. He would be flying in Europe and working one month on and one month off. He could live here and commute every other month and the airline had some sort of allowance for that. I was overjoyed! I thought that Saudi Arabia could be an adventure because I liked that sort of thing. But this way, I could keep my job and we could live in the States.

As we were talking on the webcam one day, he caught a glimpse of my mother in the background and shouted, "Hello mom!"

She quickly ducked behind the wall and said, "Hello Brayden! I would come talk to you but I don't have my makeup on."

We all laughed and I assured him that I would introduce the two of them the next day.

Wondering how it might go, my mother and I sat in front of the webcam as I dialed up the connection. When Brayden appeared on the screen I said, "Mom... I want to introduce you to the love of my life."

As we talked, my mother proceeded to tell Brayden all of the things about me that she didn't think he would know. "She's a wonderful cook and very well adjusted. We use to call her the man of the family because she can fix just about anything. Did you know that she can install a toilet?"

"No, I didn't know that," he replied matter-of-factly with a grin.

As we were talking, out of the blue Brayden said something about Julie having a lot of e-mail accounts. That struck me as odd, and I didn't really know what he meant by it. But it registered in the back of my mind as we continued with the conversation.

My mother said her goodbyes, and I asked, "So, what do you think?"

"She's cool, I really enjoyed talking to her," he replied. He seemed to be getting comfortable with the idea that she would be a new person in his life.

We began to talk about how deeply we loved each other and tears started rolling down my cheeks. I spoke about the other women and how hard that it had been for me, adding that none of it mattered anymore, because the only thing that mattered was us.

"I want to look forward and not back."

As we were saying good-bye, he looked at me full of love and said, "I've never doubted your love for me, Julie."

"I just love you so much, Brayden!"

"I love you, too."

We became engaged on October 10 and now it was October 29. Saudi Arabia is 11 hours ahead of Oregon. Brayden had called me early in the morning, but I didn't hear the phone. He called again later and we decided to get on the webcam. He was glowing with excitement and practically bouncing off the walls as he sang a little tune of happiness for me. He had just ordered dinner, so we talked until it arrived.

"Let me call you back after I've finished dinner," he said.

I didn't hear from him for a couple of hours, but it showed that he was still on Messenger so I sent him a video call invitation. He answered and I could immediately tell that his joyful mood had now turned serious. It was as though a heavy weight was suddenly on him.

"What's wrong?" I asked.

"Nothing..."

"Well, you seemed so happy before you got off the webcam to eat dinner and now you're mood has changed. Is everything OK?"

"Let's not talk, can we just be quiet and look into each other's eyes?" he replied.

I was scared and confused as we sat there gazing at each other, and in my mind I was thinking, *What is going on here? And why does he just want to look at each other?* He moved the camera so I could only see one eye for a moment and I saw a tear rolling down his cheek. *What is going on?* I thought to myself. *He must be wiping away more tears from his other eye—that must be why he moved the camera.* After a couple of minutes which seemed like an eternity, he said that he was tired and had to go.

I didn't know what to think but it couldn't be good. Everything had been going so well between us and now suddenly something was wrong. I was working from home that day and it was around 2:00 in the afternoon, which would be 1:00 AM for him. I was on the computer when out of nowhere, I suddenly got a terrible sickening pit in the bottom of my stomach. I didn't understand it, but then the thought popped into my head to look at Brayden's Myspace. There was a new woman on it. He had also changed the city in Florida that he was from to, Jeddah and dammam, Saudi Arabia.

I was more upset about the woman, but why would he change the city he was from? And why would he capitalize all of them except for Dammam? I called him to ask what it was about.

"I'm sleeping!" he yelled and hung up on me.

The next day we talked about it and he explained that the woman used to be his neighbor, but I wasn't buying it. He was still furious with me for waking him up to ask about it and nothing I said seemed to help. He stopped all communication after that.

In one of my flashes of inspiration, I remembered him telling my mother that I had a lot of e-mail accounts; and when Janis was breaking into his own e-mail, I had set up a new one for him that he never used. I hadn't thought about that account for over a year, so I decided to log on. There were updates for links to new love matches from a dating website. The dates seemed to have begun around the time that I broke things off over his last new friend. The one who it appeared he may have gone on the Mexican cruise with. I knew that Brayden was passive aggressive, and often tried to hurt me in return for the hurt that I had caused him. Because I understood that about him, it often buffered the pain.

I looked up his profile on the website, and there was an obvious message to me. I had remembered having been drinking heavily one night around that time and woke up with one of those slight panics like, *I hope that I didn't drunk dial him last night!* But apparently I did.

The message on his profile had small animated characters of a dancing pickle, beer mug, angel and devil in place of words. The title was: "Do I have your attention now?"

Well...What should I really say other than this site does need better monotoring and people should really chill out a little more 🥒 Oh! and one more thing! 🍺 can make people 😇 but most people 😈 ....

His occupation was listed as an alcohol taster. I thought it was funny at first, until I realized what he was really trying to do was hurt me by setting the account to send his love matches to an e-mail address I had access to. My thoughts shifted as I realized the link to his new matches said: "...and don't forget that your password is *flyhigh.*" Although it's against my nature to snoop, Brayden's mood had changed drastically on the 29th and I needed to know what was going on with him. I decided to try the password on his e-mail account and it worked.

I found several messages from Hilary Sinclair, who held a significant position in Saudi security. There was talk about the cruise to Mexico that they had been on, and how romantic everyone thought his proposal to her on board was. *PROPOSAL?* She went on to talk about all of the research she was doing for their wedding, and had forwarded Brayden an e-mail from her mother in England saying how they needed to set a date and get the deposits put down, because men often delay the wedding and then it doesn't happen. To me, that made it sound like she was having to put pressure on him.

Then I came across several e-mails from her updating him on the progress of the construction of their condo they had purchased in Bulgaria. *Bulgaria?* Brayden had just spent the last several years trying to get out of debt—that was why he was in Saudi in the first place. Although he wasn't a weak man, in some instances he was and I knew

there had to be some kind of manipulation on her part, to get him
to commit to something like that. She was trying to tie him to her
financially—that was clear. I found another e-mail from just before they
went on the cruise, in which she was putting tremendous pressure on
him to start trying to get her pregnant.

I was in a state of shock, mixed with utter panic and disbelief as
my body began shaking. *I know that that I'm not wrong about him, but am I?*
I sent my girlfriend Kate a 911 text message to call me, before driving
to the store for a big bottle of wine and a pack of cigarettes. She called
while I was pulling into the driveway.

"He's engaged to another woman!"

"What do you mean, how do you know?"

I told her the story about my flash of inspiration and that I had used
the password from the link to get into his e-mail. I was in the house
now, slugging down a big gulp of wine and chain smoking while I paced
the floor.

"Are you going to tell him that you know?" she asked.

"No."

"Are you going to look at his e-mail again?"

I was starting to calm down by now. "No, I don't think so." The
pieces started to fall together in my mind.

"You know, he asked her to marry him before I called and he said
that he wanted to marry me. He told me that he was tired of making
bad decisions in his life. Maybe this was what he was talking about.
That he had made a bad decision by asking her to marry him and
now he is having a hard time getting out of it. Maybe he got scared
about our talk of having children, and proposed to her on impulse. I
know he tries to find diversions from his feelings for me. Maybe that's
all it was. She's obviously putting pressure on him about planning
the wedding. I think that I'll just see how it goes because I may read
e-mails that I could misunderstand, and I don't want to make it worse
for me."

"Well, I couldn't do that!" Kate said. "I'd be all over that! Julie, you
have to write a book! This kind of thing only happens to you. The

whole thing with remembering the e-mail account and then finding the password so you could learn about the engagement?"

"These messages and flashes of inspiration happen to everyone. You just have to pay attention to the patterns in your life," I replied. "I'll write a book if Brayden and I end up together. Otherwise, the messages wouldn't mean anything to anyone, and people would just think that I was making all of this up."

I was on my way to the computer the next morning when I had to run to the bathroom and throw up. I called Sophie for an appointment and I would have called Margie too, but she had retired in the spring. Sophie answered and I was able to get in to see her that day.

What luck! Her readings about Brayden always seemed to have a negative spin and I had almost quit seeing her because of it. Margie's had always been reassuring, so I thought that Sophie may only be looking at his actions and not his reasons behind them. We sat down and I explained what I had discovered in his e-mail.

"Well if he's doing that, then it's only to distract him from doing what he really wants and that's to be with you. He won't marry her, but if he did, it would be really sad because he would be losing the only thing that's ever meant anything to him in his life. He's just so attached to you!"

Whew! I was relieved because this was the only positive reading about Brayden that I had ever had with her, even though they were almost always identical to Margie's.

Kate and I talked about the reading and I decided that I was just going to act as though nothing had happened. Brayden had a pattern of disappearing, and maybe he was just being a coward and hadn't figured how to get out of that marriage proposal yet. Maybe he just needed some time to work everything out. Kate and I both practiced the Law of Attraction, taught in the book *The Secret*. Whether positive or negative, the thoughts and expectations you have in your life are sent out into the universe, and you manifest those thoughts into your life, whether consciously or subconsciously.

"It's time to go shopping for a wedding dress!" Kate announced. "If things go south, then it's going to be bad whether we plan the wedding or not."

I left a message for Brayden saying I was going dress shopping. I had a gentile, loving tone in my voice as I added, "I want to find a dress that's soft and romantic…I can almost see you in a dark suit jacket, cuff links and no tie. I love you Brayden, and I can't wait to spend our lives together."

I hoped that I would start to break through to him or at the very least, he would tell me what was going on with him.

Kate and I met the following week to look for wedding dresses and I found one that I fell in love with. I put a deposit down and although the store normally didn't allow pictures to be taken, they let me.

Once home, I started looking at the detail in the photo, and it appeared as though I had a big, puffy tulip right in the crotch area. *Oh no! Thank God I saw this before I bought it and had wedding photos with a big puffy spot in my crotch.* As I zoomed in, I could clearly see the pattern of a joker in the embroidery. I e-mailed it to Kate.

"What do you see here?" I wrote.

"OMG!" she e-mailed back. "That looks like a devil!"

Devil or joker, that was not going to be the dress!

Disappointed, I arranged to get my deposit back and went to a few more stores, still not finding anything in my budget. The last store I went to had a dress on clearance and I knew it was "the one." Strapless and form fitting; ivory with small, blush colored flowers; and beautiful embroidery with a lot of sparkle. It had a slightly Celtic look to it and although it wasn't at all what I had imagined, it was exactly what I was looking for.

"I'm coming right over!" Kate said when I told her.

I couldn't believe that she had driven 45 minutes through rush hour just to see my dress. Only a true friend would volunteer to do that. I could tell that it wasn't what she imagined for me either, but we both agreed that in many ways, it was perfect! I called and left a voice mail for Brayden filled with love and excitement that I had just bought the perfect dress, but there was no reply.

Recently, I had set up a Facebook account and decided to see if Brayden had one too; he did. I tried the password that I found for his e-mail to log on and it worked. My heart sank as I saw several pictures of him and Hilary together. She was petite, with a ruddy complexion and straight brown hair just past her shoulders. She seemed plain looking to me, but I didn't know who she was as a person, and that still worried me. As I looked more closely, I realized that none of the photos seemed to reflect two people in love. Their energy and body language indicated distance and although they stood with an arm around each other, there were no embraces that reflected any genuine emotion. For me, it was a huge relief.

I thought about Sophie saying that he wasn't in love with her. There weren't any messages to other women either before the 29th when he had acted so strangely. But from October 30 through mid November, he had sent a message to a new woman everyday on Facebook, fishing for a date. I knew that Brayden had the ability to numb his feelings for me and put them away in a box. Now it was obvious to me that he was trying to find distractions.

I had told myself that I wasn't going to look at his e-mail or Facebook again. I couldn't bear to see anymore photos and I didn't want to misinterpret any messages between them. But I still didn't have an explanation as to why he was crying when we last spoke and why he had suddenly disappeared. I decided to look at his e-mail again and found a message from him to Hilary, asking her to take down a phone number for Jeddah Mums. *Mums?* I thought. *That sounds like a baby!*

My heart sank as my mind raced and I ran to the bathroom to throw up. Now I was terrified, and I understood why his mood had changed so quickly and he was crying. He wanted to marry me, but the night that he said he just wanted to just look into each other's eyes was the night that he found out she was pregnant. That's why he changed the city he lived in to Riyadh, Jeddah and dammam—she lives in Dammam. I knew that he had no intention of leaving another baby because he had lost contact with his son from his first marriage. *Oh God*, I pleaded. *How could this be happening? After everything we've been through?* I didn't want to believe it, but I knew this was probably the end for us.

Still in a state of shock and hoping that there was some sort of other explanation, I went to see Sophie. She said that she did think that Hilary was pregnant, but there was something very deceptive about it. She went on to say that she was trying to tie Brayden down by any means possible, and she wouldn't be surprised if the baby wasn't his.

"Do you think that she was just telling him that she was pregnant, but really wasn't?" I asked.

"No, I think that she is, she replied." Sophie went on to ask if the woman was dark.

"No, she's British," I replied.

"That's strange; she must just have a really dark aura. She's very controlling and I think that she's used to getting her way and may come from money."

"Do you think that he'll go through with it and marry her?" I asked.

"No, I think that it will fall apart by spring," she replied. "But she's putting a lot of pressure on him and she's having other people pressure him as well. Brayden doesn't want to marry her, but if they back him into a corner he might have to."

That same night, I had one of my message dreams where I'm having a conversation with someone, but I only get a short message and there's no visual.

"She's not pregnant," the voice said.

I woke up feeling at peace, but wondered if it may be my wishful thinking affecting my dream. The next night, I had the same dream.

"She's not pregnant," the voice said.

OK, that's not a coincidence, and if I wasn't listening before, I'm listening now. Sophie thought that the pregnancy was real, but she also said there was deception around it. Psychic messages are subject to interpretation and if Brayden thought she was really pregnant, then she may have picked up on what he believed to be true.

I began to wonder if Hilary had seen our e-mails after Brayden and I had gotten engaged and told him that she was pregnant to tie him down.

She worked in Saudi security and because of terrorism, they monitor all communications from phone to e-mail. Certainly they would monitor the people who worked for them and those they spent time with. Even if that wasn't the case, Janis had no problem breaking into Brayden's e-mail, and the timing of it just seemed to be too convenient for her.

On November 22, I saw that Brayden was logged onto Messenger and I let him know that I was there if he wanted to speak to me. We had a brief exchange that seemed to go pretty well, but it was too soon for me to address his disappearing, and it certainly wasn't the moment to bring up his engagement and the baby. He told me that he took a new job flying with the Saudi Prince's new airlines. He would be flying larger planes and he started training in two months. We decided to get on the web cam, but I had a lot of trouble on my end.

He finally popped up on the screen and it was a relief to see him. He immediately looked away and started fidgeting.

"What are you so busy doing?" I asked.

"Trying to charge my phone."

"Well, it seems like a lot of work," I laughed.

I could tell that he didn't want to look at me directly, and I later wondered if he was planning to drop the bomb on me but couldn't bring himself to do it.

"I have to go, I'll call you back in a few minutes," he said.

Brayden didn't call me back, so I decided to continue to play dumb. A confrontation wouldn't get me anywhere because either he was trying to work things through his own mind, or he wouldn't be able to bring himself to tell me the truth.

To: Brayden Loch   *November 26, 2008*
From: Julie Hopper
Subject: GOBBLE GOBBLE

Today I'm giving thanks for...

Having a joy for life and the resources to live it...For family that makes me crazy and true friends...

For meeting the love of my life and waking up one morning, brave enough to ask him to marry me...For him saying yes without hesitation...and the possibility that he might just love me so much, that it may sometimes scare him....and for me still being here when it passes...

For seeing in him more than I hoped to find in a man and more than he may see in himself....and most of all...I'm thankful for you.

All of my love,

Julie

I told myself that I wasn't going to look at his e-mail again, but after the Jeddah Mums message that I found, I couldn't help it. I wanted to know for sure if she really was pregnant. I read several e-mails, but there was never any mention about a baby. I read one from her that said that she was headed to Scotland in two days to put the deposits down on a castle, where they would be married. In reading all of the e-mails, I could see the constant pressure she was putting on him, but he seemed to be an unwilling participant.

The next day she sent him an e-mail that said, "I'm sorry that we didn't have a nice conversation last night. But I'm off to Scotland tomorrow to taste cakes, Oink, Oink. I'll call you when I get back my big, fluffy ball of chipstery stuff!"

You've got to be kidding me! I laughed out loud. *Big fluffy ball of chipstery stuff? Who the hell says that? And how could he leave me for her?* In the address line where the person's real name should appear, she had his name listed as Chipster. True—Brayden did have a bit of a chip on his shoulder at times, but was her term of endearment for him actually a derogatory nickname? It was hard to imagine that someone would go so far as to use it in place of a person's real name in their contacts.

As I nervously monitored his messages, it became clear that not only did she hold a high security position, but she was also very well connected and had probably helped him get his last two jobs. I was growing increasingly nervous because not only was she "pregnant," but she was putting deposits down on their wedding. *How could he leave her and save face after that?* I called Sophie to ask her what she thought and she said it was time for me to let him know what I knew. *He's either going to be supremely pissed at me or. . . I can't imagine how else he might react. Maybe he just needs to know that I know, so we can talk openly about it.* I had no idea what to say, but at this point I had nothing to lose.

To: Brayden Loch   *November 30, 2008*
From: Julie Hopper
Subject: I have to tell you something...

Do you remember when we were in Dallas and we were talking about us being together fate? That I had first been in love with a Scottish Italian Learjet pilot that was 32 and 8 years older than me, and that you were also 32 and 8 years younger when we met? That we drove the same car, in the same year, for the same reason, but you got the color that I wanted? I could go on and on... they're not coincidences. And what's between us is undeniable...you know that.

I think that I got the impulse to ask you to marry me in order to prevent you from making a huge mistake. And after all of these years...look at the timing. Do you remember telling me that you were tired of making bad decisions?

I tried to look in your wallet in Dallas but I couldn't because that's the way that I am. I got another one of my impulses though when I saw the links to the dating website with your pass code and nervously got into your e-mail. I'm truly sorry for that. But I know about everything including the baby. I have no doubt that you have feelings for her...but I believe that it's your fears that cause you to make bad decisions in order to avoid what you truly want. And it gets you into difficult situations that you don't know how to get out of.

You have tried to push your feelings for me aside for the last two and a half years and haven't been able to. In a moment of clarity and without fear or hesitation...you said yes to me. You listened to your heart and that's what you have to do now. There can be two people broken by this, or one. You are still trying to come out of a marriage that wasn't wholehearted...do you really want a third divorce a couple of years later when I've had to move on?

We WILL get through this together Brayden. I'm not angry...It's just something that we have to deal with together.

YOU...are the love of my life. And I know that you feel for me something that you may not have ever felt before. Making the wrong decision now...will only cause more harm, than making the right decision for us. We will get through this together.

I love you,

Julie

I got no reply and he didn't change his password. *Strange!* That would have been the first thing I would have done. I continued monitoring things and then sometime around December 15, I read an e-mail from his ex-wife congratulating him on the baby. My heart sank as I read the words. *She really is pregnant.*

Then I read Brayden's angry reply: "Hilary lost the baby!"

This is interesting—Hilary told Brayden she was pregnant two weeks after Brayden and I became engaged, now she's lost the baby as soon as deposits were put down on the wedding? At that moment I believed that the message dreams I had saying that she wasn't pregnant were truly what they seemed to be. And the deception around the pregnancy that Sophie picked up on was that she may have been lying about it to trap him. In Saudi Arabia, most top level people are related. *The Saudi prince who Brayden is employed by, is probably a cousin to Hilary's employer. Now there's money down on a wedding and how is he going to explain walking away from her after she just lost his baby?* I felt it was an impossible situation for him, and I felt numb by the thought of it.

I watched the steady pressure that she was putting on Brayden through her e-mails. This woman was on a mission to get married but she seemed to be having to pull him along. I hated to witness her doing that to him. She pleaded with him several times to give her the e-mail addresses of his contacts to send out "Save the date" invitations. The addresses were right there on the same account that he was receiving her requests from, but he wouldn't send them to her. Finally I read an e-mail from her saying that she had gotten them from his mother.

I knew where they were getting married and the date, but I didn't have the time. The invitations that she sent said, "We're getting hitched." It certainly wasn't a card that I would have chosen if I was marrying a man that I was in love with. They were to be married on June 5, 2009.

My future life with him was in the balance and although I was getting reassurances from Sophie as well as my own guides, I wanted a third unbiased opinion of what was unfolding. I fully believed that Brayden and I were destined to be together, but everyone has free will and out of fear or disregard for their own intuition and guidance, they can choose to take the wrong path.

I had never had a reading with anyone as accurate as Margie and Sophie. But with Margie retired and no other resources, as much as it pained me, I Googled psychics in Portland. I was a skeptic and knew what not to say before determining if someone truly was gifted or not. Up popped several, but none of them felt right. Then I saw the name Renee Madsen. *I remember her! I had a reading with her back when I was devastated about Duff. She didn't tell me what I wanted to hear, so I didn't go back. I know better now, and that's exactly why I should see her!*

I didn't remember much about my very first reading with Renee, except that she told me Duff wasn't the one who I was going to marry and she said that I would have two sons. Sophie had also told me that she thought I would have two sons, and they would be twins. Either that, or I might have one child right after the other. But she also qualified it by saying that the baby could be a Gemini, for which the astrological symbol is twins.

Renee who is a medium/intuitive, was now somewhat of a local Portland celebrity, and appeared regularly on several TV and radio stations. Although I was nervous about what she might say, I didn't want to carry false hope—I needed to know the truth about the situation. Renee was young, with shoulder length dark hair. She had a joyful spirit that was almost electric, and she giggled a lot.

When she opened the door, the first thing that she said was, "You're here about a relationship."

"Yes," I replied, as I thought to myself: *that question would probably apply to 75 percent of her clients.* Until I knew without question that she had a true gift, I would remain skeptical and tell her nothing.

"What is it that you want to know about," Renee asked.

"I just want to hear what comes through," I replied.

"No problem," she said casually, "I understand."

The next thing out of her mouth was, "There's been talk of marriage, but he disappears on you."

I didn't react. She went on to say that he could use some counseling.

"I don't normally recommend someone do a remodel on another person," she said, "But he would be worth it. You understand him in ways that others wouldn't and you're the right person to do it."

I was happy, relieved and dumfounded at the same time. She was so accurate. I was able to understand Brayden to the core, regardless of what he put out there on the surface.

She continued by saying, "Although you've talked about marriage, he uses other people to distance his feelings for you, but he's not a player."

Margie had told me that he wasn't a player either. As much as I believed that, it was reassuring to hear it from two very gifted psychics. The guides must really want me to know that, regardless of how things appeared on the surface. Renee was rattling off information so quickly that I couldn't write it down fast enough, but I didn't need to. It was like listening to someone who understood the dynamics of our relationship so perfectly that I didn't need to explain anything to her. I had told her nothing, and yet she was very specific with details that no one could have ever guessed.

I had heard enough. She was the real deal, so now I could ask her questions. Gifted intuitive aren't vending machines. Sometimes you have to ask specific questions and even then, if the guides don't believe that it's in your highest good to know, they either won't tell, or they'll speak in riddles. I told her that I found out that Brayden was engaged to another woman.

"Do you think that he'll marry her?" I asked.

"Stop holding your breath!" she urged. "You'll break the cord between us and I'll lose it! No, I don't think that they'll marry. I think it will fall apart by spring. I don't even think that they like each other all that much. *Wow! She's a piece of work!* I think that she's just tired of being alone and wants the wedding. I keep seeing the movie *Maid of Honor.* Are they getting married in Europe?"

I could not believe she said that! In the movie, the woman is marrying a man at a castle in Scotland, a man she knows is wrong for her. At the last moment, her best male friend who's acting as her "maid of honor" but who she's also repressing her feelings for, shows up and the wedding doesn't happen.

I left feeling uplifted and hopeful. Sophie had given me the same timeline: it would be over sometime in the spring.

Not long after that, I had a dream that Hilary, Brayden, and I were sitting in the front, bench seat of a car together. She was driving and he was sitting in the middle between us. There was a seam in the seat, which caused Hilary and Brayden to sit on the long side, while I was on the short side. Then Brayden looked at me with a loving smile, reaching to hold my hand, before leaning over to kiss me. In the next scene, I was behind the counter of a drug store soda fountain and they were sitting across from me on stools. I said, "Brayden, it's time to start having our children." Hilary turned to him and said, "Aren't you going to tell her?"

Brayden looked at me with a mischievous smile like he had a secret, and then the dream ended.

I interpreted it as indicating the long distance between us, and that Hilary was in the driver's seat controlling everything. I was certain that it was some kind of message because there was so much clear symbolism in it. I would later have more dreams that were similar. In the next one, Hilary was working feverishly in a wedding tent. She came out disheveled and asked me in a panic if I had seen Brayden.

"No," I replied. Then in the dream I remember thinking, *Why are you asking me that? Of all people!* But I also had a feeling of emotional detachment from it all.

I went to see Sophie again for an update, telling her about my dreams and that I thought they were messages. She agreed and said it was the same thing that she was getting. She said that Brayden didn't want to get married to this woman, but that he was getting a lot of pressure. She added that he was really stressed out and unhappy. If they got a hold of him, he might have to marry her.

"I would never be able to forgive him if he did that!"

"Well, it's something that you might have to deal with," she replied. "He doesn't want to marry her and he'll regret it even before he does it. Why is he doing this?" she asked with confusion. "He loves you so deeply. He's never loved anyone in his life the way he loves you."

She thought that I would see him in February and went on to say, "If he marries her, it won't last six months before he'll know he has to come back to you. He knows that you're meant to be together in this lifetime."

I told her that Hilary lost the baby as soon as the deposits were down on the wedding and that I thought the pressure on him to marry her was work related. She had big connections in Saudi Arabia, and Brayden had just taken another job working for a new airline owned by the Saudi Prince he had been flying for. She agreed that there was a strong money connection, as well as Brayden wanting to save face.

I went to Renee for my second opinion, and what she had to say was virtually identical to what Sophie said. When I asked her about the pregnancy, she didn't believe that there had ever been one.

"Why do women do that?" she asked with disgust.

While taking a nap a few days later, I had another message dream. No visual, just a sound bite of a conversation with someone.

"*Sophie is right,*" the voice said.

"What about the negative things?" I asked with urgency.

"*Sophie is 100% right,*" the voice replied.

And then I woke up. I was trying to figure it all out. That was a pretty strong statement saying that she was 100% right when nothing seemed conclusive in her readings. But in my own wishful thinking, I thought back to the first positive reading that I had with her when I first found out about Hilary. She told me that he wouldn't go through with the marriage. That she was just a distraction from doing what he really wanted to do and that was to be with me. I hoped it meant that he wouldn't go through with it. Not that he may be pushed into a corner, and I may have to deal with him getting married.

Around this time I got another sound bite in my sleep. It was Brayden's voice in an agitated way saying, "*Are you sure that you want this?*" The next thing he said was "*I'm in love with someone else!*" When I got these messages, I could never be completely certain if it was my subconscious or not, until they were validated. Brayden had asked me many times before "If I was sure I wanted this." I would just have to see what happened. I hoped that it would be a confession that he would make to break off the marriage.

To: *Brayden Loch*   *January 13, 2009*
From: *Julie Hopper*
Subject: *I'm sorry for writing*

I'm probably the last person that you want to hear from Brayden, it's just that everything that I believed to be true is now gone without word from you and I'm trying to understand it.

I believed that you loved me as deeply as I love you...that you wanted to be my husband, as much as I wanted to be your wife. So I need to ask you if you're sure, because if you aren't and you don't love her the way that I believed that we loved each other, then no matter the reason for marrying her, you would be denying her the opportunity to find someone that would love her that way. If Duff hadn't broken my heart....you and I would have never known each other.

If you haven't married and want to talk I would like that, but if your feelings for her are stronger than what you feel for me, please just be open with me and let me know because I want someone who loves me completely and that would change things for me. Please let me know Brayden.

Julie

To: Julie Hopper   January 14, 2009
From: Brayden Loch
RE: I'm sorry for writing:

wat are you talking about? I'm divorced not married.

Brayden

To: Brayden Loch   January 14, 2009
From: Julie Hopper
Subject: I'm sorry for writing

If we're not going to talk like adults, please just tell me and it's done....but give me that at least for the love that I've had for you Brayden. I need a beginning or an end.

I had been sitting at my computer when his reply popped up. It was almost 2:00 in the morning when I sent the e-mail back to him, so I decided to call him. He seemed to have a knack for picking up when I had been drinking. He probably realized that based on the time of night, he would have the upper hand in the conversation.

"Hello?" he answered.

"Oh Brayden! I'm so glad that you answered. I miss you so much!"

The phone disconnected. The cell service in Saudi is spotty and that happened frequently. I called back, and we got disconnected again. It happened a couple of more times and I gave up.

He called me back and this time he had a sense of urgency and desperation in his voice. "Why didn't you call me back? Didn't you get my text?"

"No, I didn't." I replied with the same urgency and desperation.

The tone of his voice was that he wanted to talk to me as much as I wanted to talk to him.

"Have you been drinking?" he asked.

"Yes, but I'm OK. I'm sorry that I got into your e-mail."

"You got into my e-mail? he asked with urgency and surprise.

"You knew that. I sent you an e-mail fessing up and telling you that I knew about her and that you're engaged."

He went silent and didn't say anything further; as though he didn't get the e-mail and didn't want to acknowledge that someone may have deleted it before he read it.

"I am not engaged," he said flatly.

"Brayden, I know that you are."

"I'm not engaged!"

OK, *he's not going to admit to it.* I went on to tell him how much I loved him and miss him, and that maybe all of this was happening the way it was supposed to because otherwise, I wouldn't have gotten the urge to ask him to marry me after he asked her. I began to cry, but they were happy tears because I just loved him so much.

"It's 3:00 in the morning, you need to go to sleep," he said tenderly. "I'll call you later."

In a little girl voice I replied, "You don't mean in February or March do you?"

"No," he laughed, with love and amusement in his voice. "I don't mean February or March. I'll call you tomorrow OK? I love you."

"I love you, too."

He hadn't gotten my message telling him that I had been in his e-mail, so someone must have intercepted it. I checked his account and he changed his password after we got off of the phone. I knew that it was strange that he hadn't changed it sooner.

The next day I called him because I was on my way to an appointment and had to get on the road. I also thought that if I was driving, then it might be a distraction for me. I was fearful of how the conversation might go. Brayden answered and he was now trying to be mad at me.

"I can't believe that you broke into my e-mail!" he reprimanded.

"It's a good thing that I did. I needed to know that you're engaged."

"I'm not engaged!"

"Brayden, I know that you are."

"I'm not engaged!"

Here we go again, I thought to myself. "We haven't seen each other in a year, Brayden. Is there any way of making that happen?"

"I'm training in London in February."

"I could meet you there," I replied.

"OK," he said in an earnest and loving way.

I went on to press him for an answer. "Just answer me this—is your love for her stronger than your love for me?"

He was trying to change the subject and he didn't want to acknowledge that there was anyone else. So I asked the question again, but decided to pull over.

"What's that sound? Are you standing next to a clock? Stop it!" he said, in an angry tone.

"No, it's my turn signal. I'm pulling over."

"Why are you pulling over?"

"Because I didn't think that I should be driving if I'm disappointed with your answer."

I stopped the car and asked him again. "Brayden, I just need to know if your love for her is stronger than your love is for me. It's OK—you can answer. It might hurt me, I may be upset, but I need to know the truth. Can you answer my question?"

"It can be answered," he said lovingly. "Look, I have to go, we'll talk later."

Brayden had an amazing ability to avoid questions and I always seemed to let him off of the hook. The fact that I gave him full permission to tell me the truth and the desperation in his voice the night before when we couldn't connect, spoke volumes to me.

I was hopeful about London but my excitement quickly faded when I couldn't get a response from him. I was reaching a point where I no longer had anything to lose. The closer it got to the wedding date, the more likely it was he would go through with it. But part of me still believed that at the very least, he would have a last minute meltdown and the marriage wouldn't happen.

To: Brayden Loch   February 4, 2009
From: Julie Hopper
Subject: Hello

Brayden,

I know that you've climbed into your cave again and so I'm guessing that seeing you is out of the question. There's still time, but I think that you know that it would be very difficult for you to marry her if we did see each other again. You know how much I love you and so I still hope that you'll change your mind.

It's because I love you that I want you to think about something.... In some ways it's none of my business and I understand that, but in a way it is because it affects our relationship.

Do you remember the e-mail that I sent to you saying that my friend thought that there was a lot of deception around the baby and that she was trying to tie you down in any way she could? It occured to me and I could be wrong....but did she tell you that she was

*pregnant shortly after we got engaged and then lost it about the time
the wedding deposits were put down?*

*Brayden, even if I'm not the one that you want to be with....I want
you to be happy and be with someone who deserves you.*

Love,
Julie

Two days later I had another message dream.

"There will be ten," the voice said.

That's all I heard, but somehow I knew that it meant ten women
on his Myspace. There were five now and as I watched his page, sure
enough, the next day there were three more. But that didn't add to ten.

A few days later there was another one. *OK, there's nine.* A week went
by and another one popped up. *OK, there's ten.*

What I said about the possibility of the deception with the
pregnancy and the deposits must have pissed him off. Now he was being
passive aggressive and trying to hurt me in the only way that he knew
how. It made me angry, yes. But aside from a momentary reaction at
times, I really had no fear of losing him. A baby was an entirely different
scenario and it terrified me. That would be the Kryptonite to our
relationship.

Even now as I was being faced with the possibility that he could
marry someone else, I knew that I wouldn't lose him forever. There
was no feeling of jealousy. It just made me angry that he would do the
things that he did. I think that may be the difference in a soul mate
connection with someone who you're truly meant to be with. There's a
pure confidence in the union and almost no fear—*almost.*

The number of women stayed at ten until mid-summer when my
nieces' boyfriend deleted all of her friends and she was no longer on
Brayden's page. Looking back, I think that it was my guide's way of
letting me know that they knew the outcomes. But I also began to realize
that they speak in riddles.

Time was passing with a lot of unanswered attempts to get a response from him. My intuition had been telling me that Brayden wouldn't get married, just as Sophie and Renee had agreed. And as the time of the wedding grew nearer, their message remained the same: Brayden did not want this marriage and he was trying everything that he could do to get out of it. But he was getting a tremendous amount of pressure from Hilary and the others around them. Brayden was worried about saving face. And although they had both thought that things would fall apart by March, it was now the end of April and the wedding was just over a month away. Aside from a last minute meltdown on his part, it wasn't looking good. I still felt strongly that I would never be able to forgive him if he married her. Even though Sophie said that it wouldn't last six months and Renee said that it wouldn't last either. *How could I forgive him for asking me to wait years for him, only to marry someone else?*

To: Brayden Loch   *April 27, 2009*
From: Julie Hopper
Subject: Road Trip

Hi Brayden,
*   I hope that you're well and that you will please reply to this. I wanted to know if you still intend to marry her?*
*   The reason I ask is that if that's what you want to do, then I plan to buy my ticket at the end of next week. I would start in Ireland and drive the coast into Scotland. It's money that I had set aside for us and I don't know why I feel the need to go...I'm losing my belief in what I thought was between us and I don't think that there would be anything left by the time that I would get there. I guess that's the point though.*
*   Everyone thinks that you and I are still engaged....only a couple of people know the truth. They think your brother is getting married in Scotland and that you and I are using the time to make decisions*

about our future. I didn't know what else to say until I knew if it was final.

Please let me know.

Julie

Still no reply. I got a call from a client who I hadn't talked to in a year and a half. Tim Santacroce had a very kind soul and was easy to talk to. I began to open up more about my relationship with Brayden. I told him that I intended to go to Scotland, but that I didn't know why. I just felt strongly that I needed to be there. My jaw dropped at what he had to say next.

His sister had been seriously involved with a Scotsman who had disappeared on her. She tracked him down in a pub in Scotland five days before he was supposed to marry his ex-girlfriend. She beat the crap out of him, put him on a plane, and brought him back to the States.

OK, that's it! I'm definitely going. Why would Tim pop up just at the right time and have a story that was identical to mine? The synchronicity of it all was so bizarre, that I almost questioned if the story was true. But everything seemed to be telling me that I should go, and now this was the final stamp to seal it.

It was becoming so obvious to me how my guides were working in my life and overall, the messages were clear. They had given me signs of encouragement to stick it out with Brayden through all of the obstacles. They wanted me to go to Scotland although I couldn't really afford it at the time.

I had sold my house and moved into a rental three years earlier, and would get pressure and jokes from the other people around me that I needed to buy a house. But it just never felt right, as much as I wanted to. The real estate business had tanked with the recession, and I was able to live off of the equity from the sale of my home. There were many ways of looking at it, but I thanked God every day and I felt blessed. Yes, I was living off of the money that would have been my down payment to buy another house, but I had money to live on. I still had my credit and I wasn't losing my home like a lot of other people were. Had I not sold my house when I did, I wouldn't have had the money to stay afloat. I was so grateful for that.

Because the market had been slow, I went back to work selling manufactured homes with my old boss, while trying to keep my real estate business alive. A couple of weeks after I spoke with Tim, I started working with a couple of ladies from California. They wanted to find a house in a manufactured home park and I mentioned that I had one in mind for them. I would preview it before we set an appointment to see it. The following day, I was on my way to lunch when I suddenly thought that I needed to go look at the house. I didn't want to, because I was hungry and I wanted to go to lunch, but I felt a strong pull to go there first.

As I drove into the park, I saw them sitting in their car right in front of me.

"Fancy meeting you here!" I said as I pulled up beside them.

We laughed at the coincidence, and they said that they were on their way to Walmart and just decided to drive up this street for the heck of it and found the park. I showed them the house and then later that day, I sent Brayden my last ditch effort to try to stop him from marrying Hilary.

To: Brayden Loch   *May 18, 2009*
From: Julie Hopper
Subject: A friend gave me this advice once

Brayden,

    I just wanted you to think about this. I had something happen once that was devastating and humiliating to me even though I was doing the right thing…a friend said to me, Julie…in six months to a year, will this still have an impact on your life? It wouldn't and it didn't.

Where I'm going with this is if you know that she's the one that you want to spend your life with...then you will forget me and never seeing me again won't matter. But if it doesn't work out and you do this to avoid the fall out...you'll never forget me and you'll question if it was worth avoiding something that people won't think about in six months.

I'm getting on a plane on the 31st with no idea if there is any hope...but I feel that I need to in case that there is.

I love you,

Julie

That night I had a dream and one of the ladies from the manufactured home park was in it. We were sitting on the floor, face-to-face and cross-legged inside of an old Turquoise single-wide trailer. We looked out the window at the same time to see Hilary running into the forest.

"She's running to find Brayden," the woman said with a laugh. "They're getting married like nuts in a shell!"

In the dream, I reasoned with myself and I wasn't sure if that was good or bad. I envisioned a cracked open pecan while I tried to figure it out. Suddenly the house started to wobble and it tipped over in the opposite direction from where Hilary had run to. I could see the shocked look on my face as if I was seeing myself from above. My expression was that of confusion like, *"What just happened?"* I was laying on the right side of the house on my back looking up. The next thing I knew, I was outside looking at the foundation. It was a single stack of cinderblocks running down the center of where the trailer had been, which was now tipped over on its right side.

The next morning, I woke up and pondered the dream. I would soon find out what the message meant, and the timing was unquestionable. I logged onto my e-mail and had this reply to the message that I had just sent to Brayden the day before.

To: Julie Hopper   May 8, 2009
From: Brayden Loch
RE: A friend gave me this advice once

Hello Julie,

  I don't want any more hurt or grief for either of us, and showing up will only make it worse.. I don't think that is the right desicion.
  I am truly sorry for all the hurt and pain. However, you showing up can't wont remedy the situation.
  I do care.

Brayden.

I didn't respond. What would be the point? He was going through with it. The honorable thing to do would have been to call me and break the news, but I knew that would be too difficult for him. It's easier to hide behind an e-mail, but he couldn't bring himself to say the words that he was getting married either. In his mind, that would have been too final and he didn't want it to be. The wedding was June 5 and it was now May 18. "Showing up can't, won't remedy the situation?" He sounded like a man whose fate was sealed and didn't have a choice—I didn't either. So I booked my flight, feeling perfectly calm and almost detached from it all.

  Tim suggested that the timing of the dream was meant to soften the blow of the e-mail. It made perfect sense to me. Not only being informed that he would marry her, but also the dream itself. Hilary running to find him represented Brayden trying to get away from her. The house wobbling meant turbulence in their relationship, the house tipping over meant the marriage would topple, and the foundation of a single row of cinderblocks represented that they didn't have a strong enough foundation for their relationship.

I talked to several other people to get their opinions on what they thought that the dream meant, and everyone agreed. Sophie asked if the house in the dream was mine, and I told her it wasn't. The message was as clear as it could possibly be. But I also thought that by not seeing the actual marriage happening in the dream, gave me a glimmer of hope. I would still go to Scotland, otherwise, why wouldn't they have gotten married in my dream?

I had never heard the term like nuts in a shell before, so I Googled it. I found one reference to it as being the opposite of peas in a pod. Tim said that his father who grew almonds used the saying on occasion. It meant that they would never fully be together because some nuts have a membrane separating the two halves. I agreed with that definition, because in my dream, I saw a pecan and there was a membrane between the two halves. None of my other dreams showed them happily together, she was always chasing after him. There had to be a reason.

As the time grew near, I began to question my decision and thought about canceling the trip. I tried to imagine how he would be able to back out with guests invited and everything planned, unless he had a last-minute meltdown. But then I decided that if nothing else, I needed to have a distraction and I still felt strongly that I was supposed to go.

The week before my flight, I felt perfectly at peace, although it made no sense to me or the others around me who knew what was happening. A friend told me that I was probably in shock, but I didn't think so. It was as if subconsciously I knew what the bigger plan for us was. I was at peace about it but I still didn't know what the final outcome would be. I still hoped that Brayden couldn't go through with it knowing I was in Scotland.

Our relationship confused my friends and family and I would explain to them that Brayden was like a fish. He knows that he's going in the boat, but he just has to wear himself out first. I would explain why he did the things that he did and although they tried to humor me, they

just thought I needed to meet someone else. Only a few of my closest
friends and my mother knew the whole story about his engagement and
the pregnancy. I told everyone else that Brayden's brother was getting
married in Scotland and that I was meeting him there. That we were
going to use the time to make decisions about our future or, move on. I
still felt very strongly that I could never forgive him if he got married.
Even if it wasn't going to work out like Sophie and Renee had said, I
couldn't wait until the relationship disintegrated to the point that he
had no choice but to divorce. My story to everyone added up and if he
married her, then it would be easy to explain that it was over between us
when I returned.

I e-mailed Brayden with my itinerary and what hotels I would be
staying at and when. I would be at the Glasgow City Hotel June 1,
checking out on the 4th, the day before he was to be married. I would
then be at the Aston Hotel in Dumfries on the 4th and after that, it
didn't matter unless it mattered to him. Dumfries was about ten miles
from the castle.

In an earlier reading with Renee, she asked me if they were getting
married in Europe. I hadn't even told her that Brayden was Scottish.
When I told her that they were, she said, "Because I'm seeing that movie
Maid of Honor." With Renee's question about the movie still in my head, I
had a small measure of hope that just as in the movie, Brayden's wedding
wouldn't take place at the last minute either.

I had one more reading with Sophie before I left. She said that I
would see him face to face, or talk to him face to face on a webcam.
That there would be delays on the trip due to a dark woman, but they
wouldn't be long. Things that should have happened a year ago would.
And things that hadn't been previously revealed, would be. She also
saw me getting pregnant mixed in with that. In my fantasy, I imagined
Brayden showing up at my hotel room and asking me if I really wanted
this, like I had heard him say in my dream. Then he would call Hilary
and tell her that he was in love with someone else, also as it was in
the dream. His voice had just been so clear—I hoped that it meant
something.

Sophie and I went on to talk about work. Real estate wasn't going well and I told her that I may need to consider another career. She said that the guides thought that I would be good in PR. *Public Relations?* Instantly I thought that it was the guide's way of making a little joke, but I didn't tell Sophie at the time. I had told Kate all along that I wouldn't write the book unless Brayden and I ended up together. And I thought the PR statement might be a clue that things would work out for us in the end and I would write the book providing PR for the spirit world. Sometimes little things only make sense to the person hearing them, and I thought that it was as amusing as it was interesting.

The week before I was due to leave, I had a few more unusual things happen. While working at the manufactured home lot, I got a call from a guy from Kuwait looking for a house. *Strange*, I thought. That someone from the Middle East would be calling about manufactured homes in Oregon City, Oregon. A couple of days later, the only call that came in that day was from Jenny O'Brien, who was calling from Ireland. I told her that I was just getting ready to leave for Scotland. She went on to tell me that she and her Irish husband had been in a long-distance relationship and now they had been married for three years and living in Ireland. It may have been pure coincidence, but the only two calls I took right before my trip, came in from foreign countries that were places nearby Scotland and Saudi Arabia. I hoped that it was a positive sign.

Flying to Scotland was a long shot and I didn't fully understand why I felt so compelled to go. I didn't even know where Brayden would be staying and he was in this so deep, it was hard for me to imagine him backing out at the last minute. A few days before I left, I had a short dream that I was standing in front of a white door and then as it opened, I saw Brayden standing there with a big smile. *What did that mean?* I wondered. That Brayden will be the one to open the door back up to our relationship and it may happen while in Scotland? I couldn't be sure.

Then the next night, I saw the same door open and Brayden was walking out of it as a woman holding a baby was sending him off with a big smile. She was about my height and her hair was pinned up the way that I just started wearing it again. The smile and hair color were like mine, but there was something different about the eyes. They weren't clear in the dream, so I couldn't be certain that it was me. But everything else matched. I was standing in front of the door in the dream the night before and it was the second similar dream in two nights. *It must have been me.* I wondered why it wasn't clearer, and then I remembered that the guides often speak and send messages in riddles. They wanted to give me a sense of encouragement, but they didn't want me to be overly confident. Too much confidence might change how I reacted to the situation.

The one thing that I knew for sure—the woman holding the baby wasn't Hilary.

*"Being deeply loved by someone gives you strength, while
loving someone deeply gives you courage."*

~ *Lao Tzu*

14

I was just putting a few last minute things together on the morning
I was to leave for Scotland, when I suddenly felt the most beautiful
feeling that I had ever experienced before. It was indescribable—but I
knew instantly that I was feeling Brayden. The knowingness of it was
unmistakable—it was him. But almost like the essence of his soul. It was
euphoric and beautiful beyond description. As I absorbed it in complete
awe, I remembered Renee saying once that she could feel him and she
could understand why I loved him so much. I wondered now if she had
felt the same thing that I did.

When I boarded the plane on May 31, I was still calm. I almost
didn't think about my reasons for going to Scotland, and what I might
have to face there. I changed planes in Amsterdam and as I rode the
elevator to the upper level, standing beside me was a beautiful and exotic
East Indian woman in her early thirties, with big dark eyes wearing an
elaborate lavender sari. On the other side of me was a mountain of
a man from Africa, who looked as though he may have been royalty.
His deep saffron yellow boubou, a traditional wide, flowing robe, was
intricately embroidered with bold colors of deep purple and red with
gold thread detail. I felt as though I was standing in the United Nations
elevator with two very important people. It was amazing!

As I walked through the busy concourse, I noticed several people who looked famous. I could have sworn that I saw Ed Koch, the former mayor of New York City eating breakfast. And when I arrived at the boarding gate, I had to do a double take. Sitting down waiting to board the flight, was Brayden 30 years from now. I couldn't believe it! I wondered if it might be his biological father because they were so identical.

In Glasgow, I searched the airport terminal wondering if I had met those women in the manufactured home park as a sign that I would run into Brayden somewhere. As I stepped outside of the airport, I wasn't expecting it to be so hot. Scotland was in the midst of a heat wave and although I had read that you should pack clothes you can layer, I was now wishing that I hadn't brought my two heavier coats that I had slung over my arm.

Approaching the desk at the car rental, I was surprised to see that the young man behind the desk could have easily been Liam Neeson's son. During my time there, I would continue to be amazed at how many people looked like they could be related to someone famous. Unlike America, you could clearly see the genes having been passed down throughout the generations.

He pointed me in the direction of a black car and handed me the key.

"A Mercedes?" I asked. "Do you have anything else?"

"That's the only automatic that we have available right now," he replied.

I don't want a Mercedes! I thought to myself. They're more expensive to repair and I was already scared about driving on the wrong side of the car and the wrong side of the road!

"Do you have a list of road signs and what they mean?"

"No, I'm sorry we don't."

OK, this is going to be interesting, I thought with a feeling of panic. *Not only am I going to be driving on the wrong side of everything, I don't even know how to read the street signs!* I slid behind the wheel, took a deep breath and pulled out of the parking lot. *Stay on the left! Stay on the left!* That became my mantra throughout the whole trip. I had printed directions from the airport to the Glasgow City Hotel before I arrived, but now I was so focused on the road and my driving that I didn't have a chance to really look down at them.

In Scotland, instead of having stop signs at intersections, they have roundabouts that allow you to turn off of the circle that you're driving around to take the road that you want. As I approached the first roundabout, the road signs for the highway that I was looking for didn't match my directions. After a 20-minute tour of the airport, I finally stumbled upon a sign that said Glasgow. *OK,* I thought. *I'll just head in that direction and hope for the best.*

I found myself drifting too far away from the center line and, in Scotland, they have curbs instead of shoulders beside their roads. I found myself bouncing off of them several times. *Ouch! God, I hope that I didn't just scrape up the rim!*

I was starting to get the hang of driving and managed to arrive at the hotel pretty easily. I was definitely on a budget and didn't anticipate having to pay for a parking garage as well. I had absolutely no idea where Brayden was going to be. All I knew was that his family was from Glasgow and if God wanted us to run into each other, then that might be a good place to stay for a few days.

The hotel was an old stone building as most of them are in Europe. The hotel lobby had a small wooden front desk and the hotel clerk was young and cheerful, although I could barely understand her thick Scottish accent. I checked in and walked up the stairs, struggling with my bags.

The room was stifling hot and so small that there was just enough room to walk around the bed. They didn't have air conditioning because it was very unusual to have this type of weather in Scotland. I opened the narrow, horizontal windows but that didn't help much. After settling in, I went down to the front desk for a beer. I was tired and wanted to relax and feel as though I had arrived. I wasn't going to be the crazy stalker ex-girlfriend disrupting someone's wedding. I just wanted Brayden to know that I was there if he wanted to reach out to me.

To: Brayden Loch   *June 1, 2009*
From: Julie Hopper
Subject: I wanted you to know that I'm in Glasgow

Hi Brayden,

*   I shouldn't be writing this when I'm tired because it's far too important and it's the last that you will ever hear from me. I've written and rewritten it too many times and so I have to hope that I've found the right words.*

*   I want you to know that I came here for me...because it would be too unbearable sitting in the States wondering if had I come and you wavered at the last minute, that maybe things might have gone differently.*

*   Please be clear that I won't be showing up at your wedding even though I told you in a previous e-mail that I wouldn't. It surprised me that you didn't know me better than that after all of this time. If this is a mistake, then it's yours to make and both of us to live with. There won't be another second chance for us if you get married. No matter how much I love you.*

*   I don't even know if you're here, but I may not stay in Glasgow. Even if fate wanted to bring us together again, it doesn't seem like a city that I'm comfortable spending time alone in.*

*   I will love you and be here for you until or unless..you belong to someone else.*

Julie

Leaving the room, I walked up the street to find something to eat. Glasgow was more industrial than I had expected it to be, even though I read that it had improved in recent years. It wasn't littered, but just seemed dingy to me like a downtown street in the 60s. Maybe it was just the area that I was in, I reasoned with myself. I was a seasoned traveler and I'd been everywhere from Honduras to Norway, but I just didn't like the vibe here. Brayden didn't like Scotland but I thought that it was the weather. If he grew up here in the worst neighborhood, it really gave me a better insight into what it must have been like for him growing up. Just to think about it along with the abuse he suffered in his childhood made me hurt for him.

I grabbed some Indian take out and went back to the hotel, asking the front desk if they had a fan. The bellman offered to bring one up and as he came into my room he said, "It's hotter than Saudi Arabia in here!"

Did he just say Saudi Arabia? Not an oven, not a kitchen, or hell, but Saudi Arabia? I checked it in the back of my mind. Maybe it was just a coincidence, but an interesting one. Even with the fan, it was so hot in my room that I couldn't stand it any longer and the staff offered me another room that had more windows. It was more like a suite and I was much happier there. But between the city and the heat, I had no intention of staying in Glasgow.

To: Kate Logan   *June 1, 2009*
From: Julie Hopper
RE: I'm going to Scotland on Sunday

Hi Kate,

Well I managed to get here without an accident in the car although, I'm still not confident and the streets can be tricky. Glasgow is kind of industrial/commercial and I'm in the center of town. There is nothing appealing whatsoever about what I've seen and I don't want to hang here even for a few days.

The hotel is a Best Western and it's not great, has no AC and it's hot! They won't give me a refund because I prepaid to get a discount. I feel like I'm supposed to be in Scotland, but maybe not here. I sent Brayden an e-mail letting him know that I probably wouldn't stay in Glasgow, but that I came here for myself because I couldn't bear wondering if he wavered at the last minute, if me being here would make a difference.

I'm going to get on line and maybe go to Edinburgh for the next couple of days. Then I'm in Dumfries on the 4th and they're supposed to get married on the 5th. Not much time for miracles, but I do think that I'm supposed to be here. I'll let you know if anything happens.

Julie

After a rough night, I headed to Edinburgh promising that I would treat myself to a hotel with a pool and air conditioning no matter the cost. I was starting to get the hang of driving on the main freeways and I was feeling much more confident. Scotland seemed flatter than I expected, but I hadn't been to the Highlands yet. I thought that I would see quaint, little villages with thatch-roofed houses, but I didn't.

Driving into Edinburgh was a confusing but the city was far more beautiful than I ever expected. There were narrow cobblestone streets and old, stone buildings with multiple chimney stacks. It was a mixture of architecture styles from throughout the centuries and you could really feel the history.

I managed to arrive at the Barcelo Edinburgh Carlton Hotel, which was in the center of town. The lobby was bright and sunny with white marble floors and pillars. The hotel staff was very friendly and I felt as though I had just arrived at a sanctuary. With all of the white marble, I half expected to hear harps and choir music in the background.

Edinburgh was several degrees cooler than Glasgow and the city was magnificent. I was still a little tired from the flight and so I had brought a bottle of wine with me to relax with as soon as I got to my room. After I checked in, I picked up my bags and I suddenly heard the sound of glass and liquid exploding—I didn't even feel it. My bottle of wine had slipped out of my hand and onto the marble floor in this beautiful hotel lobby. Standing there in shock, I suddenly smelt the odor of alcohol and then wine permeating the room. I was supremely embarrassed but fortunately for me, there were no other guests in the lobby. The woman at the front desk joked and was sympathetic, but the bell man didn't look happy, although he tried to conceal his agitation. I began picking up the pieces quickly, all the while apologizing profusely.

In a thick Scottish accent I heard, "Don't worry about it, I'll take care of it."

I looked up to see the ginger-haired bellman looking in my direction. I was grateful for permission to disappear.

I settled into my room, which had a beautiful view of the city. Opening the tall windows, I breathed in the cool, refreshing sea air. I just wanted to relax and quit moving for a while, so I decided to make one last push to bring take-out dinner to my room. Down in the lobby, there was no trace of smell or glass from my mishap. I approached the woman who checked me in and handed her a few Euros for the bellman.

"Is there a grocery store nearby?" I asked.

"Do you need another bottle of wine?" she replied. We both laughed.

I returned to the hotel with dinner and two new bottles of wine. As I walked through the beautiful white, marble lobby, I had never held onto bottles that tightly before in my life! After dinner, I poured another glass of wine to take to the indoor pool. The water was cool and refreshing. Finally relaxed, I floated on my back with water swirling around my ears in a dull, tinny, echo. Kicking my legs just enough to stay afloat, I gazed up at the high, white ceiling, noticing all of the little blemishes that had appeared over the years.

As I did, I thought about everything that was happening and why I was there. Brayden was getting married in three more days. But yet I still had this unbelievable calm about me. No anxiety, no sadness or tears. I was confused by it, but grateful because I felt that it must be my guides comforting me with their energy.

To: Kate Logan   *June 2, 2009*
From: Julie Hopper
Subject: Ahhhh Edinburgh

Hey there,

Just killing a little time. Couldn't stand Glasgow and the hotel didn't have AC. When the bell man came to move me, he said it's hotter than Saudi Arabia in here...hmmmm. Then moved me to rm 206. Decided to come to Edinburgh for the night to escape the heat and ended up in rm 406. Wonder if I'll be in 606 next ;)

I was going to spend two nights here, but got suprised with extra parking expenses. Figured Brayden would probably be there a day or two before, so went ahead and booked two in Dumfries which is nearby. Although my last e-mail said he wouldn't hear from me again, I did e-mail the numbers to the hotels without a message.

I think that you would like Edinburgh. Lots of narrow, windy, cobblestone streets with interesting shops. I'm SOOO glad I left Glasgow. Much nicer atmosphere and ocean breezes. Doesn't feel like a vacation whatsoever. I just walk around and don't even go into shops.

Anyways..the next two days are critical, but with the way things have gone, it's like I'm being pushed south sooner than I planned. (I hope)

More soon,

Julie

The next day I loaded up the car and headed for Dumfries. As I drove, I found it to be more reminiscent of what I envisioned Scotland to be: rolling green hills, some of them like small mountains, with white, shaggy sheep grazing in the pastures and stacked stone fences. I was amazed by how many small stones were used in the construction and how many man hours over the centuries it must have taken to build them.

The roads were narrow and windy. Sometimes I drove through what seemed like tunnels created by trees overhanging the road. In the movie *The Holiday*, there's a scene where Cameron Diaz is driving in a small red car, passing a truck from the opposite direction on roads just like this. Her eyes half closed she says, *"Please don't hit me! Please don't hit me! Please don't hit me!"* I had to laugh, because I had that same experience more times than I would care to remember.

I arrived in Dumfries to a small town that was a mixture of stone houses and newer business fronts. A wide river flowed through the center, so I decided that it wasn't going to be a bad place to spend a couple of days. I found the hotel with the help of the tourist information center and checked in. It was a modest, but nice, hotel. Nothing fancy, but it fit my budget. I settled into my room and set up my laptop. I normally didn't travel with it, but I hoped that I might get a message from Brayden.

My time in Dumfries was uneventful and I passed it in any way that I could. Until finally, it was June 5, the day that Brayden was to get married. It was the first rainy day since I had been in Scotland and I couldn't help but be happy about that. I was imagining him getting ready and wondered if he was nervous or throwing up. Brayden carried his stress in his stomach and I was certain that he didn't want this marriage. I knew where they were getting married but I didn't know what time.

To: Kate Logan   *June 5, 2009*
From: Julie Hopper
Subject: It's morning here

Hi,

Well, I'm not sure how I'm feeling. Just a little anxious. No dreams...nothing. Strange that I had one for the first time in months *the night before he e-mailed me and then the night before he's supposed to get married, nothing.*

I shouldn't be happy about this, but the weather has been really nice here. Out of the ordinary from what I understand. But today it's dark and raining. You know that someone is going to say that they hope that's not a bad sign. I was hoping that maybe yesterday when they would have been rehearsing, that the reality and panic would start setting in.

I'm going to have to just move forward with my day because check out is 11. I'll e-mail you again when I get to the next hotel. Fingers crossed!

Julie

I only felt slightly anxious while I waited to check out, and I may have created it myself because I knew that my calm wasn't normal. I wasn't crying, upset, or sad at all. My mood just didn't make any sense to me. I should be curled up in a ball under the bed, but I was fine. I calmly waited in my room until check out time, just in case I heard from him at the last minute. Then put my bags in the car and drove away.

Because I had no idea what would happen in Scotland, I didn't have a plan but I was going to be there for five more days. If Brayden got married, I would have to find a way to fill my time. I decided to head to the Highlands because I had nothing else to do and driving gave me time to think. Someone suggested Port William, so I headed in that direction.

As I made my way through the Highlands, the landscape was unlike anything that I had ever seen before. I was from the Columbia Gorge area of Oregon and Washington and it was magnificent, but this was magnificent in its own unique way. Tall, craggy, green mountains that sprung up out of nowhere, surrounded by rolling green hills. I reminded myself to come back when the heather was in bloom.

Port William was a large, quaint seaside village. Not knowing where to begin, I saw the tourist information office and decided to ask about a hotel. There was a big event going on and every room in town was booked. The woman asked me what direction that I was headed and I replied Loch Ness. She suggested that I try Inverness, which was just beyond Loch Ness. As I left the office, across the street from me was a business with the name out front "LochHoppers.

That's strange, I thought. It's Brayden's and my last name put together. Don't read too much into it Julie! Just take a picture.

As I passed Loch Ness it was starting to get late and I was tired. I expected there to be much more going on there, but I only saw two small hotels and a tourist center for the Loch. I continued on to Inverness and had difficulty finding a hotel. Loch Ness wasn't too far away, so I decided to take my chances. I arrived at the Scotsman Hotel expecting something very touristy. To my surprise, it had the feeling of a bed and breakfast and the price was reasonable.

The sun was just beginning to set as I walked into the bar, and the exterior wall was made up of large windows, with nothing between the Loch and the hotel but the narrow two-lane road. It was overcast and dark, but the view was still spectacular. I didn't want to go into the dining room, so I sat at a table in the bar by the window. The innkeeper/bartender seemed somewhat of a character and I could hear him cracking jokes in the background. There were only three other people in the room as I gazed out onto the Loch and drank a glass of wine.

In a soft, reflective tone I heard a man's voice say, "You can see your future out there."

It came from behind me and although I didn't turn to look, I thought that the statement may have been directed at me. It was the innkeeper. If he only knew that the love of my life—my soulmate, just married another woman today. I will never forget that statement, and he will never know what I was experiencing at that moment.

To: Kate Logan   *June 6, 2009*
From: Julie Hopper
RE: It's morning here

I couldn't log onto my e-mail last night. I'm in Loch Ness and have no idea where I'm going next. You know, I know that those dreams were trying to tell me something, even if he married her, it was not what he wanted to do at all.. I don't have the feelings of dread etc...and you would think that with everything, they would at least let me know the outcome, but maybe I'm not supposed to know yet. I'm not sure that whatever I'm here for is done yet. If by chance he didn't go through with it, he's still afraid of his love for me and he would probably have his hands full with the fall out. If I leave here without hearing from him, then I'll know.

I agree with you though, I think that a lot of my calm is that I know that I've done all that I could and if it's not enough, then I have to let go. Even though I really don't think that I would take him back if he married her, what would I do if he showed up after a week? I know that I would forgive him as stupid as it would be.

If nothing changes on this trip, then I need a story that will end it, but leave it open. And also explain why I have no pictures of him. I thought to say that his brother didn't go through with it and we spent the time dealing with fall out.

That we didn't have time to resolve things, but it's time for me to move on and be open to other people. What do you think?

I almost couldn't believe that those words just came out of my fingertips. *I would probably forgive him? Was I being a fool? Why had my opinion changed? Or was this bond so strong between us that I would love him through anything?* Kate thought that having to make up stories for other people was crap and I had to agree. But I was tired of explaining.

She was my rock, the one person besides my psychic friends (and my mother, of course) who I could completely confide in. Because of her background, she seemed to understand Brayden almost as well as I did. At the very least, when I explained his behavior and why I believed that he said some of the things that he did, it made sense to her. Kate was not only my sounding board but also my reality check. And through everything, I tried to make sure that I was being realistic and wasn't fooling myself about my relationship with him.

I decided that there would be two stories. I would tell my two other closest friends Judi and Michele, that Brayden didn't get married and that he was dealing with the fallout. To everyone else, I would say that Brayden's brother and fiancé had a fight and didn't go through with the wedding. That we were so busy dealing with that, that we didn't have time to talk about what the future held for us. I have never been one to tell stories and this was going to be very difficult for me. I just couldn't try to explain the whole, "We have lessons to learn" thing to people who just didn't seem to get it. So why bother?

It was June 6 and now what was I going to do? I had driven from one end of Scotland to the next in one day. There didn't seem to be much more to see and this certainly wasn't a vacation.

As I sat down for breakfast, there was that gorgeous view of the Loch again through every huge window. Dinner the night before had been delicious and not at all what I was expecting in a little Scottish hotel. The restaurant was serving the traditional Scottish breakfast which I had really grown to enjoy. Two eggs, sautéed mushrooms, half of a grilled tomato, two strips of cottage bacon, a link sausage and a slice of black pudding. I'm very squeamish about organ meat with the exception of paté, but I had decided to try black pudding in Dumfries, which is a sausage made of oatmeal and blood. I was surprised to find that it was delicious.

Rain sprinkled lightly outside the hotel as I brought my bags to the car. The innkeeper stopped to ask me where I was headed. Although no one ever said anything, I could read on their faces that they were curious as to why I was traveling alone. He went on to introduce himself as Willie Cameron and seemed to take a genuine interest in me. I told him that the only plan I had was to see Eilean Donan Castle near the coast.

Knowing which direction I was headed, he gave me several suggestions of places nearby that I should see, mentioning other places that weren't worth my time. He went on to talk about the weather and that an Italian film crew was there last spring, and they had four seasons in one day: the sun shined, it rained, it hailed, and it snowed. There was something about him that was enchanting, and I appreciated his interest and suggestions.

Eilean Donan Castle is one of the most recognizable and iconic castles in Scotland. It was built on a small island just off of the banks of Loch Alsh. The castle itself is also small, but beautifully designed and unique. Built just as you would imagine a fairytale castle would be, with large, square blocks of rustic stone and turrets that served as watchtowers. What added to its beauty though, was a long, narrow, stone bridge with three arched pillars below connecting the island to shore.

The castle reminded me of Edinburgh Castle and although I had a list of places that Willie had recommended, my heart wasn't into sightseeing, so I decided to drive to Edinburgh for the night. As I got closer, I looked for hotels off of the freeway and didn't see any. Scotland was completely different from the US in that respect. It was almost 10:00 at night and I was getting worried because no one seemed to be able to point me in the direction of a hotel. These little mom and pop hotels close up early, so I decided to pull into a small town where someone suggested that I try Dumfirmline.

The sign for the Davaar House Hotel was a huge relief and a welcome sight! I pulled up to a three-story stone house with windows softy glowing yellow and said a small prayer as I walked towards the door. Before I reached the front steps, the door opened. It was the innkeeper and he ushered me in with a warm welcome and a proper Scottish accent. Yes, they did have a room for the night and it was not only affordable, but included breakfast too. He introduced himself as Jim and then directed two young boys who I believed to be his grandsons to retrieve my bags.

The Davaar House Hotel would be my home for the next three nights. The hospitality extended to me by Jim and Doreen Jarvis was unlike anything that I had ever experienced before. They were lovely people. I drove into Edinburgh each day to explore, now feeling more like I was on a solo vacation. But although I was still at peace, I knew that my reason for being in Scotland was done, and I felt that I was just killing time until I could return home.

In the evenings, I would pour myself a glass of wine and walk down the street past the hotel and process everything. On one of my walks, I started playing with the wooden key chain and turned it over in my hand. I hadn't noticed it before, but the street that the hotel was on was named Grieve Street. I hoped it wasn't one of my signs, but I knew that Brayden had probably gone through with it. I wasn't sad or upset, but still felt very calm. I had continued to e-mail Kate saying that the way I was feeling wasn't normal, and my calm didn't make sense to me. She was equally confused by my mood.

"Let the winds of heaven dance between you"

~Kahlil Gibran

15

When I returned home on June 11, I felt a quiet knowingness that this wasn't the end of my relationship with Brayden. There must be a bigger plan for us that I was yet to understand. I had no pit in my stomach, or fear and anxiety that's normally felt when you know a relationship is over. Those feelings can't be suppressed, even when you try to remain in denial. I decided that it was time for me to face the truth. I looked up his friends on Facebook and found Hilary Sinclair. She hadn't changed her last name, which I found to be odd. But her profile picture was now of her and Brayden sitting in separate high back chairs that were some distance apart, holding hands in their wedding clothes. It didn't surprise or hurt me, but what did surprise me was that she would choose a photo that was so cold and formal.

For some reason, I decided to Google Brayden's name and up popped a blog. The primary photo was of Brayden and Hilary standing with their wedding party and again, they were standing several feet apart from each other, holding hands. I thought it was so strange that they had just gotten married and yet, if they hadn't been holding hands, you wouldn't have known that they were the bride and groom. Something about the expression on his face didn't look right. I couldn't put my finger on it until I saw another photo of him and his best man standing by themselves, dressed in formal Kilts. His face was pale, his smile wasn't genuine and he looked like he was going to throw up.

Then I read what I felt was the final indignity that I could experience: they had honeymooned on the island of Bora Bora. My heart felt empty as I witnessed her living my life and all of my hopes and dreams. She had married a man who I was deeply in love and connected with, in the castle wedding that I had always dreamed of, and now they've spent their honeymoon at the same destination that I've always wanted. She now had everything—except for his heart. That would forever belong to me.

When I returned to work, I told everyone "the story" but tried to avoid elaborating too much. If Brayden did come back into my life, I didn't want people to know what he had done. The way that he had conducted our relationship had already cast a negative impression of him, and I wouldn't give them any other opinions to look past. I knew there was a higher power at work in our relationship. But people don't generally grasp the concept of being here to learn lessons, let alone that Brayden's lesson could be one enormous mistake in order to knock some sense into him.

I told everyone that Brayden had delays getting to Scotland, so I spent the first half of the trip doing the touristy thing. That his brother had a fight with his fiancée before the wedding, so they postponed it. Brayden and I had been so busy with the fallout that we didn't get anything resolved, so I would just have to see how the next couple of months went with him. I hated telling a story but I felt like I had no other choice. I loved and respected him with all of his faults, and I wouldn't dishonor him by giving people who didn't know him the opportunity to pass judgment.

I had seen Sophie one last time before the trip and the message had been the same. He didn't want to marry her and was doing everything that he could to get out of it, but it wasn't looking good. She said that there would be delays on the trip due to a dark woman, but that they wouldn't be major. That things would be revealed that hadn't been previously and something that should have happened a year ago would. She referred to Hilary as having a dark aura before, so I thought she must be the dark woman that she was referring to. Obviously, I didn't have any delays on the trip and nothing was revealed to me because I didn't see him. Some of the detail was so specific, that I wondered if she may have gotten information that would it happen later. Psychics aren't good with time frames and I had been told many times before that things would happen that didn't occur for a year or more.

I believed she may have misinterpreted the delays she saw for me and that it was quite possible that the marriage would cause a delay for our relationship, but it wouldn't last. That the something that should have happened a year ago was him breaking things off with her and us getting back together. I had heard his voice in a dream say with urgency, *"Are you sure that you want this?"* And then saying *"I'm in love with someone else."* Was that yet to come? Or were these things that should have happened, but Brayden had used his free will to go against his own guidance and intuition, by making the wrong decision? Twice, I had a similar dream of Brayden opening a door to me with a big smile. *Maybe I need to open the door to him.*

To: Brayden Loch   *June 15, 2009*
From: Julie Hopper
Subject: *I didn't expect to feel this way...I thought that you should know*

Brayden,

I told you that you wouldn't hear from me again and so I apologize if this is unwelcomed.

I feel completely different than I expected. I don't even feel anger, which confuses me. My love for you is unconditional and I don't believe that you ever intended to hurt me. Maybe it's denial on my part, but I feel that this might have gone differently if you felt that you could have changed things. If I'm wrong and you're truly committed to a future with her, then please...there is no need to reply.

I still can't help but wish and believe that it should have been us. I couldn't wait for you the way that I have in the past and I would need to hear from you soon. But if you would like to talk, then I just wanted you to know that I'm completely open to that.

Julie

He didn't reply and I wasn't surprised. It wasn't realistic for me to believe that he wouldn't at least give the marriage a shot. At this point he would be committed to a future with her.

I hadn't had any dreams or messages since before I left for Scotland. And aside from seeing the man that clearly could have been Brayden's father, the only unusual things that happened on the trip was the bellman commenting that my room was hotter than Saudi Arabia and the innkeeper at Loch Ness saying, "You can see your future out there." Both of which I thought were strange, but could have been coincidence.

In July, I had another message dream and as usual, I first questioned if it was only a dream. But it was very similar to the ones that had come true before, just dialogue, with no visual.

"She won't let him move his stuff in," the voice said.

Would my guides use the word stuff? I couldn't know if it was my wishful thinking or not, but it did make sense.

Brayden was based out of Jeddah, which is on the opposite side of Saudi Arabia from where Hilary was working in Dammam. They both had housing provided to them by the companies they worked for, so they would have two apartments. I knew that she was a Virgo, which, depending on where all of her other Astrological planets were, probably meant that at the very least, she was organized and a perfectionist. That might also explain her powerful position in Saudi security. If she was the way that Sophie and Renee had described her—used to getting her own way and feeling like she was a princess—then I could see her controlling her home environment and not wanting Brayden to move his things into her space or changing anything.

I had so many messages before the trip and I wanted more insight, so I decided to see Renee.

"This was a business decision for him. How could he choose that over love? That is so wrong, and she is something else!" she added.

"What do you mean?"

"Oh, she's just like a princess that's used to getting her own way all the time. He is really going to regret this! I mean... *he is REALLY going to regret this!* You can have some satisfaction in that."

But in my heart, even though I didn't want Hilary to make him happy, I loved him too much to have any satisfaction in his unhappiness.

Renee went on to say, "He has the ability to turn his feelings off for you doesn't he?"

That was true. I knew that about him. But I also knew that he could only do it for so long and the business decision was his way of resolving himself to his own fate.

"He's testing out the marriage like he's driving a new car, saying, 'Yes, dear' and being agreeable. You'll hear from him in the next few months. He'll tell you what a huge mistake he's made, etc... But he thinks that he'll just keep you in a box. He's really going to freak when he doesn't hear from you!"

Renee went on to lecture me about being a doormat, and no matter how much he loved me, I knew she was right. When and if I did hear from him, I had to take a stand. She told me that the marriage wouldn't last but the guides wouldn't tell her how long it would be.

"Well, I wish I hadn't gone to Scotland and that I had my $3,000 back,"

"You were destined to go to Scotland."

"Why?"

She cocked her head in confusion before saying, "They won't tell me."

The last thing she said was that Brayden came into my life, so that I would know how much a man could love me. *OK, that makes no sense whatsoever.* He'd barely given me anything throughout the relationship, and he had just married someone else with complete disregard for my heart—although I knew that wasn't entirely true. A couple of weeks later though, what she said would make more sense.

Messages from our guides are personal and sometimes they only make sense to us, if we can figure them out at all, because they usually come in the form of a riddle. If we had clear answers, then that would be too easy because we have to learn the lessons on our own. Our guides are only there to keep us on track with small hints of encouragement or guidance. It's like parents watching a child try to put a square peg into a round hole. They give them time to figure it out on their own but when they don't, they move their hand so they teach the child what they're supposed to do. When they stop giving you those little prompts, it may be time to leave things as they are for the time being.

I had been pondering what Renee said to me. "You were destined to go to Scotland.

OK, maybe I was supposed to go in order to show Brayden my level of commitment to him, and maybe I knew subconsciously that it was all part of the higher plan, which would explain how calm I had been. Why would I have woken up with a strong urge to ask him to marry me, after he had already asked Hilary? Why not before? Either their marriage was part of the plan, or it was an opportunity for Brayden to finally learn how to make the right decisions and if he didn't, then he would learn by making a monumental mistake.

Then there was the part about me meeting him so I would know how much a man could love me. That made no sense to me until a few days later when I had another dream.

I was alone and had just given birth to a baby boy who was sick the moment he was born. He had big, sapphire blue eyes and his face appeared older looking than it should. The baby started coughing and I tried desperately to help it.

"I shouldn't have had a baby on my own!" I said, as if I had made a terrible mistake.

Just then, I looked up to see a young man around 18 years old, with the same blue eyes, pale skin and the lightest of blonde hair, just like the baby. He was grinning, almost smirking at me and wearing a light colored plaid shirt. Then the dream ended.

Just as there had been two of my dogs in a previous dream and one had the same sapphire blue eyes, I thought that the young man I saw might have been the soul of the baby that I was going to eventually have. That I met Brayden so I would know that I could have both the love of a man and a child. Otherwise, I may have gone through with having a baby on my own, just as I had planned before I met him. This dream was telling me that I wasn't supposed to do that and the young man was grinning in confirmation. It didn't occur to me at first, but the plaid shirt he wore, may have represented Scotland, although I couldn't be sure. It wasn't a Tartan plaid, it was just a light colored shirt with a plaid pattern on it. But even in my dream, I thought that it was a strange shirt for him to be wearing.

Although I saw Renee when I came back from Scotland, I didn't feel the desire to go to one of my psychic friends for frequent updates like I had in the past. They had become spiritual mentors more than anything else by confirming what my intuition was already telling me and filling in details that I wasn't aware of. I was beginning to understand that I had gotten all of the encouragement from my guides in the preceding months to give me hope so I would take the trip for whatever reason. Now, if I had too much encouragement, I might jump the gun before it was time and before Brayden was ready. I had a sense that it was time for me to let things unfold as they should.

I may have felt the need to torment myself and release the pain that was buried inside. It was late July and the Highland Games were taking place at Mt. Hood Community College in Portland. I had just come back from Scotland and was feeling very connected to my time there. As I walked toward the game area centered on the football field, I found myself in a sea of people dressed in kilts and medieval Scottish clothing. I began to feel as though part of myself was missing. With pain in my heart and tears in my eyes, I said a prayer. I asked God for my husband and my children. That I deserved and wanted my family and it's time for that to happen. Although the emptiness still pulled at my heart, I convinced myself to be strong and enjoy the festivities.

After walking through the booths selling all sorts of Scottish wares, I bought a meat pie and a beer to take to the grandstands while the pipers competed. I was sitting at the end of the metal bleachers when a little boy around three or four years old walked up the stairs and stopped right beside me. His mother was trailing behind, adjusting

the stroller that had to be left down below. It didn't register to me right away, but if there was "one" little boy in that crowd of people who looked like he could have been Brayden's son—this little boy was him. He had big green eyes and dark hair with a slight wave to it.

I looked at him and he looked back at me in a penetrating way with his head cocked to the side. It was as if he was measuring me up and looking deep into my soul. He looked up into the grandstands, back at me, below to the empty bench in front of me and then back at me with that same penetrating look. I gave him a slight smile and he walked past my knees and sat down beside me. He looked up at me several times as he happily swung his feet back and forth. His mother came to sit at the bench in front of us and she called him to sit down beside her.

"I want to sit here!" he said and pointed to his seat, feet still swinging back and forth.

His mother said, "No, you need to come sit here." And she tried to coax him to move down below to the bench that she was sitting on.

Now with an even more assertive voice he stood up and said, "No, I want to sit here!" Again, pointing at the bench that we were sitting on.

Surrendering, she moved to sit between us and handed him a paper container with a Scottish banger. Trying not to be obvious, I couldn't help but watch him with fascination. Part of me was wondering why he had been so adamant that he sit next to me, and the other part felt a maternal pull, wanting a son of my own just like him. His mother squeezed a packet of mustard onto the sausage and I watched as he picked it up and began nibbling on it from end to end like it was corn on the cob. I noticed every detail about him; the dirt under his fingernails, the grease and mustard on his chubby little fingers. He happily tilted his head from side to side between bites, swinging his feet as he nibbled the sausage.

I felt a strong pull toward him and thought that I would never let my son eat with such dirty fingers. But I found even his greasy little fingers adorable and I felt a sense of envy—*I wish that he was mine.* I turned my attention to his mother and analyzed every detail of her. The straw hat with long, strawberry blonde hair pulled back into a braid, her freckles and the wisps of hair blowing around her face. I wondered what his father looked like.

I reflected back that it was strange he would be so insistent to sit by a stranger, when there was a long empty bench in front of me. Like the little boy in the store who bought the strawberry milk and Chinese food, it was as if someone had tapped him on the shoulder and told him what to do. The little boy at the Highland games and my dream about having a baby seemed like they meant something.

It was now mid-August, and I still hadn't had any clear messages from my guides. The dreams that seemed to be trying to tell me something usually happened right before I woke up in the morning, and I read several books confirming it. But I also knew that we had dreams that meant nothing, they were more like the defragmenting of information retained in our minds, and some were possibly past life memories. I knew that our guides communicated with us in our sleep to let us know what is going to happen as our lives progress. But usually, we only retain the information subconsciously. I believe that when we experience déjà vu, it's a memory flash back of what we've already been shown.

Margie and Sophie had previously told me that my life would be settled by my 43rd birthday, so I set that as a goal to finally try to move on from Brayden if I didn't hear from him by then. It was time to check in with Sophie to ask if there had been any changes in my situation. She said that the marriage was already falling apart and that it would be over by February, March at the latest. But that Brayden would be so embarrassed that he would stay out of sight and talk to as few people as possible. Sophie didn't think that I would hear from him until late the following summer. But I knew if the marriage ended, he wouldn't wait to contact me. She said that he might have to leave the country to get away from her, and thought there were financial ties to Hilary's parents. She also said that Hilary may be pregnant again, but she may only be saying it because she was doing everything that she could to hang on to him.

One morning, I finally had what I felt was a clear indication that my guides hadn't stopped giving me encouragement after Scotland. I had a crystal clear vision that I was an observer in Brayden's hotel room. He was lying in bed leaning against the headboard with two white pillows tucked behind his head. He wore a white t-shirt with one knee exposed from under the covers, overhanging the bed at an angle. The headboard was dark wood with a row of stacked vertical knobs carved across the headboard towards the top. The bedspread was yellow, but with a pattern that looked like colored paint brush strokes.

It was as if I was where the TV should be, but he wasn't watching it. Instead he had his head turned away gazing deep in thought. I saw his eyelids move slightly and he had a pensive look on his face. I know that I was in the room because it was unmistakably clear. I called his name in excitement and the vision was gone.

I explained what I had seen to my friend Kate, and as supportive as she normally was, she didn't say much. It was understandable because until you've experienced something yourself, it can be difficult to believe other people's experiences. But it was no different than psychics seeing a picture of something in their mind. We're all psychic, it's just that the ability is more developed in some than in others. I felt lucky to have been given a chance to see him again, and I suspected that his deep thoughts were about his situation... and of me.

At times I was certain that I could feel Brayden. It didn't happen very often, but I could just be sitting there watching TV and a wave of emotion would come over me from out of nowhere. Kate hadn't been sure that she understood that either when I first told her about it. I explained that it was similar to the connections that biological twins have. They just know when something is going on with the other one.

One morning before I went to Scotland, I sent Brayden an e-mail that might have freaked him out, although I didn't look at it that way at the time. I woke up the next morning and for absolutely no reason, I felt like I was having a terrible panic attack and I felt a heaviness in my chest that made it hard to breathe. I called Sophie at home and she didn't answer. I called her cell phone, no answer. I called her house again to leave a message, but she picked up and I was able to get an appointment later that day.

The feeling of panic and anxiety continued for a few more hours and then it just disappeared as if nothing happened. I felt ridiculous that I had called Sophie so many times, and when I saw her, I apologized by explaining that I thought that I was feeling Brayden's emotions. She wasn't able to confirm it, but she agreed that I probably was. She thought that the e-mail would have freaked him out with all of the pressure that he was under.

An ex-boyfriend who was very dear to me, but that I hadn't heard from in years, contacted me around the time that I first found out about Brayden's engagement. Frank had been married for 20 years and was now having serious marital problems. Although he and his wife were Catholic, I talked to him in depth about my spiritual views and reincarnation. Just as Kate had been skeptical about some of my experiences, it had taken me a long time before I could wrap my head around past lives and reincarnation. It was only through processing the concept and reading other people's near-death experiences that it began to make complete sense to me.

I suggested that Frank read *Many Lives Many Masters* by Dr. Brian Weiss. When he did, it struck a chord in him and the more we talked, the more some of the dynamics in his marriage began to make sense to him. I talked about going to psychics and how I had begun to realize that the information wasn't always clear, and they all had difficulty with accurate time frames. It was as if the guides gave them pieces to a puzzle and then it was up to us to put that puzzle together. It was only after much trial and error, that I realized if I was asking about another person, they could only tell me what that person was feeling or intending at the time of the reading.

Unfortunately, you never know if it's the moment, or the outcome that they're giving you. We all have free will and can go in another direction depending on our fears, etc. I believed that I had developed my own intuition to the point that I was able to decipher their messages and know when it might be the moment or the outcome.

Frank decided that he wanted to have a reading with Renee. He had never gone to a psychic before, but because I told him that I always felt like I had been through therapy afterwards, he thought that it couldn't hurt. He's a police detective with a healthy skepticism, which was good.

"If she tells me about my brother, Tom, who was killed, I'll believe it," he said.

"Well, just as I did with her the first time that I went, I would recommend that you not tell her anything. Just see what comes through and then you'll know if she's accurate,"

Renee is a Karate instructor, and her office is located above her studio in a questionable neighborhood. I decided it may be best to deliver Frank to her office so he wouldn't be put off by first impressions. Renee has a joyful glow and serenity about her, with big expressive brown eyes that light up when she talks. I knew he would be comfortable with her from the moment that they met and he was.

Although I felt that I needed to be patient with my situation, and give it time to develop or unfold, I decided to set up a short appointment with Renee later in the day to get an update. My car was dying, real estate was dying and maybe she could give me some direction.

When Frank came out of his appointment, I asked him what he thought. He said that his grandparents came through and essentially told him not to have guilt about leaving the marriage and it was OK to move on. Renee went on to tell him that she felt a spirit keeping just enough of a distance that she couldn't connect with it clearly. Although she sensed that it wanted to come through, it was ashamed by how it had passed because they had been self-medicating heavily with drugs and alcohol, and were partially responsible for their death. She said that she felt there were multiple impacts in their upper and lower chest, which caused their passing. As the reading ended, Renee told Frank to book another 25 minute reading over the phone at no charge. It was really important for this spirit to communicate with him, but she wasn't able to coax it forward at this time.

Frank and I both knew who Renee was talking about, but he didn't tell her. He wanted to see what she had to say when he made the appointment by phone. Frank's brother Tom had fallen heavily into drugs and alcohol, and was sitting on a curb in a dangerous part of town intoxicated, when a transient came up from behind him and stabbed him multiple times in the back of his chest. Coming from a law enforcement and Catholic background, the chances of Frank having a reading with a psychic medium were very slim. We obviously reconnected for a higher purpose as people often do. So he could get not only reassurance about his thoughts of leaving his marriage, but also to reconnect with his brother who had passed.

Frank tried to play the recording of his reading for me, but he wasn't able to slow down the playback speed. I was able to hear a few bits and pieces that were very specific. Renee told him that he would be meeting another woman and then added, "You've been talking to Julie a lot lately haven't you?"

Julie? I thought. I had been to see Renee probably three or four times and her schedule was so busy that appointments are booked on line. I was surprised that she said my name, because I couldn't imagine that she would remember me, let alone my name. She went on to tell Frank that the woman who was to come into his life wasn't me.

My own appointment was scheduled for 3:00 and I got a call from Renee's assistant asking if we could move it to 4:00.

"Sure," I said. "Is there any chance that I can get a longer appointment?"

"No, I'm sorry. Renee won't be able to do that."

"OK, that's fine. I'll see her at 4:00 then."

A few minutes later, I got another call from Renee's assistant. "Renee just thinks that you're wonderful! And for you, she'll make an exception for a longer appointment."

"Thanks, I really appreciate it!"

When I got off of the phone, I thought it was strange. I never got the impression that she liked me that well in the past. Although she was always really friendly, just as I would imagine her to be with her other clients.

I said a prayer, just as I always do before going into a reading, asking that my guides be there with me, and their messages be clear. In a polite way, I added that this time, I didn't need to be lectured about taking a hard stance with Brayden when he came back. I understood that my lack of messages from them meant that I wasn't to make any attempts to contact him at this time. But if there was still a possibility that we would be together, then I did need some encouragement so I could leave my heart open to him.

Renee was full of enthusiasm when I arrived for my appointment. She told me how connected and like minded she felt we were, and then the next thing out of her mouth was, "You're going to be an author."

An author? I thought. My friend Kate had told me on several occasions that I needed to write a book, and I replied that I wouldn't unless Brayden and I were together in the end. Was this a clue that everything was going to work out between us? I could only hope.

As Renee began telling me again how intuitive I was, a message popped into her head and she giggled, "Oh, this is good! They say to repeat this to yourself, 'I am like Renee, but I do things my way.'"

She went on to say that real estate was my back-up plan and that I would be mentoring or teaching others. She said that readings were her back-up plan as well and that she planned to move more in to teaching. But that she would continue to read for certain clients like me.

Me? I was surprised that she was feeling so connected with me and I thought that it was wonderful! Renee can read your personal barcode. Who you are and the true essence of your being, both positive and negative. I took it as a real compliment, and felt a sense of validation that she would think so highly of me. Talking to her was a lot like talking to my friend Kate, but I could speak freely to her without explanation, because our spiritual belief system was the same.

She told me that even if I wrote the book as fiction, that I needed to write it. I thought to myself, *There's no way that I'm going to write it as fiction. All of this really happened to me and I can't treat it as fiction.* She went on to say that Brayden had already had a mini meltdown, and was drinking a lot.

"Has he reached out to you?" she asked.

"No."

"Then he's been reaching out to you psychically."

Renee had mentioned in a previous reading that she herself wasn't really into the whole Karma concept. But now her eyes narrowed and she shook her head.

"The relationship between the two of you is really Karmic. You were so drawn to each other, that you found each other before you were supposed to meet. It's really rare, like a shooting star. Your cords are connected and intertwined."

Renee was referring to the silver cord that connects our physical body to our astral body, or higher self and said that due to Hilary's high connections, Brayden may have to flee the country. In a recent reading with Sophie, she had told me that Brayden was trying to get assigned a new base in order to get away from Hilary.

Sophie also said that because they were having problems, Hilary was doing everything in her power to keep Brayden, including getting pregnant, or pretending to be pregnant again. Sophie had gone on to say that there wouldn't be a baby born to that union. I asked Renee if she thought that Hilary would have a baby and she shook her head no. That was a relief! A baby would complicate Brayden leaving her.

Renee said suddenly, "The guides say that you're not crazy."

Well, that was another relief! If I had been imagining the messages and signs that had been happening in my life, I certainly would have been crazy. At least I knew that I was on the right track.

She next said that my uncle appeared in hip waders saying, "'We've been through this before." "And they're trying to help you sort through the situation with Brayden from the other side."

When my uncle was alive, he had helped me previously with my relationship with the first pilot, so I knew what he meant by, "We've been through this before."

"They're saying that you need to tell them what you want."

"Well, isn't that pretty obvious to them?" I laughed.

"One would think so by now," Renee agreed. "But they can't help or intervene in ways that you don't ask them to. That's why you have to tell them what you want."

It kind of makes sense, I thought. *In the future when I pray, I'll make sure to tell them specifically what I want, and never forget to end it with please, because "I want" just sounds too demanding.*

With a smile, the last thing Renee told me was, "They say that you're going to have your happily ever after."

That excited me because not only was it a reference to our relationship, but also to the book, which would only be written if the *ever after* included Brayden. I was hopeful again!

Although I had been trying all along to put the pieces together as to why things had happened the way that they did; it all began to make sense to me after this reading. There weren't just lessons for myself and Brayden, there was a big lesson here for Hilary as well. After all, she was one of the players in this scenario. Sophie had told me that Brayden and I had the same problem in past lives together, because he wouldn't commit and truly open his heart. Although Brayden was solely responsible for getting himself into this situation, I believed that I had asked him to marry me after he asked Hilary, so that if he didn't make the right choices, then his colossal mistake would cause him to finally learn his lesson in this life time. In the e-mails prior to the marriage, I had seen what I believed to be a lot of pressure and manipulation on her part. Now it appeared that the marriage was going to fall apart, because she forced her will on him when he didn't want it.

I called Kate after my reading and told her about the conclusion that I had come to about the lessons for both Brayden and Hilary. It would also explain why I was destined to go to Scotland, and why I was so calm during the trip, adding what Renee said about writing a book. Kate had been telling me that all along, and now it appeared to be validated. I decided to follow both of their advice, and Kate was excited that I was finally going to write it all down.

The first time that I sat at the computer, the words just flew from my fingertips as quickly as I could type them. I sent Kate the first several pages of the rough draft and a she e-mailed me back saying that she thought that it was glorious! It was really encouraging for me because, up until then, I had written little more than a resume, or some advertising. I certainly wouldn't have ever guessed that I would ever write a book. Kate knew everything that had happened between Brayden and me, including the spiritual messages. But now she was getting the details that aren't always shared in a conversation.

About a week later, she and I got into a conversation about soulmates. I told her that I believed that Brayden and I might be Twin Flame soulmates and she didn't know what they were. I explained that just as biological twins are created in the womb, when a soul is created, it divides into two, incarnating into life separately, to accelerate our spiritual growth on the physical plane. It's rare that they come together in the same lifetime, but when they do, they often find that they have unusual synchronicities, and similarities between them, just as the stories you hear about biological twins separated at birth, but who have the same likes, dislikes, jobs, etc. Twin Flames are somewhat telepathic with each other, just as Brayden and I are. Renee had told me that our cords were connected and intertwined, so now it made even more sense.

Twin Flames often have very difficult relationships, because one half is usually less spiritually evolved than the other; and the deep connection between the two can be so intense that it frightens the twin who is less evolved, causing them to run from the relationship. Twin relationships are as beautiful as they are painful, but to others on the surface, they only appeared to be a dysfunctional relationship. It all sounded so accurate about Brayden and me.

A few days later, Kate called me with a business question, and we started talking about the book.

"I'm so excited that you're writing!" she said.

"It's amazing how it's just flowing out of my fingertips as fast as I can type! I think it's because I don't have to make anything up, all that I have to do is remember everything and try to piece together the timelines and sequences of events. I also believe that because I'm supposed to write it, I may be getting some divine help. I feel really strong energy around me while I'm writing."

Kate mentioned that she had a dream about a friend of hers who had been killed recently in a motorcycle accident. I explained that my understanding was that when you have a dream about someone who has passed, it's not just a dream, but a visitation from them. I knew that I must have told Kate before about my own experience, but I explained it to her again.

"I had a visitation from my dog Gypsy a couple of months after she passed, and it was so vivid, that I was more surprised to wake up than I was to see her. In the dream, there were two of her sitting side by side. One with sapphire blue eyes that seemed younger, and one with brown eyes that seemed older. Gypsy was big and white with brown eyes. These dogs were identical except for the eyes and age."

Suddenly our call got disconnected. Kate called me a few minutes later and said with excitement, "I swear that I'm not making this up! You're not going to believe me when I tell you this, so I had to take a picture with my camera phone! The reason that our call disconnected was because my phone exploded. I got a loud sound like a fax machine in my ear and then it died and I couldn't get it to turn back on again. I looked up to see a man walking two big fluffy white dogs. I finally got my phone back up and I took a picture of them. *I have a picture, I swear!* If that wouldn't have happened to my phone, I would have never seen them!"

Kate and I were always having the argument that these things only happen to me. But what were the chances of us having that conversation, at the same moment that her phone rings like a fax, shuts down, and a guy is walking by her with two big white dogs? Spirits often interfere with electronics and because the tone sounded like a fax machine, I thought that it may be a humorous reference to them sending her a message.

To: Kate Logan   *October 1, 2009*
From: Julie Hopper
Subject: *This might freak you out more*

Did your phone really sound like a fax machine before it disconnected? Aren't messages sent by fax? Maybe they wanted to drive the point home with you and make it super obvious that it was a message... I really do think that they have a sense of humor over there. Just thought to share that with you.

PS..I had major energies as the fax connection clicked in my head.

She sent me the photo saying that she was frustrated because the picture was taken from too far away to be clear, but the dogs were a large breed that she wasn't familiar with, adding, "Weird creepy voodoo stuff happening I'm telling you!"

To: Kate Logan   *October 1, 2009*
From: Julie Hopper
Subject: *This might freak you out more*

That's too bad because it's hard to see. There aren't that many all white larger dogs. That would be so crazy if they were Kuvasz or somethng similar. How often do you see someone walking two big white dogs anyways?

Welcome to my world. Lol!

I had a couple of glasses of wine before I replied, and wasn't sure if I could spell Great Pyrenees. Not wanting to take the time to look it up, I just said, or something similar to a Kuvasz. My phone rang and it was Kate. She said that she Googled Kuvasz.

"That was the dog! Only the dogs I saw had straight hair that was a little longer."

Laughing I said, "The dogs that you saw were Great Pyrenees. You don't see two of those walking around together very often, but I happen to have two that walk past my house also. I saw them for the first time after Gypsy died, and I had to do a double take, because my first thought was that they were Kuvasz."

It was wonderful that Kate's visitation got an undeniable validation. I truly believe that if you pay attention, you'll see these patterns and signs in your own life. But not everything is a sign and you have to use your own intuition and logic to discern between wishful thinking and a validation, or message.

Kate went on to say, "Julie, my mother is Catholic and I wasn't raised around any of this stuff. But the way that you explain things and what I've seen happen with you, well... it just starts to make sense."

Timing can be interesting. Margie had retired and was traveling the country with her ex-husband in an RV. They were just friends, but had a better relationship than most married couples. I hadn't heard from her in over a year and just figured that she was having a great time and enjoying retirement. Out of the blue, I got an e-mail to my business address telling me that she had been thinking about me and wondering how I had been. I gave her a recap on what had happened with Brayden and she replied:

To: Julie Hopper   *September 30, 2009*
From: Margie Anderson
RE: Hello

The whole thing with Brayden is such Karma Julie. It's just too weird with all of the feelings and the whole thing. I wonder how it will all spin out. I always felt that what was between you was too strong to lose energy until whatever was supposed to be worked out in your life was.

M.

We decided to set up a time to get together, not for a reading, but because we had known each other for 20 years and truly cared about one another. Although I would have loved her psychic opinion on my situation, I wouldn't ask that of her. I was meeting her as an old friend, not as a client.

Margie was incredibly smart in the way of people and relationships. Aside from her natural, psychic gift, she had seen and heard it all. She was camping at an RV park in Garibaldi, Oregon, not far from my sister's house, so I drove over for a visit. She hadn't changed a bit, except that her mountain of red hair was now blonde, and she was still seven inches shorter than me even with the height from her hair. Her big, expressive blue eyes were just as beautiful as I remembered, having the same reassuring and calming effect on me.

We talked about my reason for writing a book and I told her that over the years, I had begun to learn how to piece together the messages in psychic readings with my own messages. The guides spoke in riddles, and I was beginning to figure out how to decipher them. Although I was still learning, I believed that I had some insight that could help others. We had a great time catching up and she told me about all of her adventures on the road. There wasn't much talk about Brayden and I, but that was fine with me because I needed to talk about something other than my own drama.

We ended up in a humorous conversation about people's belief systems and our own, which were very much the same. She recounted stories about the religious people who would show up for a reading toting a bible in hand, as though the devil was going to show up at the door and Margie needed to be on notice that he had better not. Then there were others who thought that she had put some sort of curse on them when their lives started going badly.

Every psychic that I knew had a firm belief in God, but our beliefs were more spiritual based and similar to that of Eastern philosophy, not the fire and brimstone teachings that we were all born sinners.

They also have a strong belief in reincarnation, which should help people who have difficulty wrapping their head around the concept try to consider it. These are ordinary people like us who have a natural gift from God, and/or have developed their connection with the other side. If reincarnation didn't exist, or if life was all about fire and brimstone, then surely they would know it.

We talked about the bible speaking against going to psychics and mediums. Margie didn't recall that there was a true reference against it, but possibly references that could be interpreted that way. But we both agreed that at the time it was written, religious leaders had ultimate power over everyone, including Kings and Queens, I believed they didn't want that control taken away by people with the gift of prophecy. Margie said that her mother had the gift, but she was religious in the biblical way and tried to reject it.

As our conversation continued, we also agreed that the purity of the bible had been compromised throughout the centuries, not only by man's desire for power and control, but also through translation into different languages. *The Gnostic Gospels* are a good example of how many of the true teachings of Jesus and other prophets had to be hidden away and protected. They taught a form of spirituality that was very similar to Eastern philosophy, which differed from that found in *the Bible*. After all, how can you have "versions" of *the Bible?* It's either "*the Bible*" or it's someone else's interpretation.

As a reader, I would be unable to judge the character or motivation of the person doing the writing. Just about any sentence can be manipulated into meaning something entirely different. I wasn't aware of it, but Margie told me that the Vatican had the largest astrological library in the world, but astrology isn't taught in Christianity. There is just so much that we don't know or understand, and there seem to be gate keepers censoring what we're allowed to know. It made me think about a vision that a great Native American spiritual leader had:

"I looked ahead and saw the mountains there with rocks and forests on them, and from the mountains flashed all colors upward to the heavens. Then I was standing on the highest mountain of them all, and round about beneath me was the whole hoop of the world. And while I stood there I saw more than I can tell and I understood more than I saw; for I was seeing in a sacred manner the shapes of all things in the spirit,

and the shape of all shapes as they must live together like one being. And I saw that the sacred hoop of my people was one of many hoops that made one circle, wide as daylight and as starlight, and in the center grew one mighty flowering tree to shelter all the children of one mother and one father. And I saw that it was holy."

~ *Black Elk, Oglala Sioux Holy Man*

In one of the many books that I read years ago, they had interpreted his vision as each individual hoop representing a religion or spirituality. And all of them were valid and an equal part of the entire circle. That depending on your soul's level of consciousness in this incarnation would determine which form of spirituality that you would be drawn to in this lifetime.

Margie and I had a great time catching up with each other and the next day, she asked me for the time, date and location of Brayden's and my birth. She's a very gifted astrologer and I wasn't going to say no. I had recently tried to go around the psychic element, by consulting with an astrologer. I wanted to find out when and if Brayden and I might come back together, because the guides weren't giving Sophie and Renee firm answers. *Sneaky?* Yes. But you can't fool the spirit world.

The astrologer who was doing the reading over the phone was admittedly having difficulty with the interpretation and didn't charge me. Which to me, is a sign of someone who takes pride in the accuracy of their readings. Instead, he e-mailed me the information that was pulled off of an advanced astrology program he had. The only thing I was missing was his professional explanation. The chart wasn't going to give me the predictions that I was looking for, but it said that my relationship with Brayden was unusually Karmic and written in the stars. But I already knew that.

Margie did our charts and said that I had been under a strong influence of Saturn. She added that she was surprised that I wasn't under my bed sucking my thumb. I had to laugh because that's how I happened to feel that very day. She told me that things would continually get better as we ended the year. That Brayden's marriage would end by February, but no later than March. She went on to say that I probably wouldn't have much if any contact with him until the spring. Well, that was almost exactly what Sophie had told me. But at least Margie thought that I would at least hear from him in the spring. Sophie thought that it would be the end of summer because after the breakup of his marriage, he wouldn't want to have contact with anyone. I wondered later though if I might hear from him, but that we may not be together full-time until spring or summer. Although I knew Brayden's free will could change everything, at least I could hope!

I conveyed the message to Kate who cheerfully reminded me that something could still happen, and I could hear from him sooner. I appreciated her reminder, and it seemed as though she was beginning to understand how the universe works. A couple of years back, we had a party at one of Kate's friend's house and Margie came to read for us. She had been with a cancer patient earlier in the day and only had the energy for two readings. The two that got the readings were both skeptics and one of them was a close friend of Kate's. The information had been so accurate that on another outing with Kate the woman saw a psychic with a sign in the window and she decided to get a reading for fun.

The psychic went on to tell her friend that her husband was having an affair. Margie's reading had been so accurate, that she was ready to end her marriage. But Kate told her that she had listened to me enough to know, that a good psychic wouldn't deliver destructive information in that manner, unless specifically asked. Even then, they would probably say something like, "I think it's possible."

Although they may have websites, intuitives with a true gift develop their clientele through referrals and word of mouth. In my own experience and those I've heard of others, it's the psychic readers who set up shop with a sign in their window who tend to fabricate scenarios that will cause the person to want to come back for information. Taking advantage of their suffering and desperation, so they can make more money. In my early 20's when I made that mistake, the woman convinced me to bring back $250 that she would pray over, and it would bring the man that I was in love with back to me—It didn't work.

"We must be willing to get rid of the life we've planned
so as to have the life that is waiting for us."

~*Joseph Campbell*

16

My days were unbearably painful at times, mixed with moments of hope and reassurance in the confidence I still had in our love. Now I was writing our story, and it was a welcome distraction. But with each new chapter, I was also reliving all of the frustration. At times I felt myself begin to hate him, and I would sit under the stars drinking wine and wondering what purpose of all of this could possibly serve. The phrase "Breathing Underwater" popped in my mind from out of nowhere, and I realized that my guides had just given me the title of my book.

As I turned the phrase over in my mind, I realized that the metaphor couldn't be more perfect. I had been on a scuba diving trip when I met Brayden, and when we kissed for the first time at the airport in Dallas, I felt a sensation of suffocating without his lips on mine. But it also represented the connection I had with my guides, and how they helped me when I felt that I was drowning in our relationship. They truly were the lifeline that kept me sane and be at peace with the journey.

Now I was becoming more excited about writing, and began going through old e-mails and filling in little details. I credited the book *Guardians of Hope*, by Terry Lynn Taylor for helping me to transform my life by teaching me one of my most important lessons: how to recognize your ego and the way it interferes with your perspective on life. I wanted to find the chapter that taught about it, but thought that I may have learned it from one of her other books. Still living out of boxes in a rental home, I decided to look for the book online with the hope that it would allow me to read that chapter.

There was a glowing review by a guy from Dumfries, Virginia. *Dumfries? That's the name of the town I stayed at in Scotland, near the castle where Brayden was getting married. OK, that's odd. Coincidence? I don't think so, but I'm not going to call it a sign either.* I also wasn't going to tell Kate because she was just getting the hang of all of this message and sign stuff, and this was so subtle, that I didn't want her to make the same mistakes that I had in the very beginning, by making everything unusual into "something." The guy had written a very funny line and I decided to post it on my Facebook profile:

"I've been there and done that, I wrote the book, drew the pictures and ate the crayons while watching the video."

Kate commented:

I love it, LOL!
It's my new motto ;D
FYI, I was researching a book that I read years ago, and that was part of a review from a guy from Dumfries Virginia. You know... DUMFRIES. I wasn't going to tell you that ;) It was the town that I stayed in by the castle.
You wouldn't think that these things would continue to shock me, but it does!!
Kinda weird that I was doing research for the book huh? I don't know, could be a coincidence. But I loved the saying!!
Just curious - If you were in a bar, how many coincidences would you be allowed? They would Sooo cut you off! You're cracking me up!
Just doing reality checks.

On my way to bed, I turned off all of the lights but there was just enough ambient light to find my way into the bathroom. As I sat down, I began to think about what Kate said. How many coincidences was

I allowed? Just when I started thinking *Yeah, but it could all have been a coincidence,* I noticed a light out of the corner of my eye. I looked out of the open door to the hallway. Instead of the little button on the smoke detector flashing red, it was glowing white and increasing in size. I didn't have time to blink because right before my eyes, it increased to the size of a nickel in seconds.

I started to reason with myself, *I'm sitting in the dark, watching a light that should be red, but it's white, and it's five times bigger than it should be.* Still watching with fascination, I thought about what I had been thinking when I first noticed it. I realized that I had been questioning if the Dumfries reference was a sign, and I didn't want Kate to think that every coincidence was one. I knew that this glow was completely out of the ordinary and it was a sign for me that the Dumfries reference was a validation. So I acknowledged it and thanked my guides. As soon as I did, the light slowly shrunk until it became dark again.

The next day I realized that I had all of these major things going on in my life, but I hadn't mentioned it to one of the people who had been the most supportive of me: Sophie. I attached the pages about Paris and the paragraph that introduces her and sent her an e-mail.

To: Julie Hopper   *October 17, 2009*
From: Sophie Douglas
Subject: This is exciting.

Good Morning,

It was great to hear from you and reading what you have written you are definitely an author. The guides say you will be very successful and I agree with them that you are most certainly gifted.

You have been through many lifetimes and will also draw on the information from those as you do your writings. I have no doubt that within a short period of time we'll be seeing your books (the guides say there will be at least three)at the top of the best seller list.

Again, it was so good to hear from you. Please keep me posted on your progress and if there is anything I can help with feel free to ask. Have a good weekend.

Love & light,

Sophie

I was excited by her reply, but I still needed my "happily ever after."

The real estate office I worked in was having a pumpkin give away party on October 24 and I was dressing up as a water fairy. I wore a white velvet dress with long sleeves, elf ears, and blue sparkly lips and nails. I looked great and everyone loved my ears! While sitting beside another agent in our office, she asked me what I had been up to.

"I'm writing a book, believe it or not." I explained that it was about recognizing the synchronicities in your life, so you can learn how to receive messages from your guides. Her response was quite positive and it surprised me.

Then she turned to me and said, "Are you still dealing with that guy?"

Dealing? I thought to myself. *That guy?* "I don't know Kathy—are you still dealing with your husband?" I asked sarcastically.

She apologized several times, but the statement pissed me off.

"Have you heard from him?" she asked.

"Brayden is off the table for conversation," I replied casually.

She apologized again, but it was too late and I was still angry.

Brayden was my soulmate and I loved him regardless of his faults, but I also understood how things looked to people on the surface. They had no idea about the marriage, and Kathy's comment was a good example of why I hadn't told anyone. When others were critical of his behavior, I would explain that he was afraid to love deeply because of the abuse he experienced in his childhood but it always seemed to bounce off of them without registering. Brayden's behavior and our relationship exhausted me and to make it worse, I had to constantly defend both of them.

I hadn't dressed up for Halloween since I was in my early twenties and I loved my costume. I had several pictures taken in it, but didn't have one that I felt captured it well. I knew that Brayden had Googled me in the past, so I was sure that he had seen that I was on Facebook. I wanted to get a rise out of him and give the impression that I was moving on with my life without him. I took a close up photo of myself that showed only half of my face with the elf ears and sparkles. It was sort of artsy, so I made it my profile photo. He and I both liked science fiction/ fantasy, so I knew that the costume would have some appeal to him.

For the next two days afterwards, my mood was angry and hurt, but with no explanation for it. I cried frequently and my first thought was that maybe Kathy's comment had finally broken the dam to my pain. Maybe I was finally letting out all of my pent-up emotions about him getting married because up until then, I had been so calm. My second thought was that I may possibly be picking up on Brayden's emotions. I had recognized it before when an emotion would come over me for absolutely no reason, and I knew that somehow I was feeling him.

I reasoned that it must just be my imagination before deciding to look at his Myspace page. While going through yet another process of trying to let him go, I hadn't looked at it as frequently. Although they didn't communicate, my niece Mikala had been listed as one of his friends for a couple of years, and in July when her boyfriend deleted her page, she sent him a new request. She didn't know that Brayden had gotten married, but I told her that she shouldn't be hurt if he didn't accept it. Myspace publicly showed the date when someone logged onto their account, and Brayden hadn't been on since long before he got married. Now it was four months after Mikala sent him the new request, and he had suddenly accepted it just at the same time that I was feeling all of this anger and emotion.

The timing was unmistakable and I considered it to be a good sign. When I questioned her about it, she said only that he had accepted her request, with no mention of communication. Brayden had used Mikala as a way to open the door with me in the past, and now he was doing it again. She adored Brayden and wanted us to be together more than anything, so I decided that it was time for her to know the truth about the marriage, with the promise to keep my secret. She was stunned and disappointed, but reassured by my faith as I explained all of the synchronicities and messages of encouragement that I had received.

I often reassured myself knowing that every time Brayden and Hilary got into a disagreement, he would resent her and regret his decision. It was now obvious to me that he was beginning to break. And after what Sophie and Renee said in the last reading, it all made sense. But the problem was that if Hilary was pregnant, or was pretending to be, Brayden wouldn't contact me. I knew that he wanted me to make the first step, that's why he'd accepted Mikala's request. But that would only make him feel safe, and be able to disappear again knowing that he still had my affection. I couldn't get into the same cycle with him.

Growing weary with the real estate market, I had to wonder if I was having my worst year ever in order to push me in a new direction. I hoped that Renee's reading saying that real estate was my back-up plan and that I would write a book and mentor others was true, because everything that I loved about my job was beginning to fade.

I was working with a couple who had a very similar spiritual belief system to mine and I thought that they were wonderful in the beginning. But instead, the husband's ego and sense of self-entitlement made me hate what I was doing and I had to pull from every bit of strength that I had to keep working with them. My friend Kate, who was servicing their loan, was having an equally difficult experience. As we were talking one day, she told me that she had started seeing the patterns in her own life. Kate had been very successful financially, but she also tended to over extend herself. And because she had experienced abuse in her childhood, she had chosen to marry a man who was predictable, although she herself was very dynamic.

Kate had already decided to leave her marriage when the economy tanked, but now she couldn't afford to. I had begun to realize that one of her lessons to learn was financial and because of the economy, she was now in danger of losing her home. She had previously told me that she was looking for an owner contract on a new house that her husband could afford on his own if she left. She wanted a payment of around $1,800 per month, and as gently as I could, I kept telling her that she should find something with a much lower payment.

When I was in Scotland, I sent her a link to a website I had found years earlier that described how your guides teach you lessons. She didn't reply, so I didn't think that she was ready for the message. But now in our conversation, she agreed that if I hadn't said some of the things that I did, she wouldn't have gotten into a house that was so affordable. I asked what would have happened if she had the $1,800 per month payment that she was originally looking for.

"I would now be delinquent," she replied.

A couple of days later, I got a full page e-mail from her describing in great detail a dream that she had about the two of us. In it, we were going shopping for a dress to wear at a formal event, but I was determined to shop for something else. While she tried on dresses, I disappeared for a long period of time, and returned with a small tree strapped into a child's seat on a shopping cart. She continued by saying that I was so happy to have found this tree, that I was glowing with a fairy like appearance, because I had been looking for it for years.

We went to the formal event, and she was freaking out but I calmed her. I had the tree with me in the shopping cart, and was wearing an expensive, silver dress with a long train. We got separated but she saw me from across the room. I was eating fruit from the tree and it appeared to be lemons, but I ate them as though they were apples. I was happy and at peace over the tree, and the fruit transformed me into an angelic presence. As I left the room to walk down a corridor, the train from my silver dress stayed in place, growing longer as I walked away.

TO: Kate Logan   *November 13, 2009*
From: Julie Hopper
RE: Oh man, too cute!

*Wow Kate, that dream is amazing!!! I think actually that it could be
a message dream because there is so much true symbolism in it. In
fact... I'm almost positive!*

*I'm going to have to process it because the parts about me, I think I
completely understand. Your dress and what you're going through in
the dream, I'm not sure of. And why you would have a dream that's
so much about me and my life, confuses me and so there has to be a
connection there for both of us.*
    *Maybe if I tell you what I think that my part means, then maybe
you will figure yours out. I have to qualify my interpretation by
saying that it's also based on my expected and hopeful outcome with
Brayden and the book. By the way, blue is a very spiritual color.*
    *There is a tree that I have wanted SO bad at my next house. I
think that I have pictures of it in my yahoo web folder and if I do, I'll
send them to you. You could easily say that it looks like a silk tree.
Anyways, my interpretation of this would be that I won't be around
all the time because I'll be setting up a home (the household goods)
The tree represents home and family and the car seat is of course
a baby. I glow and I'm so happy because I finally have it, but me
helping you means that I'll always have your back even when I'm
gone.*
    *The room surrounded by a ton of people (the book?) possibly
teaching like Renee said? And then leaving down the hallway with
my tree (going back home to my family), but leaving a trail of me
behind. The dress could represent the silver cord that I told you
about. You can connect it to other people. I bet that's it! With the
color and it being long, it makes sense. But also, if I had "money" my
wedding dress would probably be a 1940's style satiny cocktail dress.*
    *This is a real stretch, but a couple of readings ago Renee thought
that I might be going to Italy. Last reading she thought that I would
be working in Europe and Brayden would have to flee Saudi Arabia*

to get away from Hilary. Lemons are a really big deal in Southern Italy and so I thought that the lemon might indicate Italy and eating the fruit from the tree symbolizes happiness and rewards. Fruit from the tree also symbolized a baby to me at first thought.

Wow! That's really exciting. We need to figure out what all of the focus on your dress was about. This might be one that would be validated in the future. I'm saving all of our e-mails because I realized that I was missing a few that I had wished that I had saved. One of these days, lets get together and you can help me back up Messenger, etc...

To: Kate Logan   *November 13, 2009*
From: Julie Hopper
Subject: The tree

This is the tree. It's some form of Eucalyptus and I just love it!

In her reply she said that the photo of the tree I sent her could have been a miniature version of the tree she saw in her dream, adding that the trunk was two separate trunks that had been entwined into one. For me that represented two people becoming one, and it fascinated me as I realized that other people can have symbolic message dreams for one another. She wouldn't have known anything about the dress, silver cord, or tree that I wanted in my next home, and yet I understood all of the symbolism in the story very clearly.

Halloween had long passed and I thought about changing my Facebook photo on the chance that I might evoke another reaction from Brayden. I wanted to post something that would bring his feelings and thoughts of me closer to the surface; I thought about taking a photo of the two of us and cutting him out of the picture. I knew that it would hurt him, but I decided that it could also send the message that I was cutting him out of my life, causing him to be more reluctant to contact me.

I found a picture that he took of me at the top of the Eiffle Tower. Even if he didn't recognize it as a photo that he had taken, there were other things that would stir his memories. I had a big smile on my face and was looking into the camera with an expression of genuine happiness; I wore my black leather jacket that he had been so fascinated with in Paris, and the scarf I had purchased there that he liked so much.

Just as I had woken up in an angry mood after posting the Halloween photo, the next morning I woke up even angrier and for absolutely no reason. My first thought was that I was just in a bad mood, before realizing that the only time that I had been in this mood for months was after changing my photo. I knew that he watched everything that I posted publicly, just as I had watched what he did.

Why we were still apart and doing this is absolutely ridiculous to me!

"To reach the fruit of a tree, you must be willing to climb out on the limb."

~ Unknown

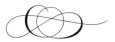

17

I felt as though I had been running a three-and-a-half-year marathon since the day that I first met Brayden. I had not only climbed out on the limb, but had climbed to the end and dangled off the tip. I always told people that if he couldn't pull it together, I would always love him, couldn't be angry with him, and would not regret the time invested—and I meant it. But I also couldn't wait for him forever and if when I next contacted him he wasn't fully prepared to end the marriage and start a life together, then it was time for me to release it.

Renee told me in a previous reading that I needed to include in the book that, "Free will sucks!" She's right. I believe that if more people looked at their lives as if they were on a spiritual path verses being upset when things don't go their way, then their lives would flow in a more peaceful way. We can love someone, give everything to them, but if they choose not to receive it or if the connection was only meant to be temporary, then there's nothing that we can do to change or control it. We have to accept that it was what it was and take what we've learned and move on to possibly a better relationship in the future. My psychic friends were as much spiritual mentors as they were sources to provide me insights into probably outcomes. Their words provided wisdom to help me to understand my journey from a higher state of consciousness, instead of a human level.

I had seen Sophie recently and she said that things were starting to fall apart in Brayden's marriage, adding that there was new talk of a pregnancy, but that a baby wouldn't be born to that union. Regardless, baby news scared me so I thought that I would get Renee's opinion.

Renee agreed with Sophie that things were getting screwy in the marriage and there was "talk" of a pregnancy. I told her that I thought that things weren't going well, so she suddenly became "pregnant."

"Based on the timing, she'll have to lose the baby by the holidays and then she knows that Brayden won't leave her at that time of year. I don't know how I know this," I said to her.

"You know these things because you're so connected with him. You're not the type of person who sits around making stuff up."

Whether the talk of a pregnancy was true or not, I was relieved to hear that it was likely just her way of keeping him tied to her.

I knew in my core that Brayden and I would ultimately be together. I also knew that his fear of my rejecting him after what he had done would be so overwhelming, that he may not make the first contact. I just had to be patient and wait to test the waters until I knew that he feared that he had lost me forever. I imagined he might expect that I would use the holidays as an excuse, and if I didn't contact him by then, he might think that I would send him a message on his birthday, January 6. That meant that I had to give him sufficient time to feel the pain of loss. It would have been seven months since he last heard from me, and we hadn't gone nearly that long before without speaking. Our pattern had been that we always seemed to reconnect around the first of the year when there had been a separation.

I would wait until January 14 and then send him an e-mail. That would be the time of the new moon, which is supposed to carry positive energy for new beginnings. I wasn't sure how deeply I believed that it would have an effect, but I needed all of the good energy that I could possibly manifest. I woke up on January 10 and my first thought was that it was OK to send the e-mail I had prepared. Because it was my first thought without thinking, I realized that it may be my guides letting me know that it was time. I found something on moon phases that said that the waning last quarter moon is a good time for letting go of negativity and bad relationships. Well...he needed to do that too.

To: *Brayden Loch*   *January 10, 2010*
From: *Julie Hopper*
Subject: *Hello*

Hi Brayden,

I hope that this message finds you well. I just wanted to ask if you're happy? If you are...I won't ask again. Please let me know.

Julie

To: Julie Hopper   January 11, 2010
From: Brayden Loch
RE: Hello

Hello Julie,

It's great to hear from you. I've been thinking about you a lot, trying to think of how to apologize for hurting you. I wish I had dealt with things a lot better. I did try calling you the night you where in Dumfries, but you never answered the phone.

How are things with you? are you happy? Let me know what you have been doing with yourself lately. I really do miss talking to you and seeing you smile. Wish that I could see and hear that from you. Let me know how you are.

I am currently training for an Iron man event this year. Swimming a mile a day and then running two hours daily, or at least most days. In between working of course. I am no longer working for the Prince, I am now working for his airline flying 737.

I hope to hear back from you soon.

Brayden Loch.

By using his full name with a period at the end, I knew that he was pretending to be more confident than he was feeling.

———

To: Brayden Loch　　　　　　　　　　　　　*January 11, 2010*
From: Julie Hopper
RE: Hello

Hi Brayden,

I'm glad that you're well...There is no reason to apologize for loving someone else more. I just wish that you would have told me so that I didn't believe in something that wasn't true.

It's hard to be happy when you feel as though a part of yourself is missing...but I try. It wouldn't be good to see or talk to each other if there was no hope for us. I still love you too much and it wouldn't be possible for me to separate myself from that. Thank you for the nice e-mail though.

It sounds as though you're happy and your life is full. That's what I needed to know. Please take care of yourself.

Julie

———

To: Julie Hopper　　　　　　　　　　　　　January 11, 2010
From: Brayden Loch
RE: Hello

Julie,

Please don't be that way, I know it is deserved though. My life is far from happy or full. I miss you. I spend countless hours running and I can help feeling that I'm running from something.... I do still love you also and I feel terrible for the hurt I've caused you. What we had was great and I know I didn't give it the respect it deserved.... Please don't stop talking.

Brayden.

TO: Brayden Loch   *January 11, 2010*
From: Julie Hopper
RE: Hello

I can't talk to you until you're prepared to make things right... and then it would need to be in person. This is too hard for me.

Julie

PS...I miss you too.

I didn't get a reply. Was he not prepared to leave her? Or, was he just satisfied that he hadn't lost me and so now he could leave me hanging again? Off the hook for the moment so he didn't have to do the difficult thing and tell her? I had to be more direct to evoke some sort of emotion from him. I sent my messages based on the time difference in Saudi Arabia giving him plenty of time to reply.

To: Brayden Loch   *January 13, 2010*
From: Julie Hopper
RE: Hello

Brayden,

After all of this time and everything that you said...do you still need time to think about this? Or were these just words that you knew that I wanted to hear? And you still choose her instead of me? It's important that I know.

Julie

<hr/>

To: Brayden Loch   *January 14, 2010*
From: Julie Hopper
Subject: Never mind....

    Today I was imagining how it would feel like to hold and kiss you.... And that's not good because I have never loved anyone else as deeply as I love you.
    Before you got married, I truly didn't think that it would be possible for me to ever forgive you for going through with it. And so before I contacted you, I was honest with myself and I came to some realizations. I know that however you respond...it will always be. And that if you don't want us now...then I can't risk my heart to you again in the future. You haven't answered the question that I've been asking you indirectly and so if your answer is no, then I think that e-mail is best because I want you to always remember me for how happy that you made me...and not the tears of losing you for the last time.
    I only want to know if you will leave her so that we can be together? If your answer is no, then we both move on without looking back.

Julie

<hr/>

To: Julie Hopper   January 14, 2010
From: Brayden Loch
RE: Hello

Julie,

    I'm not sure what you are saying but what I say I mean. If I didn't care or feel anything then I wouldn't have replied. My feelings for you have never changed. They surely never will.... It's probably easier to lie and not tell each other our true feelings, than it is to face the truth. Then again, we don't do that easily....... do we!

Brayden.

To: Brayden Loch   January 14, 2010
From: Julie Hopper
RE: Hello

The last line confuses me a bit...but I think that we should talk. Do you want to?

To: Brayden Loch   January 17, 2010
From: Julie Hopper
Subject: You haven't responded

Brayden,

Sometimes doing the right thing isn't easy and so you just have to make the jump if it's what would make you happy...It's different for me this time and so I'm not going to spend a lot of time trying to convince you to follow your heart. It's too frustrating and you didn't listen to me before.

Will you leave her so that we can be together?

Julie

To: Julie Hopper   January 17, 2010
From: Brayden Loch
RE: You haven't responded

   Would you trust me if I did? I really want you..

Brayden.

To: Brayden Loch   *January 17, 2010*
From: Julie Hopper
RE: You haven't responded

Brayden,

   You've given me no reason to trust you in the past. But I believe that I know why you did the things that you did. Otherwise... I would have been gone long ago. Above anyone else...I truly believe that I know you and your heart to the core. And you are most certainly a beautiful person worth trusting.
   I've told you the things that I must have in a relationship....do you remember them? And if you still do and you told me that I can trust you...then I would with my whole heart. But with that understanding and after everything that's happened if you betrayed that trust...I'm not certain that I could ever forgive you again. Because it would tell me that I was wrong about who I believe that you are.
   I've wanted no one else the way that I want you...but if we're going to be one with each other then I need to know that I will from this point forward be a part of your decisions and what happens. I would need to be assured that it's been ended and there would have to be a definite time line and plan for us to be together. Please let me know if that's what you want.

I love you Brayden...
Julie

To: Brayden Loch   *January 20, 2010*
From: Julie Hopper
Subject: I'm not sure what to say

    Except that I had expected to hear from you by today. It really shouldn't take as long as it has for your replies. I hope that you haven't taken my willingness to forgive for granted. Sometimes · being a bigger person comes at risk for that and I know that if you're not ready to take an active role in a reconciliation...then it's just best that I accept that now then come to that realization weeks from now.

    Please let me know where you're at on this so that I don't wait any longer.

Julie

It had been 11 days since Brayden's last response and his last two e-mails had gone from his smooth poetic way of speaking to his choppy nervous sentences. As I stayed up late one night pondering everything and drinking too much wine, I began to question if my reply to his last e-mail was too demanding and if the one that I had just sent was too harsh. It was 1:30 in the morning and I was certain that I had read and re-written this enough times that it was right and the wine not reflected in my tone.

To: Brayden Loch   *January 21, 2010*
From: Julie Hopper
Subject: What we both want

    I'm not sure that I liked the last e-mail that I sent to you. And so I truly hope that I'm happy with this one.

    Brayden...I waited for you because I loved you and you asked me to. I believed in you...but then you proposed to and married someone else. You had the fairy tale wedding that I've always dreamed about...but will never have. I'm certain that you know my heart and what I'm feeling. Remember Paris when we told each other what we wanted and needed in a relationship? Can and do we choose to give that to each other or do we go through life incomplete?

The next morning now sober, I realized what I had done. I was falling into the same pattern of attempting to keep the conversation afloat until there was closure, and trying to soften things when in reality, I had only been telling him what I needed if this was to be a relationship. I was angry with myself, but I also wondered if he was silent because he was trying to gain the emotional upper hand, which had always worked so well for him in the past. He knew my patterns and weaknesses just as well as I knew his. I refused to allow it—even if it meant losing him. What I told him that I needed from our relationship was not an ultimatum, but simply what I needed for myself.

To: Brayden Loch　　　　　　　　　　　　　　　*January 21, 2010*
From: Julie Hopper
Subject: I can't repeat the past

And this is beginning to feel like the same pattern. I won't put myself through that again Brayden..no matter how much I love you. Your words mean nothing to me if you don't follow through. And your silence to me is completely disrespectful under the circumstances. I allowed myself hope...and I shouldn't have contacted you. I'm sure that you and Hilary are very happy together. I'll find it again too.

Julie

If he thought that I was pulling back, it may invoke a response, but I also intended to follow through by not contacting him again. I still felt certain that everything would work out in the end. Two days later I woke up feeling uncharacteristically agitated. I spoke with my friend Kate who has similar issues to Brayden's, and she thought that he may not have opened my e-mail until that morning. Adding that she often didn't open mail until she was prepared to read it. Kate thought that once again, I was probably picking up on Brayden's agitation after reading my messages.

Four days later, Sophie popped into my head. I thought, *If she answers her phone, I'll go see her and check in on what was going on with him.* She didn't answer and then five minutes later I got a call from her. Sophie said that she thought that Hilary had intercepted our e-mails and either knew that we were talking, or he may not have gotten them. That was no excuse for the length of time that it had been since I heard from him. But if he had only received the last one and not the others, then it may make sense. Sophie was able to see me the next day.

Sophie was about as accurate as you could expect a psychic could be, and that was proven to me over the years when comparing her readings with Margie and Renee's. But through the last 20 years of learning to tap into my own inner guidance, and how the spirit guides often speak in riddles, I had learned to objectively combine her information with what my own intuition told me was true. It wasn't that I would only believe what I wanted to. I had discovered that you have to use both and sometimes I would have a different first impression of what a message meant. Or sometimes after processing it a bit, I would be confident that the message meant something slightly different than her interpretation.

Whether Brayden had gotten my e-mails or not, she was certain that Hilary was aware of our conversations and that she would now try to get "pregnant" again and pull out all of her tricks. She seemed to me to have an evil streak and Sophie agreed completely, adding that Brayden and Hilary were separated due to work, but mostly by his choice. He had pulled back from both of us and was processing everything. She said that the intensity of his feelings for me scared him and he was trying to decide if he should get involved with me again. But that it looked more positive for us than it ever had before. She also thought that I would see him late spring and that we would finally be together by the end of summer.

"I'm not going to send him anymore more e-mails, I'm going to call him."

"The guides say to wait a week, but use your own intuition because you've been so accurate in the past."

"I'm going to start calling today. It feels right to me."

We talked about how people need to tap into their own inner guidance and combine that with what a good psychic tells them. Adding that I wished I could teach that to people who dwell on and believe every word in a reading, because the information that psychics get is only part of the puzzle. She thought that it was a good idea and believed that I could help others learn how to do it.

It was January 27, 2010, when I called Brayden a few times with no answer. The next morning I tried again. I knew that he must have seen me on his caller ID, so I decided that I would wait the week that Sophie suggested before trying again. That evening I got a call and I almost couldn't believe it. It was Brayden and he sounded depressed. Between the background noise and his Scottish accent, it was difficult for me to understand him. He was driving when he called (my trick to stay distracted) and he was on his way to the airport.

"Why are you so down?" I asked.

Immediately he started venting about how his ex-wife was trying to take financial advantage of him and that he had gotten upset with his mother. The entire conversation was about him and nothing about us really. He arrived at work and said that he had to go.

"So, you're just going to vent and get off of the phone?" I asked.

"I'm sorry for venting," he replied.

"Oh, no. You can vent to me anytime. It's just that we haven't spoken for a year and I had hoped to talk about other things."

"I'll call you tomorrow, sweetheart, and we'll talk more then."

Brayden knew that he was overdue to call me but he wasn't ready to have "the conversation." He also knew that I would pick up on his tone, which would give him the opportunity to take the conversation in a completely different direction.

I was disappointed but happy that he had obviously pushed himself to do something that he was uncomfortable with. I remembered him saying in his second e-mail that he ran for countless hours and couldn't help but feel like he was running from something. Although they were baby steps and a long time coming, he was making progress with himself.

I tried to call him the next day when I didn't hear from him, but he didn't answer—it didn't surprise me. He was trying to push past his fears and I had to go at his pace. I didn't want to e-mail him again because I didn't know if he would get the message and I was concerned that Hilary might intercept them before Brayden was ready to tell her. But if he wasn't taking my calls, then I wanted to give him some reassurance.

To: Brayden Loch
From: Julie Hopper
Subject: Hello

January 30, 2010

Hi Brayden,

I know that we were both nervous when we spoke, although we shouldn't have been. It's more important than ever that you follow through when you tell me that you're going to do something. You didn't do that before and I want to be able to trust you with my whole heart.

You said that you were going to call me the next day after we spoke and although I understand that things happen, it's been almost 3 days now. If our words were true to each other then there should be no reason to be nervous about talking. I won't be in the same pattern that our relationship was in before. I need to be able to believe in you completely. Please call me when you get this. I'll do the talking if you're not ready.

I didn't tell you the other day that I love you...I do with all of my heart.

Julie

I waited for several days with no reply, trying to find the balance between giving him time to absorb the situation, while keeping some pressure on him so he didn't withdraw. It had already been a month, so I decided to call him. He knew it was me but he wasn't picking up, so I called five more times on the half hour with no response. A couple of days later, I tried again and it just went to the Arabic message saying that the caller was unavailable.

Brayden had never set up a voice mail on his overseas phone. I figured that it was either so he could pretend that he didn't know that someone had called him, or so he wouldn't get angry messages from all of the women he left dangling when he dropped out of sight. I decided that it may be time to drop out of sight myself. Much more of this and I was going to be faced with a difficult decision. A few days later on February 2, I tried one last time and he answered.

"Hello?"

"Hi..." With road noise in the back ground and a little nervous I asked, "Are you on your way to work?"

"It's midnight here," he said sharply.

OK, I see how this is going to go, I thought to myself. *He's setting the tone so he has the upper hand, knowing that I'll be careful what I say. Either that or he's trying to put himself in the frame of mind that he doesn't care about me, so he's going to find reasons that I'm annoying him.*

"Oh, I guess that I misunderstood," I replied. "I thought when you called me the other day that you were just getting off of work."

"No, I was going to work," he answered with annoyance in his voice.

"Oh, OK. Brayden, I just need you to tell me if you are willing to leave her so that we can be together. Otherwise, I need to find some way to move on with my life."

His tone was now soft and vulnerable, "I thought that you had already moved on.

"You don't just move on after seven months when you're in love with someone," I said, emotion and tears now welling up in my eyes and voice. "I love you so much, Brayden. I would be there with you tomorrow if I could."

"I thought that you probably hated my guts."

I was silent for a moment. "Brayden, I just know how you get yourself into these situations."

"Get myself into these situations?" he replied sarcastically.

"Brayden, I figured that you probably weren't spending all of your nights alone over there, so either you got yourself backed into a situation that you didn't think that you could get out of, or you married the woman you wanted to. I wasn't the one that you asked to marry you."

Silence.

"Look, I know that you can be a complete and total pain in the ass, but I love you and at least life would never be boring."

"Boring's good," he replied quietly.

"Brayden, I need to know if you're going to leave her so that we can be together. If you don't have the strength to do it, then I need to know that right now."

"I just hate to disappoint,"

You hate to disappoint? I thought to myself. *Listen very carefully to what he's saying Julie. When it came down to him disappointing you or her, he married her! Maybe you need to cut the cord right now.* Big sigh in my head. *See what he does this time. You've come too far. You have nothing to lose and you've been in this for years. If he doesn't make the right decision, then you're done anyways and you know it this time.*

"We'll continue to talk won't we?" he asked vulnerably, without answering my question.

"There's nothing else to talk about Brayden. I know what I want," I replied firmly. "I was the other woman for three and a half years, and I won't be the other woman for one more day. Brayden? Do you love me?"

"Ohhh! You know that I love you!" His reply was agitated as though I had asked a ridiculous question.

"Well, sometimes it's nice to hear," I said calmly. "Can we see each other?"

"I want to but I have to work."

"Yes, but you work eight days on and eight days off right?"

"No, I changed my schedule. I only have three days off now."

Silence.

"Well, you can take vacation days can't you?"

"I would have to request them and then it wouldn't be until July. There's a chance that I wouldn't even get them."

Longer silence.

I thought to myself, *This is it! No hope, I'm done!* when Brayden interrupted my thoughts.

"Julie, I can schedule the time so I can come to see you," he said softly in earnest.

Come to see me? I thought. I wanted desperately to believe him, but I knew that I couldn't.

"Brayden, I just love you and I miss you so much."

"I miss you too, Julie."

"I need to know if you're going to leave her so we can be together."

"Will you just give me a day to process all of this?" he asked with apprehension in his voice.

"Yes."

"Julie, I have to go to work, but I'll call you tomorrow or the next day OK?"

Tomorrow or the next day didn't come. *It never does.* But I understood that he was now in a position that he not only had to face his fears about his feelings for me, but also the reality of having to end the marriage, which was huge. Besides the normal complications of a divorce, it would be especially embarrassing for him just having come out of another divorce prior to marrying her. He can't seem to ever make a decision until he's backed into a corner and has got no other choice. That's how he ended up married to someone that he didn't want to be with in the first place.

We were talking about having a baby together, he got scared and to distance himself from dealing with our decision, he got himself wrapped up in something else that he knew he wouldn't fully commit to. He impulsively asked her to marry him, realized his mistake, we got engaged and then he put off telling her. She conveniently became pregnant within days of our engagement, and I'm sure that her working for Saudi security probably had something to do with the timing. They monitor everything over there, so she would certainly have access to his phone and e-mail. His ex-wife had tapped into his phone and e-mail and she didn't have the connections that Hilary did. Her potentially fabricating a pregnancy to make it more difficult for him to leave hadn't helped.

No matter what, this is it!. But I can't draw the line until I'm ready to accept the consequences. I can't cut the cord just because I'm impatient—I'll see how or if things progress.

To: Brayden Loch   February 6, 2010
From: Julie Hopper
Subject: Something that you said.

Brayden,
When we last spoke, you said twice that you hate to disappoint. That statement is really gnawing at me.

If you're trying to decide if you would rather disappoint me a second time rather than to disappoint her once, then I don't want you back in my life. If you're still processing what you need to do in order to be true to yourself and to me...then you are just going to have to take the leap because the longer that you think about it, the harder that it's going to be. You asked me for a couple of days but in reality, it's been almost a month.

Call me and let me know which it is so that we can both move on or move forward.

Julie

He didn't reply and I needed closure, so on February 9, I decided to call.

"Hey Julie, can you hold on a minute?" I heard Brayden speaking Arabic to someone in the distance. "I'm sorry, Julie, the guy is messing up my car. I'm just on my way to the mall to meet some people."

"Brayden, we need to talk about what we're going to do."

"I'm off for a few days and I'll be back Friday. I'll e-mail you."

"You'll e-mail me?" I asked in disbelief.

"I'll call you Friday when I get back," he corrected. "It's just that you want everything *yesterday* and it's not black and white. *It's complicated.*"

"Well, then explain it to me so I can understand."

Silence.

"Julie, I have a good job here. I just got Janis paid off. I have my housing paid for and money going into the bank."

"Would you lose your job if you left her?" I asked with confusion.

"No, but you want me to come back to the States and I'm finally getting my life under control."

"Brayden, I told you in our last conversation that I would be there with you tomorrow if I could."

"You would come here?"

"Yes! I've already told you that I would. Brayden, the longer that you draw this out the harder that it's going to be."

He laughed. I wondered if someone had already told him that.

"Well, things just don't happen quickly here and you want this to happen right now."

"Brayden, if you don't get things started for a month, then it just means that it's going to be one more month before we can be together. It has to get started at some point."

"What was it that you were saying you could do for work here?"

"I don't want to talk about that right now. Is that what it's about? How much money she's making?"

"Who, Hilary? That has absolutely nothing to do with anything! I could care less how much she makes!" He had a tone of complete disdain in his voice for her, which took me by surprise.

"What about your mom?"

"My mom will be fine without me. I can't live my life around her."

"Maybe we should do what's best," he replied.

In my head, that statement made me panic. And then there was a long silence. "Brayden, are you not going to leave her so we can be together? I need to know."

"I sure have a way of screwing my life up!" he said with a big sigh. "Look, we'll talk about this more, but they're waiting for me in the mall."

"They can wait!" I replied adamantly. Tears started welling up in my eyes as I processed again what he had said. The "Maybe we should do what's best" statement along with his line of questioning wasn't good. Although in my heart, I still believed that everything would be OK. "Brayden, I'm scared. I'm scared that you don't have the courage to leave her. I'm also scared that she's *suddenly* going to become pregnant and I'm not going to be here three months from now when she *suddenly* loses it," I said, my voice now trembling.

His tone turned soft and comforting. "Don't be scared."

"Brayden, I am because this last year was *really* hard on me."

"Don't you think that it was hard on me too?" he asked, with his voice now raised in emotion, as if I should have known that it had been just as difficult for him being apart too. "Look, I'll be honest with you, I'm scared."

I heard a call coming in a couple of times on his phone, and I couldn't help but wonder if it was her and if she was the one he was meeting at the mall.

"I have to go but I'll call you later."

I knew that we weren't going to be able to resolve things in this conversation, so I had no other choice but to agree; later could be that day, or a month from now. His laters didn't mean anything to me anymore.

Brayden's words kept playing through my mind:

You want things yesterday but they're not black and white.

What are you going to do for work?

What about your mother?

Maybe we should do what's best.

I really have a way of screwing up my life.

Don't be scared.

Don't you think that the last year has been hard on me too?

I have to be honest, I'm scared.

He was trying to find reasons not to face a situation that he knew would be complicated, so in his mind he was trying to convince himself and me that it was too difficult. Regardless of what he said, it was still inconclusive as our conversations frequently were. I couldn't be sure that he was going to be able to find the courage to do what needed to be done. If he hurt me again, there would be no turning back this time. He said that he would call me but from past experience, that could be weeks. I couldn't do that again. Four days later it would be Valentine's Day. It was just another day to men but to women, it meant something.

To: Brayden Loch　　　　　　　　　　　　　　*February 10, 2010*
From: Julie Hopper
Subject: I don't think that you realize this

But when we spoke...you gave me several reasons that might make it difficult for us to be together and not one of how we can be together. I know that you're scared and what you need to do would be difficult. But if it takes you more than a month or two to figure it out, then no matter what you say...I think that you'll just continue to find reasons for delay. You told me not to be scared, but looking at it from my perspective. I just can't wait much longer only to have my heart served back to me like it was before.

On Valentines Day she's probably going to get roses and a sweet message from you. What would you think about that if you were me? I love you Brayden. I just can't draw this out only to have the outcome that it did before. Please let me know if you have solutions as to how we can finally be together and if you're ready to make it happen for us.

Julie

After several days there was still no answer, so I called Sophie to get her opinion as to if I had pushed him away in my previous e-mails. She said no, but that the guides thought that my last e-mail was good. Brayden was just afraid of seeing me in person again. I knew that he must realize that our next conversation had to come to some resolution. He was avoiding telling Hilary and trying to grasp the reality that he would have to deal with his fears of being emotionally vulnerable to me.

It was around this time that I began to realize how many people were going through similar situations. And just how many walking wounded were around me. There was my friend Judi, who was involved with a man who loved her deeply, but also found reasons to keep her at a distance. She had been going through the same thing longer than I had and the man that she was involved with was finally admitting that he was in love with her. He told her that he was beginning to realize that no matter how things had gone, he knew that she would always be there for him, she wouldn't leave him. But that didn't mean that he expected her to be his doormat, it just meant that she had been so patient and consistent with her love, that he was finally allowing himself to begin to trust and believe in it.

Then there was my other friend Kate, who kept herself in a position so she wouldn't get involved with men who could hurt her by leaving. She admitted to me that it was her 48-hour rule. If they left and she knew that she couldn't be over them in 48 hours, then she wouldn't go there. She was now in communication with a guy that she knew as a teenager and he understood her like I understood Brayden. He called her "a runner."

He recounted to her a situation that she didn't remember. When they were young, they were making out when suddenly she ran out of the room. Probably because her vulnerability was becoming too strong, so she left. After watching me go through with Brayden what I had, Kate was working hard to conquer her own fears but it was still baby steps for her. Even with as much as she now understands about herself, she told me that the thought of seeing him causes her waves of panic that make her physically sick.

My own emotions were going through waves of missing Brayden so much that it hurt, along with having brief flashbacks of the things that he'd done in the past that made me almost hate him. The other women, keeping me on the line while he's been in a steady relationship with someone else, his proposal to her and their fairy tale wedding at a castle in Scotland, and to top it all off, a honeymoon in Bora Bora. All of the things that I wanted, he gave to her. And then I would have to remind myself, as I had throughout the last three and a half years, there's only *one* person who has his heart—and that's me.

I knew that with conviction and nothing else mattered if I had his heart *and* him in the end. It was a constant play on my logic but I wasn't in denial. This man truly loved me and his actions were a result of his fear of losing me. Better to push me away now, than to love me and I choose to leave him later. My frustration at times was almost unbearable. But I still had this quiet calm and knowing telling me that it was my patience that would to take me through the home stretch.

My sister was visiting me on the 23rd and we had been up late talking. It was around midnight when I got a call from Brayden. As soon as I answered, he hung up the phone. I called back with no answer. I thought that he may have dialed me by accident, but later realized that it probably wasn't him but likely Hilary who had called. I imagined her with his phone in her hand confronting him on who I was and then dialing my number as he snatched it out of her hand.

Sophie would eventually confirm it for me, and it would also make sense after a reading with Renee saying that "the heat is on him now."

Sophie sent me several e-mails. One each week, saying the same thing, which was something that she had never done before. I must have needed to have the message reinforced to keep me strong in my belief of what we had: "He's just afraid to see you in person because he knows that he won't be able to control his feelings for you the next time."

To: Julie Hopper   *February 28, 2010*
From: Sophie Douglas
Subject: Hello

The guides seem to think sometime around Memorial Day, (end of May) things will be resolved between the two of you. Hopefully you'll hear more from him soon. He is just avoiding the face to face meeting because he knows his emotions will overcome his trying to be aloof and detached.

Hope you are enjoying this beautiful Sunday afternoon.

Love,

Sophie

I tried to call Brayden several times but he still wouldn't answer. He's a lot like a kid with chocolate on his face who says that he didn't have any candy. When we do talk, he'll say that he didn't know that I tried to contact him, even though the evidence was on his caller ID.

It was March 8 and almost a month since we'd spoken. My frustration and temptation of sending him an e-mail telling him what a rude and selfish bastard he is by ignoring me was becoming stronger. After a barrage of e-mails suggesting that we compromise and/or see each other again and doing the "take away" by giving him the impression that I was finally walking away if it didn't happen (which he'd grown too smart for), I realized that I was not only out of ammunition, but I had been doing what I had promised myself that I wouldn't: trying to maintain contact when he had shut down. I knew when he did that, there was nothing that could draw him out.

Once again, I reminded myself of the May resolution that Sophie mentioned and that she and Margie thought that it would be over between Brayden and Hilary by February, March at the latest. And last year's prediction by Renee that it would be over by spring. A prediction along with others that I believed might have been a year off. In my heart though, I knew that when free will was involved, timelines meant nothing.

Still, I had to keep myself going mentally, so I decided that I would do nothing and hope that everything would fall into place by then. I needed to set small goals for myself with a man that rules his life by fear. *So spring it is. I have to be patient and understand that things don't always happen on my time frame.* When I decided on the spring resolution, I got the familiar tightening and energy sensation in my temples that I recognized as my guides. It didn't mean that he was magically going to show up, it just meant spring. Through all of these years, I hadn't been able to determine if the sensation in my temples was reassurance, or my guides just letting me know that they were there, even though I still try to find distinct patterns. But even if it was confirmation, there was always Brayden's free will that could change the outcome.

I hadn't had any message dreams since before I left for Scotland but I started having dreams that made me curious. In one of them, I was in a hotel and I was having difficulty finding Brayden. We encountered each other briefly and he said that his house in Florida would be empty when Janis, his ex-wife moved out. We ended up separated again and then I found one of his business cards that he left for me. On it he had written the words "The next time will be on my knee." I assumed, or hoped that it was a reference to a proposal the next time that we met. In the other dream, I was wearing the jersey of his favorite football team the Tampa

Bay Buccaneers. I didn't feel strongly that it wasn't any more than just my subconscious, although the only time that I had dreamt of him in the past were messages.

But there was the little boy after Scotland, the one who insisted that he sit next to me in the bleachers at the Highland games. I had also had a vision that I know was real, when I saw Brayden looking pensively in his hotel room. Those were all last summer and why hadn't I had anything significant recently? *I could use some spiritual reassurance about now.* If stuffing your face with handfuls of Special K Strawberry like it's popcorn after downing two liters of red wine is coping—then I was coping. But as much as I wanted a message or some sort of sign from my guides, I realized that I must not need it. I must be on the right track because I'm not feeling any strong nudges, other than a calmness that tells me that it's time to let it go and leave it to God and Brayden.

I called Kate who had some of the same issues that Brayden did and asked her what I should do.

"Bombard him with phone calls and if he doesn't answer, then disappear."

Reluctantly I agreed and for one phone call, Brayden picked up. I didn't know if he picked up by accident or decided that he shouldn't have after he did, because he pretended to be French and answered "Bonjour." I tried to get him to acknowledge me but he wouldn't. Like he wanted me to think that I had dialed the wrong number or something.

OK, maybe this guy is just broken, or maybe he's retreated into his protective place. I later realized that she must have been with him when I called and not answering would look suspicious. He pretended that someone French had dialed his number by accident to cover up. Regardless, he had hung up on me in the process of protecting her and I was pissed.

Messages from your guides usually come in quick, short and unexpected thoughts or inspiration. I was trying to process him not returning my calls after the whole French thing and then out of the blue, the idea that he had set the ring tone assigned to my phone number as silent popped into my head. This whole thing was making me crazy and that's exactly what I promised myself that I wasn't going to let happen.

But this just had to be our last shot at this and I kept poking at it trying to find the magic button. I looked at the sent folder in my e-mail and was embarrassed for myself by the number of messages that I had sent to him. I had been beating my head against the wall and found myself exactly where I promised that I wouldn't be.

As the weeks passed, letting go felt unnatural and moving on impossible. It would have been one thing if Brayden had ever told me that he wasn't ready or didn't want to be with me. But trying to move on from someone who you know has the same love for you and who wants and needs you just as much, if not more than you need them, is like asking yourself to stop breathing. Sophie and Renee were consistent in their opinions. They both felt that Hilary knew about me and was keeping a tight leash on Brayden. But although he missed me and wanted to see me, he couldn't because he was being watched and monitored closely. My guess was that because of Hilary's high position, he was probably also being monitored by people in the Saudi security. Surely they would need to know what the people around her were doing.

Sophie and Renee were also consistent in saying that the marriage was falling apart, but that she would hold on to him at any price. Brayden had become financially tied to her family, and they just weren't sure if he could get himself out of the situation. Sophie went so far as to say that his life could be in danger if he left. It was all sounding like some international spy story. But it did make some sense because in the previous fall, they had both told me that if he left her, then he may have to flee the country because of her high connections.

Renee added that he went through with the marriage because not only did he feel like he had no other choice, but that he felt it would increase his social status. That he would finally feel like he was "someone." It made sense to me because having come from an impoverished childhood, I could understand why it might be important to him. At the time that they married, our relationship and my enduring love was still unproven to him.

Renee went on to say that when he and I spoke, "It was gorgeous, just like the old times. Brayden feels safe with you because you're the only person who he's ever loved this deeply, and the only person in his life who's ever been consistent in their actions towards him. You're like a lifeline for him and almost an antidote because you calm him. When you're out of touch with each other, he becomes agitated and uneasy."

The following month they would be celebrating their first anniversary and if he didn't end things with her before that, then I had to face the possibility that he may be in a situation he truly couldn't get out of. Another month from then would mark the fourth year of our involvement. I also had to consider the possibility that he could be broken and not just damaged. If either of those were the case, I had to find a way to move on with my life. Hilary's profile photo on Facebook for the last several months had been one of her in her wedding dress. Knowing that Brayden's and my communications had likely been discovered, I looked to see if she had the same photo posted, but she didn't. In its place was a casual photo of the happy couple, and it was painful to see. Although they weren't touching and there was no sign of affection, with no word from him it was time to truly let go.

I hadn't told him about the book because I knew that it may make him angry and I didn't want to upset him. The book was never intended to be published without my "happily ever after" with him, because I didn't think that it would have the same meaning or impact on others as it would if we came back together after all of the struggle. I just couldn't imagine that our love would dissipate into nothing, and I prayed for a message or sign that it all work out, but got nothing. Why did I have so much guidance before Scotland and virtually nothing afterwards?

Although I still believed that something would happen to change the situation, I had to face the agonizing possibility that it may not, and I would be left to feel connected and without him for the rest of my life. If that was the case, then I had to decide if I would move forward with the book or not. Being loving and nice to Brayden wasn't working and I had nothing to lose. *It's time to poke the bear!*

To: Brayden Loch   *April 29, 2010*
From: Julie Hopper
Subject: *I wrote a book about our story. You'll want to read this.*

Brayden,
    *I should probably be addressing this to both you and Hilary
because I'm certain that if she isn't just reading my messages, that
she may be intercepting them. No need to reply via e-mail. I wouldn't
believe that it was you anyway.*
    *I had planned to wait to tell you about the book until we saw
each other so that you could read it and censor anything that you
were uncomfortable with. Because I thought that initially you would
be upset at the idea. But there are some things that I didn't include
out of respect to you. The messages in this book will help other
people. Even if they didn't help us. It's very good and should be quite
successful. Understanding why you make the decisions that you do
has already helped me to help others better understand the people
that they're in relationships with. I won't explain everything because
I'm not certain that you'll even get this.*
    *I've had 3 of my psychic friends use the same words
independently to describe your marriage. That she has you "on a
tight leash." And that you're being watched closely among other
things. A marriage is in the heart and mind. Not in the physical or
on a piece of paper. And I know that your heart is with me. From
what my friends tell me, she's not a very nice person at all. And how
someone could be satisfied with binding someone else to them like
that is beyond me.*
    *I wasn't going to move forward with the book until after we
spoke. But under the circumstances I've decided to. The cover and
title are done and it just needs to be edited. I will change your names
but anyone who knows you will likely figure it out. People will love
and understand your character just as I do. I promise. But they won't
have the same opinion of your wife. This is not written as fiction.
Everything is true and factual. Just as it happened.*
    *I hope that you find your happiness Brayden. I've watched you
live your life without fulfillment before and know that you're capable*

of it. You will only be able to do that for so long though. I'm sorry that things turned out this way for you.

With love always,

Julie

"A river cannot flow against its current."

~ A message from my spirit guide

18

Brayden had been struggling against his current from the beginning. He knew that we belonged together and yet his fears caused him to try to run from his feelings for me. What he got as a result of it was a marriage that he didn't want and the possibility of losing me forever. I knew that there was no way that he could ever truly let go of me; but in many ways, I enabled his behavior by being available to him whenever he decided to drop in. But it was a balance, and difficult to determine how much time needed to be invested in order for him to feel safe enough to let the walls down and trust his love with me. For some, you can never invest enough time. So now, with no word from him for months, it was time for me to attempt to release him.

As juvenile as it may be, Brayden had always used his Myspace site to poke back at me in a passive-aggressive way. He hadn't been on it for over a year, other than the time he accepted my niece's friend request in October, and that was an attempt to reach out to me. Keeping an eye on his web page was a little like interpreting code and watching a car wreck at the same time. I just couldn't help but look. The day after he would have received my e-mail, he had a new woman on his site. I could usually judge how much he wanted to get my attention by the number of new friends he added.

A dialog in my head began: *OK, you jerk I get it. I pissed you off and fuck you too for doing that after everything that you've put me through! Do you really think that posting someone on your stupid freaking Myspace page is going to upset me after you've married someone else?* I had a strong feeling of disgust for him under the circumstances, and it surprised me that he would dare to consider using that as a weapon, after everything that had happened. I had poked the bear and now he was poking back.

I felt the connection that I had previously felt so strongly with him begin to disintegrate. Maybe this was it. I had told Brayden before that I would give him everything that I had until the switch flipped. And from past experience, I could never turn it back. I had gone to Renee for a checkup after the e-mail and she said that if he knew that I was reaching, then it was "Game on" and he felt OK to disappear again. I knew that to be true all along, but I had never had the strength to let go until now. Walking away from me again after I gave him another opportunity was enough. And each day that passed was another day that he was choosing her first and me second. No matter his reasons—I was worth more than that.

It was rare that I dreamed about Brayden and in the past when I did, they were clearly message dreams. Since right before I left for Scotland, I had only two others that were faint, and I wasn't sure if they were my subconscious or not. Recently though, I had two more in the same week that caused me to pay attention. In both of them, he was franticly trying to convince me that he was trying to get out of his situation to be with me. In the last one, Tiger Woods was sitting on a couch with Brayden and I, and as I slid my hand up the back of Brayden's shirt to stroke his back, I could feel the conflict of his fear and desire for me.

I told him, "I was with Tiger last night and now I'm with you. Isn't this much better?"

The symbolism in the dream made me laugh because I believed that it meant Brayden wanted to be with me, but he was still scared of his feelings; and Tiger Woods was an obvious symbol that Brayden was a womanizer before, and he no longer would be once we were together.

Interesting... Do the dreams that we have sometimes reflect what the person involved with us is feeling and not just the situation? Maybe the dreams that are faint but have symbolism and meaning are not exactly message dreams, but are connected to the consciousness of those involved.

I told Renee I had a couple of dreams about him in the same week and thought it was odd because I rarely dreamed about him. She said that it was because we were still so connected, that I was picking up where he was at in our relationship.

A few weeks passed and then it all became obvious me. He had to know that he may have blown his only chance at my forgiveness for marrying Hilary and the opportunity to win me back. He had handled the situation badly by disappearing on me instead of acting like an adult and being honest with me. I didn't react to his Myspace antics the way that I would have in the past, so he needed to make sure that I was still available to him. He wasn't prepared to leave her, but he wasn't able to let me go either. So now he was going off the deep end to get a reaction from me with the hope that I would open the door again.

Suddenly a parade of thirty five women began popping up as friends on his Myspace page. They ranged from porn stars to huge naked women in bath tubs. He was going for shock value, but he didn't realize that the dominatrix woman that he added was actually a cross dressing man. I had to laugh because it served him right for being such an idiot. Particularly amusing was a heavily tattooed white trash–looking girl who was lying on her bed passed out drunk with the caption "Quit chewing on my name." What the hell did that mean? It was as if he was poking around asking himself, "OK, what will she react too? Alright, I'll tryyyy this one!"

I hated myself not only for watching the train wreck, but also for checking my e-mail constantly with the hope of hearing from him. I was at work when I looked at his profile and all of the women were deleted. I checked my email, and found a request from Brayden to be his friend on Facebook, followed by a message:

Subject: Make things right

I wanted to talk to you and try and tell you how sorry I am for acting like a child and not living up to my responsibilities. I hope that you will let me try and explain things and talk to you about how I can apologize for my past behavior.

I understand if I don't get an answer, I don't deserve or even expect it. From the bottom of my heart I am truly sorry for the hurt, pain and tears I have ever caused you and hope you can find it inside to try and let me heal things over with you. You truly have made every effort to be a friend and more. I can't find the words to express the regret I have with the way I have treated you and dealt with situations in the past and I have to make amends with you and redeem my character and before it is too late.

I can't apologize enough for my behavior, I am deeply and truly sorry for all my actions.

Brayden X.

I flushed hot and the energy in my body began to buzz as my anger and excitement began to clash. *After everything that has happened, I was sure that he wouldn't contact me unless he was ready to do something about it. And now he's sent me a fucking friend request? After all of the deep love and understanding of why he does the things that he does? And torment that I've been through? He wants me to be his Facebook friend and be subject to updates and photos of his marriage? Responsibilities, amends, friend? And he signed it with an X after his name just like I had seen Hilary do before. I can't think anymore!*

I got into my car to drive home before I responded. The numb, aching, buzzing reached a point that I didn't think I couldn't bear it any longer. Had everything that I had gone through come to this? I knew that his words and apology were truly heartfelt, but they meant nothing to me and also something at the same time. Once home and computer booted, I thought, *Calm down, Julie. This is what you've been preparing for. You know that he dangles a carrot and then disappears once you bite. Keep it simple, but leave the door open.*

Brayden,

I will always care about you. If the day comes that you're ready to tell her that you want a divorce, I would talk to you if I haven't already moved on by then.

Julie

---

can I at least be added as a friend to FB?

With that message, he sent me another friend request from Facebook. I exploded with rage and anger as I thought, *You rip my fucking heart out of my chest and serve it to me with a cocktail fork? And then you want me to be your "friend" so I can see everything that's going on in your life without me? You fucker!*

I called my friend Kate who was giving him more of a benefit of the doubt than I was.

"Julie, you've come this far, don't cut the cord until you see how it may play out."

I didn't think that I cared anymore, but knew in some ways she may be right.

I hoped the first one was an accident.

You write me an e-mail apologizing for the hurt and pain that you've caused me. And then you want me to be your FB friend so that I can be witness to updates and photos of your marriage? Did you stop to consider how cruel that was before asking a second time? I'm not capable of being your "Facebook friend" Please read my reply to your original e-mail again.

---

it wasn't a case of me trying to be cruel. I just wanted to see you and how you were, not wanting you "to be witness to updates and photos". I apologize for being inconsiderate.

I'll stop hurting you. I was trying to heal the damage I have caused, not hurt you further. I will stop contacting you. Again, I seem to do the wrong thing.

I had no intention of responding but around the time when Brayden and I first reconnected, my computer was hacked and I was pretty sure that it was Hilary or someone close to her. I had been working on the book and watched in horror as line by line the words were quickly deleted. I was frantic as I realized that I had lost control of my computer and I couldn't do anything to stop it. My last hope was to disconnect from the internet and thankfully it stopped. My e-mail had also been sending me strange notification codes around the same time, and at one point Yahoo UK/Ireland popped up on my screen. I knew that was the site that Hilary used, so she must have been logged into my mail when I signed on.

Now, the day after Brayden's last message to me, I logged on to my computer and it said "Messenger has been disconnected because a second viewer has logged on." My first thought was that she could be spying and/or possibly sending messages in my name. But I also wondered if it was one of those electronic interferences from the other side so I would send him another message. I couldn't take the chance.

I just wanted to tell you that someone is hacking into my messaging and I think my computer. Be cautious if you get anything from me because my first reply is where things are for me now.

Who do you think is hacking into your computer... and why? Or do you simply want me to stop all communication?

And every time I reply to you I have to put in codes as you will not add me.

I don't want to say...But Brayden, you don't seem to understand that I can't communicate with you unless you've left her. I'm sorry, just you talking to me like you want to re establish our relationship as a friendship causes me great pain. And that will never happen. I can't talk to you anymore.

---

you can't talk to me anymore?... It upsets me that you can't talk to me until conditions are met. I know and understand I have hurt you and I just would like the chance to start from the beginning to try and work things out.

You know what the biggest obstacle is and so nothing can be worked out until that is out of the way.

ADD ME NOW!....LOL

I knew that he wasn't thinking when he sent the last message. He was going into his playful protective zone because I was finally drawing a line that he wasn't used to. But I also knew that he would obsessively read everything over and over again, and my statement that it was cruel for him to suggest that I add him as a friend would scare him. I was angry that he had opened a door that he was unprepared to walk through, and I began to feel disdain for him as the events of the last four years played through my mind.

I had seen the beauty of the person that I knew him to be. Not only was he kind, compassionate and thoughtful in so many ways, but he had a vulnerability about him that I was drawn to. I loved the part of him that he kept concealed from the world, but that I instinctively understood. At times his sense of humor and unpredictability was borderline crazy, but I loved that about him, too. Still, I was beginning to replace my understanding of his actions with the question of his true character. The line in between was feeling dangerously close and I felt as though I was finally to the point that I could let him go.

I don't fully understand why it is that if you release something with your thoughts and actions, it will sometimes finally happen. I had given up on love and marriage and decided to have a baby on my own, just a month before I met Brayden. And then there are all of those stories that you hear about couples trying desperately to have a child, and as soon as they adopt, they suddenly become pregnant. I don't know why, but there's something to it. Maybe it's the Universe's way of teaching us that we aren't in as much control as we think we are—that there's a bigger plan at work in our lives and we need to learn how to let go and trust it.

Contemplating it all, I sat on my back porch drinking wine as I watched flies in the distance glow from the sunlight reflecting on them. I let my mind go blank, mesmerized as they swirled around like tiny little sparks from a fire. A woman walked past me with her young son in her arms and I wondered if I would ever experience that for myself. The thought pulled at the emptiness and pain in my heart. My opportunity to have children was fleeting by the day and if moving on with my life and letting go was what I needed to do, then I wondered again if I should try to have a child on my own. Recently I had asked Renee if I would have a biological child and if I should start trying.

"The window is narrow," she replied, "But the guides say no, that you shouldn't try on your own."

To me her words carried hope for Brayden and me to still have a child together. But my 44th birthday was now approaching and it was something that I had to consider.

"I would rather follow my heart and fail,
than compromise my beliefs and regret it."

~ Julie Hopper

19

With time, peace began to settle back into my heart, but I still wondered what purpose all of this could serve. It was becoming clear to me that Brayden may not have the strength to leave his marriage so we could be together. But as much as I wanted to find the strength to let my hopes and belief go, I just couldn't and I was beginning to feel ambushed by my some of my closest friends.

They would ask if I had heard from Brayden, then seemed to use it as an opportunity to lecture me that I needed to give up on him. That regardless of what I thought he felt for me, he married someone else and that was inexcusable. As I reminded them for the hundredth time about the synchronicities between us and the guidance that I had received telling me that I wasn't supposed to give up on him yet, it was as though I was talking to stone and they couldn't absorb what I was saying.

I hadn't told many of my family members that Brayden had married, and this was why. Most people who don't follow a spiritual path and have never been aware of their own guidance, often can't see below the surface to the big picture. I felt like I was beating my head against a wall to try to help them understand, and I was becoming so frustrated that I wished that I hadn't confided in them at all. Ending one of those many conversations, I said, "I would rather follow my heart and fail, than compromise my beliefs and regret it."

I had learned to understand my relationships on a spiritual level, and less on a human level. I read a quote once that said, "When we look outside of ourselves we are dreaming, and when we look within, we are awake." I was more awake and clear about the true workings of our relationship than many of my friends could ever have the patience to be about their own.

I prayed and pleaded every night for a message or guidance to relieve my suffering, but nothing came. There were many days when I felt a steady aching sensation in my body, and it was a struggle for me to make it through work until I could be home where I felt safe. Then one morning right before I woke up, I had one of my dreams that was so clear, I felt as though I was truly there. My dog Gypsy who had passed away was running in the opposite direction of me with a black bird flapping its wings at her neck. I was horrified and screamed for her to come to me, because I was afraid that the bird might hurt her and I wanted to get it off of her. She came to sit in front of me with hesitation; squinting and blinking her eyes as she always had when she was in trouble.

Telepathically she said "I was going to help another dog cross over."

The black bird was now resting calmly on her shoulder, although I still didn't like that it was there. I felt ashamed with myself for screaming at her and that I hadn't understood what she was doing.

With love in my voice I said gently, "OK, go now and help." And she ran away.

When I woke, I Googled the symbolism for black birds in dreams and although there were various definitions, I found one that said they represented death and transition. It made sense to me and I was happy to know that my Gypsy was helping other dogs cross into the spirit world. Years before I had spoken with an animal psychic who said that although her cat often dropped by for a visit, she never stayed long because she was often going to Indonesia to do spirit work there.

Two weeks later, I struck up a conversation with Susan, a gal who worked at the local grocery store. She knew the spiritual side of my relationship with Brayden, and often asked how things were going. She always seemed to be a little on the sad and serious side to me, but this day her energy felt heavier. I asked how she was doing and as tears began to roll down her cheeks, she said her Yorkie had a seizure two weeks ago and died in front of her. I found the timing of my dream and the death of her dog uncanny, and I explained my dream to her.

"I've always believed that animals have souls and they go to heaven," I added. "I do too, and thank you so much for sharing that with me. It really means a lot"

It was now October 2010 and I was at the Oregon Coast to celebrate my sister's birthday at the new bar where she worked. Ed, the cowboy who I had been so in love with years before, had shown up around her birthday for the last couple of years to go elk hunting. He and I worked together briefly after our split, and the wounds had long since healed. But although we still had a great measure of love between us, we didn't stay in contact. Lynne asked me for his number to see if he was in town, so she could tell him where we were. At the moment she called, he had just been asking a bartender at her old work place where she was.

I looked up to see his big, beautiful, brown eyes and scruffy beard walk through the door. His face glowed as he came over to me with a wide smile and gave me a big hug and kiss. Over drinks, he asked about Brayden and I explained his abusive childhood and how much effort I had put into building his trust in order to help him overcome his fears, adding what an amazing person he was, but that our relationship had been difficult and I had done all that I could to save it.

I continued by confessing to Ed that years earlier, when he said his final good-bye to me, it pushed me to the brink of taking my own life. An expression of pain washed over his face as his thoughts turned inward for several minutes. I was confused by it but I also saw a look of compassion, as though he was both horrified that our break-up had driven me to such a point, and appreciating that I took such great measures to understand Brayden's pain.

I hadn't wanted to get involved with Ed when we did because his wife had just left him for another man. Although I believed that his feelings for me were real, I also knew that he hadn't healed from the marriage yet. When he ended our relationship, he told me that he wasn't ready to be emotionally vulnerable again. Now I felt great empathy for him because I knew at that moment, he was reflecting about what had been lost between us.

A two-man band was playing acoustic guitars on the outside deck where we were sitting. Without saying another word, Ed jumped to his feet and asked one of the guys if he could use his guitar.

"Please?" he pleaded playfully. "I'll even pay you $50.00 and take my belt off so I don't scratch your guitar."

It took a lot of convincing, but the band member finally agreed. Ed pulled his chair directly in front of mine and began playing a song and singing words of pain that I knew were about his love for me and our break up. I was uncomfortable being serenaded with a crowd of people watching, but could clearly see the emotion that he poured into the song, as he looked deeply into my eyes while he sang.

When he was finished, I was left speechless so I wrapped my arms around him and we kissed. Several people told us how beautiful it was that we still had so much love between us, and as the evening ended, I saw pain return to Ed's eyes. He knew that I was in love with someone else, and our time had long since passed. As the bar began to close and I became distracted by my good-byes to other people, he slipped silently out of the door and into the night.

Years earlier I had begun using the term "stepping stone relationships," and now it was all beginning to make perfect sense to me. I knew that soulmates come in many different forms and purposes. They're people who come into our lives not only to help us grow as individuals, but also to prepare us for the person we're meant to be with. Now I was beginning to think that on some subconscious level, either they, or we, know that no matter how strong the love is, the relationship is only meant to be temporary. And whatever the reason is for the break up, it's only a catalyst for us to move in a new direction.

Ed was the man who I almost took my life over because he had walked away from me. Now years later, he was telling me that his love had never left me, but that it was his own pain that caused him to leave. It was then that I realized that this was my pattern: Tim, one of my first loves, had recently been left by his wife and wasn't ready to be emotionally vulnerable again; and Duff, the pilot who had triggered my spiritual path, was engaged to be married when his fiancée suddenly told him she wasn't in love with him anymore. Brayden had the same pain and fear of allowing his heart to be vulnerable, so he ran from his emotions and became involved with people who could never fully have his heart or hurt him. We had come into each other's lives so I could learn to love without trying to control their fears and they could learn to love without fear. The world is full of walking wounded, and if people only took the time to understand it, maybe there would be fewer divorces and missed opportunities with people who are worth the extra effort.

Ed had become a multimillionaire and although I still had a deep love and respect for him, the love that I felt for Brayden was far more important to me than the security that Ed could provide. And even though Brayden had been manipulated to some degree and backed into a corner, I found it somewhat ironic that he traded our love for financial security when I wouldn't. Money can't buy you love and love can't cure poor, but love can make you rich in your heart. Brayden and I would have never been poor, so how much money did he need?

Earlier in the month, he had changed his Facebook photo to one of a 747 passenger jet. I cringed to click on his information, for fear of what I might see. But he had made public only his basic information without his marital status. He had left his job as a pilot for the Saudi prince's airlines and was now working for a Saudi-based international carrier. I knew that he would have signed a contract for at least a year, and I feared that it meant he would have no intention of leaving his marriage, or that job. I knew that he wanted to share it with me though, because he would have been very proud of that achievement.

It was nearing Halloween, and I thought that I would see if I could get a reaction from him. I changed my profile photo on Facebook to one of my favorites, which I had doctored with red eyes and fangs as vampire. The next day, he changed his photo to one in which he had red eye, drinking a beer. It brought a glimmer of hope that he was still trying to communicate in our own strange way, but when would it end or be resolved?

It had been months since I felt that I had received any true direction or messages from my guides, and I was beginning to feel abandoned by them. But I also knew that it may just mean that I was to do nothing. I was doing my best to keep moving forward with my life, and hoping that something would change soon.

For the last two years, the rainy climate of the Northwest had become almost unbearable for me, and I often referred to it as "rain poisoning." I had always dreamed of moving somewhere in Europe that had a warmer, dryer climate, but would allow me to still hop on a train and be in an Alpine country in just a few hours. The south of France or Italy would be perfect, and I knew if Brayden ever got the courage to ask for a divorce, the company he now flew for must fly to France due to the high Muslim population there. It was a dream that I rarely allowed myself to indulge in: living with him in a centuries old village in a stone cottage with a view of the sea. But lately, I had begun to feel a strong urge to figure out a way to move to the Mediterranean with or without him.

Flipping through the TV channels one night, I paused to watch a Halloween episode of CSI. I hadn't watched the show since they took Grissom off, but this episode looked interesting because it was about Vampires and Werewolves. I had to shake my head at what I was seeing. The detectives had gone into the room of a missing man, and pulled a Celtic knot wedding band out of a coat pocket, remarking that he was getting married. Then they pulled a receipt out of another pocket and at the top it read, "The Mediterranean" (hotel and casino) and below that it said "Julie."

The next day I went into my office and even my non-believer friend had to agree that it was unusual. She had been listening to me fantasize about moving to the Mediterranean for months now, and the Celtic knot wedding band was reminiscent of Scotland, not to mention the vampire theme and name Julie.

Weeks later, I traded in my cell phone for a new smart phone and downloaded blocks of ring tones of various musicians including the band Coldplay. I barely knew how to operate the phone, and wasn't patient enough to play with the settings so I chose a programmed ringtone until I had more time. Walking through the mall, I answered a call and as I pressed the end call button and lowered the phone to my pocket, I grazed my breast with it and heard a click. I looked to make sure I had hung up, and the song "Fix You" by Coldplay was highlighted on the screen. I stopped mid-step in amazement, looked to the heavens and with a laugh I said, "Seriously?" In the beginning of our relationship, Brayden sent me that song and added that every time he heard one of the verses, he was reminded of me. The lyrics gave me greater insight into what I already suspected—Brayden loved me but he didn't feel worthy of me. The risk that he may not be able to measure up to me scared him, but the love that he had for me was too strong not to try.

Still in amazement, I sat in my car pressing buttons and trying to figure out how the song appeared on my screen so easily, but I couldn't. When I looked closely at the block of Coldplay songs that I had downloaded, in fine print it was labeled, *Post Cards from Glasgow*. I couldn't believe what I was seeing! Not only was it Brayden's song to me that appeared out of nowhere, but the label had his home town in the title. "Fix You" was on the Coldplay album *X & Y* and I had never heard of this album before. I hoped that I wasn't reading too much into it, but these seemed to be unmistakable signs of encouragement.

I had two more of my faint dreams about him the following week. One in which we were walking down the street with his arm around me, and my friends who had been so critical about our relationship were watching in disbelief that we were finally together. As I held his hand, which was over my left shoulder, I noticed a smudge of dirt on my fingernail and was embarrassed and worried that he might see it. Without hesitation, he lovingly reached over with his right hand and wiped the dirt away.

Two days later in the second dream, we were standing in a room face to face, and not believing that he would accept the invitation, I said, "I would invite you to stay for lunch, but…"

"I'm staying," he replied, interrupting me.

But what did it mean? Was I picking up his intentions in the form of a dream story? I knew there must be something brewing, and then I got spam e-mails from Brayden's address on December 14, 20, and 30. That was a new attention getter and I couldn't be certain if his account had been hacked by a spammer, or if they were attempts to get a reaction. I no longer had any intention of communicating with him unless the messages included news of a divorce.

My curiosity was answered when on January 2, Brayden sent a message to me from my business website:

"Merry Christmas and Happy New Year. Just wanted you to know that I still think of you and miss you."

I felt that he was "bouncing the ball" again. What did he think his message was supposed to mean to me? Was I supposed to feel better just because he still thought about me and missed me, even though he wasn't offering to change the situation? I had been through enough with him— it was time for him to take action, or let me go forever. I would have to say things that I didn't believe in my heart, to make him realize that my opinion of his character and our relationship was in question.

To: Brayden Loch   *January 3, 2011*
From: Julie Hopper
Subject: Your e-mail

Brayden,

My love for you and the pain of your rejection didn't end the day that you married someone else…I have to deal with it every day. And when I contacted you a year ago, it was my hope that you would

*realize there was something special about the love between us, and that
you had made a mistake. But with each day that passes, my hope is
replaced with the disappointment and realization that I must not have
been more than a back up plan for you. I'm not closing the door...but I
sense that your e-mail was only a way of checking to see if I was still
available to you, and the next time would still be no more than that.*

*It's a new year, and a time for new beginnings. A time to let go of what
isn't working any longer, and time make room for someone who wants
to be a part of my life, and will put me first in theirs. My hope is to
start over with a new career and move South, or to the Mediterranean.*

*As difficult as this is...I ask that you please not contact me unless you
have something significant to say that will change things between us.
I will always care for you, no matter the time or the distance.*

Julie

To: Julie Hopper   January 3, 2011
From: Brayden Loch
Subject RE: Your e-mail

It's so great to hear from you.

    I would like so start by stressing that the email was not me
"checking to see if you where available to me". It was meant to be
a note wishing you well for the New Year and wanting you to know
that you are and always will be in my thoughts. Also, YOU WHERE
NEVER A BACKUP PLAN. NEVER. I made a bad decision when I
should have followed my heart.
    Like I mentioned in my previous email, I know how much
disappointment and hurt I caused you and for that the regret will sit
with me for the rest of my life. Typing my feelings out on a keyboard
is not easy, all I can say to you is that I can't get you out of my head I
don't want to. You pointed out that it's the new year and a time for new
beginnings and that's what I was hoping to do.

I can't ever stop trying to contact you. You ask me to stop and the honest answer from me is that it's impossible for me to do that. Not because I won't, I just can't bring myself to do that. Please let me know more about your possible move. I miss not knowing where you are in your life and what your doing. You deserve the best that this life has to offer and I hope you get everything you want. I love you Julie, please believe me. I love you more than I have ever loved anyone in my whole life.

Not being with you is the biggest mistake I made in my life and if I loose contact with you I know i'll be making the same mistake again.

I will love you the rest of my life Julie

Brayden.

I cried and sobbed uncontrollably with relief, my body heaving as I released all of the emotion that I had restrained to keep myself strong throughout the years; my eyes so swollen, that I could barely see through them, while I processed every word of his message.

From: Julie Hopper   *January 3, 2011*
To: Brayden Loch
Subject: RE: Your e-mail

Crying now.....but I'm afraid of the hope the tears bring. I don't think that I can say anything more because I need to absorb what you've said. I wasn't prepared to hear from you, and I wasn't prepared for your response. If you're serious, do you want to talk tomorrow after 12:00? Brayden, you must be completely certain.

But my joy was only temporary, as I began to sober up from my euphoria and question why there was no mention of a plan for us to be together.

From: Julie Hopper   *Date: January 3, 2011*
To: Brayden Loch
Subject: RE: Your e-mail

Brayden, I really need you to clarify this for me right away because I think that I may have misunderstood you. Now that my head is clear and I'm reading this...are you telling me that you're staying in the marriage but want to stay in contact with me anyways?

From: Brayden Loch   January 4, 2011
To: Julie Hopper
Subject: RE: Your e-mail

Julie..... I'm saying, I would like to be friends and see where that takes us. I live alone now and just need to take small steps with my emotions as Iv'e hurt you in the past and don't want to make that same mistake again. I meant everything I said. I do love you.
I don't want to have you shed any more tears, you are far too good for that especially over me.
Let me know your thoughts!

Brayden.

I knew what that meant. He was trying to reconnect with me without committing to a solution. A man doesn't say what he did in the first e-mail, and feel the need to be "friends" and take things slowly. But I had to play along to a degree.

From: Julie Hopper   *January 4, 2011*
To: Brayden Loch
Subject: RE: Your e-mail

Brayden,

*I agree with the small steps because there's still much that needs
to be said. But I don't think that we should have that conversation
over the phone, do you? As far as friendship goes, something inside
me has always felt strongly that you truly were my best friend...
even when you didn't behave like it. But if you mean friendship
in the context that I think that you mean, then I'm sorry...it's not
possible.*

*Moving on from you is a lot like asking myself to stop breathing,
but what I said in my e-mail is true. Knowing how I feel...please let
me know if you would still like to talk.*

Julie

I had never drawn the line so many times with him as I had that
last year. He knew that I was finally serious and I was certain that
he must be processing what I said to him. Two days later would be
his birthday and again, I struggled as to whether or not I should
say anything further. These may be the last words that I ever speak
to him if he doesn't do something now, and I felt that they were
important.

From: Julie Hopper   *January 6, 2011*
To: Brayden Loch
Subject: Happy Birthday Brayden!

I hope that all of the wishes that you wish this day come true!

I wanted to say more, but it will have to wait for your reply. Regardless of the outcome.. I will love you the rest of my life too.

Julie

He didn't reply and I wondered if this was finally the end for us, or if he was respecting my wishes by not communicating with me until he was committed to a plan to change the situation. The next day, I had one of my message dreams. A beautiful woman with dark Mediterranean features appeared to me face to face. I had never had a dream like that before. She said that her name was Deasrhianna, although there was something about the name I couldn't quite pronounce.

"I'm here to check on Brayden," she said.

"Well, you know that he's married," I replied.

"I wouldn't be so sure of that. I get my information from…" and she mentioned a name I didn't understand, and then the dream ended.

On January 17 and 18, I received two more spam e-mails from Brayden. I thought that he was trying to get a reaction from me and test my resolve so I ignored them. He had always taken every word in my e-mails very literally and he knew that I was serious. Then on the 21ˢᵗ, he sent another with no subject, but in the main body of the message was a single link to a Valentines Day advertisement. It was the first that seemed to be an actual attempt to tell me something. I wondered if he was trying to let me know that he was making a plan, or if our messages had been discovered and he wasn't able to tell me himself.

I knew that it was too soon to check in with Sophie, because I needed to give Brayden time to process what I said. If ever he was going to make a plan to be with me and get out of the marriage—it would be now.

I waited a few weeks and the reading with Sophie was filled with positive news. She had always used playing cards in her readings instead of a tarot deck, and what was curious to both of us was that after I shuffled the cards, all of the red love and money cards were at the top of the deck. I could have shuffled them hundreds of times before that could possibly happen.

As she read the cards and tuned into her guidance, she said, "He's made a plan to get out of the marriage and someone is helping him do it. But your communication was discovered and he's in danger, so whatever you do, don't contact him."

She added that my life was about to turn a corner in a positive direction, and it should happen around the end of summer. I was elated! It meant more waiting, but I had waited this long and if the end result was that we would be together, then the extra time no longer mattered. I just had to go on with my life until we could be together again.

Weeks later I began feeling anxiety attacks, followed by two dreams about Brayden. In one of them, he was filled with anxiety, asking himself if he loved me enough, because he had loved Melody too. "Why should this be any different?" I had no idea if he knew someone by the name of Melody but I suspected that he was sorting through his emotions. We had a psychic connection and I had felt his strong feelings before, even when he was on the other side of the world. Renee had told me previously that our cords were intertwined and the connection between us was too strong to ever cut it. What he was going through now was too painful for me to witness any longer, and I prayed to ask that the cord between us be severed. Everything stopped after that and I no longer felt him.

I held onto the hope that Sophie had given me, and thought that Brayden just needed to time process everything as anyone would. But I needed a distraction and became curious about Duff, the first pilot who I had felt so deeply connected to. I knew he was married with two children, because I had seen him years earlier on a classmate website. I found him on Facebook and sent him a simple message saying that I hoped he didn't think it strange that I decided to say hello, but I hoped that he was doing well and that life had been good to him.

The next day, I was driving in downtown Portland when my phone rang. It was Duff and he had that same sensual voice that I remembered. He said that he was divorced now, and that he had only dated his ex-wife for a month when she became pregnant, but they decided to get married anyway. We spent over an hour on the phone, but he did most of the talking. I felt nervous speaking to him, but I had to wonder if he was nervous too because the entire conversation was about the difficulties with his ex.

He was still living in Medford, so I tried to change the subject by cheerfully asking if he ever made it to Portland. He laughed, and flatly stated the he never comes to Portland. *OK*, I thought to myself, *just trying to open a door that might allow us to reconnect, even if it was just as friends*. I didn't believe that I could ever feel for someone else the way that I loved Brayden. But years ago, it came pretty close with Duff and I was willing to test the waters again.

Duff called me frequently, but it was always just after he dropped his kids off at school. As our conversations continued, I could see why I had been so in love with him years before. He had a degree in Physics and was extremely intelligent. He was also easy to talk to and I was fascinated by his knowledge. But as our conversations progressed, it became clear to me that he had become jaded as a result of choosing the wrong women. His biggest complaint was that women are just looking for a man to take care of them financially, instead of being an equal partner. He pointed out that when he meets female friends for lunch or dinner, they still expect him to pay the tab; adding that women want men to make them feel special and take care of them, without doing the same in return.

I countered his objections and generalities by saying that it wasn't true for all women, and it certainly wasn't true of me. Adding that I love the male/female role in a relationship, and although I expect to be an equal, I still want a man who's "the man." I like to be taken out on a traditional date, but I also do special things for the men that I'm in a relationship with, recalling the gourmet picnic that I had prepared for Brayden in Dallas. I had a sense that Duff had given up on true love, and had redirected his focus primarily on his children, leaving no room for anyone else. He was an amazing and wonderful man, so I was left feeling disappointed by it.

Duff was now in his early 50s and an extremely attractive man, both inside and out. Although I wasn't looking to replace my love for Brayden, it was important that I leave all options open. I enjoyed my conversations with him, but aside from the playfulness in his voice when he first called, there didn't seem to be any flirtation developing between us. The reason for parting years ago was never mentioned, but then, it was no longer relevant.

The Shakespeare Festival in Ashland, Oregon was only a couple of hours from Duff's home and I had always wanted to go, so I suggested that we meet and attend a play together. He seemed receptive to the idea, so I asked him to check the website and let me know what play he would like to see. He was just leaving for a flight to Malaysia, so we agreed to firm up plans when he returned. But somehow we ended up playing phone tag several times, and our communication just fizzled. It was clear to me that seeing each other in person wasn't of great importance to him, and when he was on leave from flying, his time and schedule was spent exclusively with his children.

For the last several years I had been suppressing the pain of missing Brayden so I could remain strong, and I knew that he was doing the same. For me it was just a matter of getting through one month at a time. But even when we were apart, I could still feel a sense of him with me. May was now approaching and although I had prayed that my connection to him would be severed, I was now praying that it would be returned to me, but it wasn't. I was no longer getting any messages or guidance about him and it began to scare me. I thought that possibly it meant that our relationship was over and there was no longer any hope.

My friend, Doug, had recently passed, so I decided to see if Renee could bring him through, and I could check in on what was happening with Brayden at the same time. During the reading, my friend clearly came through with his personality and sense of humor. When he was gone, I told Renee about the anxiety that I had been feeling from Brayden earlier in the year, and that I prayed for the cord between us to be severed, but that I couldn't seem to reconnect it; and I wasn't getting any messages from my guides like I had before.

An expression of concern crossed her face, before saying, "The connection is still there, but it's as though it has only been insulated."

"How do I reconnect it?"

"Just simply ask that your connection be restored."

I didn't tell her that I had already done that without success and it concerned me.

She continued by telling me the same things about Brayden as Sophie had.

"He has a plan to leave the marriage, but he isn't moving forward with it yet."

I was disappointed, but at least there was progress and he still had a plan. She also said that his life was in danger and he had to be very careful. Whenever I heard that, it just seemed so international spy crazy to me. But his wife was in Saudi security, and it made sense that the people she worked with would be protective of her: their culture had a different way of looking at things.

"Is he safe now?" I asked with concern.

"Yes, he is safe. You just need to be patient, because your life is about to turn a corner in a new and positive direction. I think that you'll hear from him in August or September."

The guides wouldn't give her any more information so I decided to ask her about my own guides and angels.

"I'm getting the name: it's not Airiella, but Ariella or Uriella? It's not a difficult name, but for some reason I can't seem to pronounce it."

I was dumfounded! I had been given that name twice years ago when I asked, and I had the same difficulty in pronouncing it using the same combination of sounds! She could have chosen any name in the universe—but not only did she give me that one, but she also had difficulty pronouncing it just as I had.

"What does she look like? I asked.

"The image of her is so beautiful," she said. "I wish that I could show this to you. She looks goddess like with flowing robes, as if she's descending from heaven."

"I know that it can change, but what color are her robes?"

"You're right, they can change, but in the image they're white."

Just as I was beginning to think about the angel with the gold dress that I saw years ago, Renee said, "She's showing me gold thread. So maybe it's embroidery, but she's also saying 'rich colors, rich colors.'"

I was amazed as I processed her confirmations. Renee had given me the same name, although I don't remember the "ella" at the end. She had difficulty pronouncing it, just as I had. I knew that the spirit world speaks to us in riddles and has a sense of humor. The angel that I saw was wearing gold, which is a "rich color." The confirmation to my own experience was fantastic!

Later that month, I attended a "Channeling your guides" class with Renee at the Oregon Coast. Lana, who had been a friend of mine from high school came with me. We had been out of touch for several years, but I knew that she was an aspiring author and although I resisted, I had been feeling a strong push to contact her. Acknowledging to my guides their insistence, I gave in and sent her an e-mail without saying what my book was about. When she replied, she said that she had felt a strong push to contact me too, and that she was feeling in need of spiritual direction. I told her that was funny because that was what my book was about.

We settled into our chairs in the conference room at the coast: a wall of windows with crashing ocean waves behind them and light meditation music in the background. Renee guided us through our first meditation and I got nothing. In the second, I clearly saw a psychic image of a patch of mud with large bird tracks in it. As I wondered what they could mean, I clearly heard "Running Bird" followed by Lakota/ Dakota. As instructed, I wrote what I experienced down on a little paper pad.

When I showed it to Lana who was sitting next to me, tears began to well up in her eyes and she underlined the words Lakota/Dakota and in the side margin she wrote Wounded Knee.

Previously, she had told me that she was drawn to Gettysburg and to the sites of American/Indian Battles, and I told her that she must have a past life connection there. Now she was expressing deep emotion at what I had written on my pad.

As Renee went around the room asking people about their experiences, she added the additional details about their guides that they hadn't experienced themselves.

When she came to me, I explained what I saw, adding, "I worry sometimes that I may be imagining these images myself."

"Would you have imagined a patch of mud with bird tracks and the name Running Bird?" she asked.

Feeling slightly embarrassed, I replied, "No, absolutely not."

"Well, that's how you can tell the difference."

I had questioned what I had seen in meditation before, but this was the clearest experience that I had seen or heard in 15 years. Why did I continually feel the need to question an experience that was obviously authentic?

Previously in one of Renee's other classes on guides, I had seen an old, weathered man with small, piercing, blue eyes and a long, curly, grey beard. He was wearing a long white headscarf with two light blue stripes across his forehead, reminiscent of the one Mother Teresa wore. He said that his name Adam, and he looked like he might be a holy man of some kind. If I was going to "create" a guide in my imagination, it certainly wouldn't have been him. I would have created one that I had seen before, like my first Indian, or the angel with the gold dress. The name Adam seemed unusually simple to me, but it was probably the English version of a foreign name that would be difficult to pronounce. Renee told us to ask our guides if any of our other guides were with us that day. I didn't put it together at the time, but Adam lifted up his arm and pointed his finger forward. It wasn't until I was on my drive home that I realized he was pointing in Renee's direction.

As we stood in line at the hotel restaurant for lunch, we agreed to share a table with a few of our classmates. One of them, Kris, had been talking to her boyfriend on the phone and was angry. While we sat at the table, I found her to be abrasive and didn't much care for her at all. But as we all talked about our experiences in class, I complained that I didn't feel that Renee validated Running Bird the way that she had for others.

"Of course she did!" Kris defended. "The name Running Bird is a Lakota name," she replied as if I should have known. "It means that he runs swiftly like a bird and it's a very honorable name. I used to date a fancy dancer." (Indian dancers who wear elaborate costumes of shells and feathers.)

After a few more statements, my eyes narrowed and I asked if she was a medium.

"Yes, I am," she replied. "I'm only here to get credit hours for a hypnosis certification that I'm taking with Renee's partner."

In a humorous, matter of fact tone I said, "Well ... let me ask you this! About 10 or 15 years ago, I was walking through a parking lot in broad daylight and it was like the lights were switched off and an Indian was suddenly in front of me. His face was painted silver and..."

Kris gasped. "That's what they do!" she said with excitement.

I continued by saying that he had indigo blue U shapes painted under his eyes from between his eyebrows and down to his cheeks, and he was wearing a black fir turban.

"That means that he was a seer," (a psychic/medium) she said casually. "He was a shaman."

I had been Googling and searching war paint of Native Americans for years, trying to understand what his paint meant to no avail. I knew that Indigo was a spiritual color, associated with the third eye (your way of connecting to spirit) but I didn't connect the dots. But I somehow knew that he wasn't the Running Bird whose name I had heard so clearly in the meditation.

We returned to class and as Renee guided us through the next meditation, we were to visualize ten steps leading up to the door of our spiritual temple. I imagined old, stone steps leading to a wooden door with ornate wrought-iron hinges. As she continued, I saw what appeared to be a wide ledge on the side of a stone castle, with ivy growing down the walls. She told us to visualize a bench, and ask that our spirit guide come there to be with us. I was getting a fairly clear image of the surroundings, but nothing else. As she began to bring us out of the meditation, the images became clearer and it was as if I was drifting away from the ledge. In the distance, I clearly saw an Indian with long, black hair, and three white feathers twisted into his hair. He had two or three white stripes painted across each cheek, and was bare from the waist up. The way that he was looking at me was as though he was curious about me but hesitant. I believed that it was Running Bird, and then the image was gone.

For the next several days when I would recall the image of him, I felt an unusual sense of romantic attraction toward him. I would dismiss it and question why I was feeling that way, but it was there. Later I would speak to Sophie who asked me if I had ever been given the name of my guides because in her 82 years they never revealed them to her, adding that there must be a reason for it. I told her about my other guides whose names I knew and when I told her about my attraction to Running Bird, she said that I must have been with him in a past life and now he was acting as one of my guides.

Years ago, when my spiritual experiences were more spontaneous and unexpected, I wished that I'd had a combined resource to help me understand them. Now that I understood, and was further developing my connection to spirit, I realized that I had also developed an ability to dig under the surface of other people's relationship issues, discovering the destructive patterns that were holding them back in ways they had never thought of before. Several of which seemed to move on to more healthy relationships after we spoke.

Jake worked at a local bar. Originally from Samoa, he was exotic and handsome with a great sense of humor, and the only man who had caught my attention since I first met Brayden. But his own insecurities caused him to sabotage the possibility of something romantic between us, although we remained good friends. As we talked one night about the book and the patterns in his relationships, we discovered that he was usually either rescuing the woman he was involved with or committing to someone just to fill the void. He admitted that he didn't like being alone long enough to wait for the right person, adding that it didn't matter because work always came first in his life.

"Well, if you met the right person it wouldn't," I told him.

"Yeah, you're probably right," he agreed.

It's interesting because around the time the bar he managed was going out of business, he reconnected with a childhood sweetheart and moved to the East Coast to be with her. As far as I know, they're now living very happily together and he may have finally chosen the right woman, for the right reasons.

My friend Mark was another man who couldn't be alone long enough to choose a woman for the right reasons. I hadn't talked to him for years, but for some reason while he was passing through town, he decided to call and invite me for a beer.

As we sat across from each other catching up on our lives, I told him about Brayden and what the book was about. Mark was now separated from his second wife, and as he shared some of the awful things she would say and do while they were together, I couldn't believe it. Although there are always two sides to every story, her treatment of him was inexcusable under any circumstance.

"What attracted you to her in the beginning?" I asked. "Because she didn't suddenly become this way over night."

"Well," he replied, "I thought she was beautiful and she was the life of the party kind of gal."

"That's it?" I asked. "What do you want in a relationship, what's important to you?"

Suddenly this big, burly logger sitting across from me had tears rolling down his cheeks and he replied, "I want to feel special. I want someone who will do special things for me to show me that I'm important to them. I want someone who is a kind and caring person."

My heart broke for him because he was one of the sweetest kind-hearted people I knew. And now he had two kids from his first marriage, and two from a second marriage that was heading towards divorce.

"Did you experience those qualities in your wife before you married her?" I asked.

"No," he replied, with tears now rolling into his scruffy beard.

"Mark, I know that it's difficult to be alone, but you need to decide what qualities are most important to you, and be patient until you meet someone who has them. No one is ever going to be perfect, and everyone wants an attractive partner, but if the package is pretty and the contents aren't, then you'll end up in the same situation again."

He agreed with me and although I haven't spoken with him since, I've heard that he's with a very nice woman now.

I was happy that my observations seemed to be helping others, but my own relationship was still unresolved and I prayed every night that Brayden was doing something to correct it. I was beginning to wonder if he ever would, because it was nearing the end of June and I still hadn't heard from him. At times when I needed to feel a connection with him, I would log onto the e-mail address that I set up for him. There were still reminders there of times that he tried to hurt me, like the matches from the dating website. And the time after Dallas when he got angry with me for suggesting that I would contact Molly McDermott to confirm that their relationship was over. He had asked her to send a request to the address for instant messaging, and had sent one from himself as well. Every time I logged on for the last several months, those requests would pop up in a taunting way, but it didn't bother me because I knew what his intention was at the time.

Now I'd logged on and they were gone. They'd been there for years, so he must have logged on and deleted them. It was a positive sign, and then I started noticing others. The previous year, the gal with a photo on a cruise ship who he added as one of his Myspace friends must have discovered that he was married because she posted an angry and derogatory comment on his page. It had been there for months, but now suddenly it was gone. It was as if he was doing some soul searching and trying to clean up his image before contacting me.

Then on June 20, I got a spam e-mail from him and the first addressee was wwtooo@. It was like he was sending me a cryptic message that he wasn't able to communicate directly with me, and the address told me that he may be going through world war two now. I checked the first addresses on the other spam he sent, and they were the same, but this one was different.

At the end of July, I got a notice from Yahoo that someone had tried to get into my e-mail account. I had no idea what was happening with Brayden, but I knew it was him. He was missing me and wanted to know what was happening in my life. I suspected that Hilary had been in my mail before, because Yahoo UK Ireland had popped up when I logged on one day and that was the site that she used for her mail. But with her connections it would be easy for her to get my password without alerting the system. It was obvious to me that Brayden was finally breaking, but when would the insanity ever end?

I knew that by writing my experiences in the book, I could help others; and any detail that I left out might be the one that would make a difference to someone else. But I also knew that if I dedicated my time and effort to developing my own connection to my guides, I could help others in the same way that Renee did. In one of my earliest readings with her when she was telling me about my life path that was yet to come, she giggled and said that the guides said to repeat to myself, "I am like Renee, but I do things my way." I decided that this may be my purpose in life, and I wanted to add as many tools to my belt as I could. Renee was teaching a class for Angelic Healing and I decided to attend.

The purpose was to make yourself a clear channel for the light and healing energy of the angels to come through to clear negativity and balance energy in the Chakras of others, as well as general healing of ailments. Before I arrived to the class, I said a prayer and asked that if this was the work that they wanted me to do, then to please make it obvious to me.

As Renee readied us, she took us through a series of steps to cleanse and clear our Chakras, raise our vibration and ground our energy, followed by prayers asking the angels to help make us a clear channel for them to work through.

In the first exercise, a classmate sat upright in a chair, while we placed our hands on different parts of their body as we felt guided to do, while sending white healing light to them. I felt a mild sense of awkwardness, as though I was playing make believe. When I was finished, the woman in the chair said that it was interesting that I kept moving back to her head because she had a mild headache that was now gone.

In the next exercise, we would be working with pendulums, a crystal at the end of a six-inch chain. I had never worked with one before, and always thought that New Age people that were into the power of crystals were just adding drama to their spiritual practice; I didn't believe that it was real. As I picked up a borrowed pendulum from the table, Renee told us to hold it by the chain from our fingertips, with the crystal an inch or two above the palm of our other hand. Then she said to visualize white light moving from our fingers, down the chain, and into the crystal. I imagined a white light with gold, Tinkerbell sparkles, moving down the chain and into the crystal.

It suddenly began to quiver rapidly above my palm, even though my hand holding the chain was perfectly still. Without moving my head, my eyes looked up at Renee and with slight humor and suspicion in my voice I asked, "What is it doing?"

She smiled and explained that it was tuning into the energy of my body, adding, "I'm not surprised, that was really cool light that you sent down the chain."

"You saw that?"

"Yes. At times when I'm working on someone and I start to move the pendulum from their body, it will remain diagonal in the air momentarily, still zeroed in on the last place I was working on."

"You're kidding me!" I said with astonishment.

"No, I'm not. It really happens," she replied.

"It's true," another student chimed in with agreement.

Next we had one classmate lay on a massage table with their eyes closed, while three of us worked on them without touching their body. As I visualized sending beautiful white healing light, with a gold sheen to the woman's abdomen, the vision became clearer as it began to swirl around her like a gentle vortex. I sensed that I should change the light to violet, the color of transformation, and imagined a beautiful violet light with the same gold sheen. The gold is god light and the violet is one of the colors of angel light. When we were finished, the woman said that she felt strong energies around her abdomen. I was surprised, and sheepishly asked Renee if the angels ever direct you to change the light.

"Sure they do!" she replied casually.

I recalled years back when I meditated, sending Duff angel light, and then suddenly found myself sitting cross legged in white robes next to a male presence. He was very pleased that I was sending this light to Duff. I began to realize that this isn't all make believe—it's real! Our bodies are made up of energy and every thought that we send out to the universe is also energy. I was becoming fascinated by it, and realized that in the future, I needed to be very careful of my thoughts.

It was my turn on the table next, and although I knew that no one was touching me, I felt an occasional buzz of energy, or a tug in different parts of my body. Next to lie down was the woman whose headache I had apparently helped, and coincidentally, her name was also Julie. She had told me earlier that she didn't have a conscious connection with her guides, because she was always in her head too much, adding that she just paid attention to the little signs and synchronicities that happened in her life. She had also mentioned having neck problems earlier, too.

As the three of us rotated around her body sending energy, I eventually made my way to her upper body. I visualized a vortex of white light swirling around her neck, and then suddenly got the impulse to send deep rose pink light around her temples, the angel chakras. Although I wasn't touching her, I noticed my hands had moved into a position as if to cradle her neck from above and below. I was surprised by how I could clearly visualize two different colors swirling around two different areas of her body. Then I got a very clear psychic image as if someone removed the back of her neck, and I could see the vertebrae that were damaged—similar to the plastic anatomical bodies that you remove the individual organs from and it shows you their placement in the body.

When the session was over and she sat up, several tears rolled down her cheeks and she seemed to be emotional. She said that she felt strong energy around her neck and temples, and she heard popping and clicking in her ears.

I was completely awestruck! I told the woman what I had just been doing and with gratitude in her voice, she thanked me. Renee had previously told me to take any pressure off of myself to do the work, because it wasn't me—it came from the angels. At the time her words brought great relief because I knew it was true. But now I couldn't help but feel a sense of accomplishment for what I had just witnessed. I had asked my guides in advance to give me a sign if they wanted me to do this work, and although I didn't know if it was just coincidence, as Renee passed out our Angelic Healer Certifications, I was the first to receive one.

A week later I was at my niece Kiley's house at the coast when I noticed a white butterfly on her living room floor, fluttering around as if it was in its final death throes. *That's strange*, I thought, *that a butterfly would find its way into the house.* So I gently scooped it up into my hands and took it out side to release it. It became still in my hands, gently opening and closing its wings slightly, as butterflies do. Then for several seconds, it looked directly at me with its little black eyes, as if communicating with me, before flying upwards and away, as if nothing were wrong with it.

I came back into the house and said to my niece, "Now tell me that wasn't unusual!"

"That was unusual alright," she agreed.

The following week I was having lunch with a client on an outdoor patio. We had been talking about her father who had been diagnosed with pancreatic cancer and along with his medical treatment, he had been going to someone who did energy work. As I began telling her that I had become a Angelic Healer and what had happened in the class, a cream color butterfly started fluttering around me, just inches from my face.

"I wonder what that means?" she said with curiosity.

"I know what it means."

Remaining silent, I recalled that during class, we were doing long-distance healing and I got the word butterfly. I was now both grateful and amused by the validation of that day and the one at my niece's house that I should be doing this work.

As I waited patiently hoping for word from Brayden at any time, I continued to work on developing the clarity of my connection to my guides through meditation. But I still wasn't disciplined enough to practice regularly and when I did, I didn't experience anything. I remembered that Renee had given me a "Connecting with Your Higher Self" meditation CD, so I decided to give it a try. She had told me previously that it was as if our guides hang back, to see how dedicated we are to developing a connection with them. I knew it was true because my most clear and amazing experiences, were when I was at rock bottom and had complete focus on learning how to connect with them.

As I meditated, she guided to ask our higher self their name, and the impression or word Rhiann came to me strongly. Next she said to ask your higher self how they connect with Source (another name for God). A very clear psychic vision of the galaxy appeared, and in the center, surrounded by stars, was a large, bright white light, which was as soft as it was intense. Around it was a soft, medium blue halo. The vision was beautiful, and as she asked another question later in the meditation CD, I saw it again, just as clearly as the first. I was excited by the experience, and knew that if I only dedicated more time, I would see spiritual visions like that more frequently.

Renee was having another class at the Oregon Coast called "Channeling your angels." Whereas the angelic healing class was more channeling their energy, I hoped that this one would create the opportunity for a personal experience. My friend Linda attended it with me and just as before, the conference room was a wall of windows with the ocean waves crashing in the distance.

Renee's guided meditations were beautiful, but I wasn't feeling anything. During the third meditation with my eyes closed, I noticed light to the right of my peripheral vision. Under my eyelids, I looked to the right and saw what appeared to be an illuminated man, with shoulder length, golden hair, and light-colored nondescript clothing. Although I could clearly see color, the image itself was soft and diffused, like he was fully illuminated but standing behind a foggy window.

I thought that I may be imagining it, because I wanted to have an experience—that's why I was there. So I turned my eyes back to the left and continued listening to Renee. I noticed a light again to my right, and when I looked back, the same image of the man standing silently was still there. I wasn't overwhelmed with amazement, but I knew that I had clearly seen something.

In the next meditation, Renee guided us to ask our angels who was there with us. I got the name Chamuel very strongly, and although I knew he was associated with love relationships, that's all that I knew. His name was followed by Uriel and Metatron, but not as strongly. Renee had told me before that Metatron was one of my guides, and the way she said it seemed to be a great honor. But knowing that any angel was watching over you was a great honor. The definition of the purpose that each Arch Angel serves seems to differ so greatly as I read about them, that it was difficult to define. But unknown to many in main stream Christianity, Metatron is said to be the highest of the angels, and serves as the celestial scribe. I wondered if he was overseeing me at this time to help me with the book.

When Linda and I returned to the house where we were staying, I checked my e-mail and had a message from Sophie.

To: *Julie Hopper*   *September 3, 2011*
From: *Sophie Douglas*
Subject: *Dream*

Good Morning,
Hope you had a fun, relaxing and productive trip to the coast.
Near the water is a good place for writing and reflecting. There
is such peaceful, creative energy around the water.

I had a dream again last night is why I am writing. I dreamed
the two of you were walking down a sandy beach hand in hand
and you were saying to him "this is the perfect honeymoon. I
knew our lives together was worth waiting for. " Hopefully this
is an omen you will hear from him soon. My guides say once he
can get out of the danger zone which should be soon, you will
hear from him.

Have a safe, fun holiday weekend.

Love,

Sophie

It was around the end of June, when she told me that she had a dream that I was walking on a beach alone, and her guides said that I was on my honeymoon. When she began to ask questions, the dream ended. Now she's had another which was similar. Progressive dreams are almost always spiritual messages, and I was excited at the encouraging news!

I came home feeling that the class was a little anticlimactic, when I should have just been thankful for what I did experience. I Googled Uriel and couldn't find what purpose he may be serving, or why he would be with me at this time in my life. The guides in our life change depending on what was happening at the time. I did find one reference to him that would make sense, it said: *Uriel can show us how to heal every aspect of lives, turning disappointments into victories, find blessings in adversity.* Well, that was certainly true: I was constantly having to find blessings in what I was experiencing, just to keep my hope intact.

I Googled Chamuel, and found something that said that he was the overseer of helping Twin Flame soulmates to come together. That—I found very interesting. I had already come to realize that Brayden and I were twins by the descriptions that I had read. Most people have never heard the term, because it's so rare that they come together in a lifetime. The descriptions differ, but the one that made the most sense was how it was explained to me by Kris, the medium that I met in Renee's first class: When a soul is created, it divides into two, just as twins in the womb are created. They incarnate into the world living separate lives, so that the soul can experience lessons at a much more rapid pace, thereby evolving to a higher level of consciousness more quickly. We all have twins, but it may be many lifetimes before they come back together. When they do, they typically experience great difficulty in their relationship because one of the twins is usually less spiritually evolved, and the intensity of the love can be too overwhelming for them to surrender to. They may not be able to sustain the relationship, no matter how great the love.

Several of the articles mentioned that a relationship preceding the reunion may act as a catalyst in preparation for the reunion. It all made sense to me. I had already suspected that I met Duff so I would recognize the similarities between him and Brayden. I believed that it was the Universe's way of telling me to pay attention, that there was something special about him, and not to give up. Duff had triggered my spiritual path and, as a result, I was much better prepared to understand Brayden on a different level. That in turn allowed him to trust in ways that he hadn't been able to in other relationships. I began to think that the purpose of our separation was to allow Brayden the time that he needed to grow in the same way I had to after Duff. I knew that he had to have been receiving his own messages and guidance, but he was likely to be slower to process the experience.

Twin Flames usually have a psychic connection and may feel or sense when something major is happening in the other's life. And just like biological twins separated at birth, it's common for them to have strange similarities or synchronicities such as driving the same car, sharing the same interests, or some other uncanny parallels in their lives. Without a doubt, Brayden and I had those things. But I often worried that we would be "one of those cases" where he couldn't overcome his fear, and we wouldn't be together in this life—as beautiful as our love and connection truly was.

I read several references to twins being the opposite, or mirror image of each other. I didn't think of Brayden and me as being that different, so I decided to read the definition of Yin and Yang which made more sense to me—twins are interconnected opposites of equal qualities, which bound together, create a "divine whole," causing them to balance and transform each other into their intended state of being.

While I had been Googling Chamuel, I came across the most beautiful definition of Twin Flame relationships set to classical music. I felt as though the mysteries of the Universe were suddenly solved because my relationship was described so clearly. It was such validation of what I knew to be true, that I could hardly believe what I was seeing. The stages that stood out to me were a deep, spiritual connection with synchronicities between the two, followed by running and crisis. And while the stronger twin released the other to grow toward them at their own pace, they often turned their focus to creative aspects, like writing. The book! All of the turmoil that Brayden and I had been experiencing seemed to be a textbook example of a Twin Flame reunion. Now what I believed in my heart had been validated in a way that let me know we weren't alone in the experience.

Later I would have a conversation with the woman who posted the clip online. She said that I should feel honored to be in a twin relationship because their purpose was to serve humanity by helping to raise the positive vibration in the world, often helping others to do the same by sharing their story. She added that it was one of the most painful soul lessons that could be experienced. As if we agreed before incarnating to have our soul scoured through pain so intense, that we could emerge from the experience to a higher level of consciousness more rapidly.

As much as she knew about the subject, I realized after questioning her about her own experience, that she herself had romanticized the twin relationship. I asked her how she knew that she was with her twin, and she said that she just "felt" that she was, and that another couple who specialized on the subject said that they saw twin energy around her relationship. Whether that was true or not, there was no mention of synchronicities, psychic connection or spiritual guidance and intervention in her relationship. When you've met your twin, there's no mistaking all of the signals. It's a relationship that is as painful as it is beautiful.

The frustration of a relationship like this was almost unbearable, and had it not been for my constant guidance and reassurance that I received from the spirit world, I could have never endured it. I had been deeply in love before, but nothing compared to the clarity, intensity, and knowing that I felt with Brayden. Many times I told myself that I wouldn't wish this on anyone, unless the end result was that they would be together. As much as I had faith and Renee told me that the guides said it was only a matter of time, I still had a small measure of fear and apprehension: was it be possible that I could have such love in the present and without the distance?

I had just turned 45 and the time that Renee and Sophie thought that I would hear from Brayden had passed, but I hoped that he was just procrastinating as was his manner. Sophie had been checking in with me almost weekly to ask if I had heard from him. She felt that good news was on its way. As hopeful as I was, I feared that it was almost too good to be true. I was afraid to allow myself to believe that we would finally be together.

To: Julie Hopper   September 17, 2011
From: Sophie Douglas
Re: Dream

Good Morning,
Have you heard anything? I had almost that same dream again
last night, except there was a small child walking with you
and he was looking lovingly at you and the child saying "now
we have everything we were meant to have."
Interesting to say the least, so I thought maybe you had heard
something.

Hope all is going well. Have a wonderful weekend.

Love,

Sophie

Three? She'd had three of these dreams, so I knew there must be
something to it. *Please God, let it be true!*

"Separation is only an illusion of the physical"

~ A message from my guides.

20

I was certain that I would hear from Brayden at any moment, but, after so many years of waiting, it felt surreal and almost too good to be true. I noticed signs that he was beginning to break over the summer and although my own intuition and sense of him didn't feel as strong as before, I had received many positive reassurances from women who had clearly given me accurate information in the past. They were as much spiritual mentors as they were sources of what was likely to unfold in my life. Sophie was still checking in with me weekly to ask if I had heard from him, saying that she felt that something wonderful was about to happen for me.

On October 2, I checked Brayden's Facebook photo as I often did, to see if he had changed it to convey some cryptic message. In its place was a photo of a newborn baby. I went into shock—my heart and mind plunged into a dark abyss.

It's a mistake! This can't be true! I reasoned with myself. I did what I hadn't had the courage to do for months and looked at Hilary's photo on his friends list. There was a pink balloon with the writing, "It's a girl!" I tried desperately to remain in denial as I reasoned with myself that a new mother would never add a photo of a balloon in place of her own daughter. Brayden's brother or some close friend must have had a baby, so they were paying their congratulations by posting photos. I turned back to click on Brayden's photo and could see his image in the baby—she was his.

An indescribable pain washed through my mind and body as I felt my heart physically disintegrating, aware of each little piece as it pulled away and exploded in slow motion. I could feel myself dying at that moment and I welcomed it. The seconds felt like hours as cries came from the depth of my soul and I waited for my life to end and everything to go dark. I knew at that moment that it was truly possible for a person to die of a broken heart, and I begged God to please let it happen.

My thoughts turned to anger and betrayal at God for the deception and what I had endured for so many years, only for it to come crashing down around me like this. I ran to the bathroom heaving and choking over the toilet with tears streaming down my face.

Sophie's dreams, Renee's reassurances, and my own experiences mean nothing! It was all bullshit! Everything that I believed in was ripped away from me at that moment, leaving in its place a hollow shell.

My mind went into a numbing shock. *This can't be true!* Again I looked at the baby, which was propped up in a woman's lap who was wearing a hospital gown and I could clearly see Brayden's image in her. I felt love cross my heart for the baby before the pain quickly returned. I knew that Brayden posted the photo because he couldn't bring himself to tell me about the baby. It could have been one of him holding her but he knew that would be too painful—too final for me to see. My life and all of the hopes and dreams that I had for the future were over. *He will never leave that baby after losing his son and wanting a child so badly!*

The anger and betrayal returned painfully to my heart as I thought about the struggle and sacrifice that I had gone through for him to reach a point that he knew that he could feel safe in my love. Now he had tied himself permanently to a woman who I knew he didn't love as he loved me, and had given to her the one thing that he had ever promised to me—a child. I had fleeting thoughts of wondering if he had used me as a pawn in some sick and twisted game, and if he had only been pretending to love me as he did. But I knew that it was only my despair searching for answers for what I had been through.

My faith was destroyed as quiet contemplation set in. Why did Sophie have those dreams of Brayden and me with a child on our honeymoon just weeks before he had a child with her? Is it possible that everything that I experienced was only a coincidence, and not encouragement to have faith in our relationship? How could it be possible to have so many? Even if my message dreams were only dreams, and the other synchronicities only coincidence, what about the ones that had been validated? The similarities between Duff and Brayden may have been like lightning striking, but what about all of the other similarities between us? Had there been a point that I was supposed to give up on him and missed it? Why had I been lead to believe that our relationship was finally about to come together, and why was I not told that Hilary was pregnant? Why had God put me through this loss for a second time? Why wasn't the pain of losing Duff not enough? I felt betrayal by everyone and everything that I had ever believed in—*I had nothing.*

I asked God, as I had so many times before, why I had been given so many obstacles to overcome with Brayden. Overcoming his fear of love from his childhood abuse would have been difficult in itself, but to meet him when we lived on opposite ends of the country, then opposite ends of the world was insurmountable and cruel to put me in a position to try to reach him long distance.

I sat trembling in the bathtub holding my head in my hands with water pounding down on me from the shower. I cried heavy sobs as I processed the final destruction of what Brayden and I had together. Our love and all of my hopes and dreams for the future had been destroyed. I had not only lost him forever, but my life was now empty and I had no direction and nothing to look forward to. I had been taking prenatal vitamins for years with the hope of having a child, and now that was now gone too. With each month that had passed for the last several years, I hoped that the next month would be the one that Brayden and I finally came back together and I would conceive. My chances would have still been difficult when he and I first met, but now at 45 they were even less likely. Not only had I lost the love of my life and a beautiful future with him, I would never have a child of my own—that hope was gone too.

The next morning I woke up to my heart pounding irregularly as if it was trying to burst out of my chest. My emotions still raw, I prayed that I would die and hoped that my heart would stop beating. I looked at the greenish blue veins in my wrists and pressed my fingernail hard into them, knowing that it wouldn't stop the blood flow—but wondering how it might be if it did. I felt indifferent to my life and was dismayed that I was still here.

I called Sophie who had become a close friend of mine, and she was in as much shock as I was.

"The guides have never been this far off before. I don't understand it," she said with concern and confusion.

I sent a message to Renee who was equally as shocked, and she agreed to make room in her schedule to see me as soon as possible. Margie had recently come out of retirement, and she was able to see me that day. She and I had been out of touch for quite some time, and she knew only that Brayden had gotten married. When I arrived to see her, I said that I didn't want to tell her anything; I wanted to hear the good, the bad and the ugly.

As she entered mine and Brayden's birthdates into her astrological program on the computer, she asked, "So, he's getting another divorce?"

"I don't know, you tell me," I replied suspiciously. As the reading continued, she said that Brayden had "a plan" and the divorce was set in motion in June, but that he hadn't put the process into action. She went on to say that he was lonely, wanted to travel, and would contact me to meet him. A look of confusion appeared on her face and she asked, "Why is there such a distance between them?"

I explained that Brayden and Hilary lived on opposite sides of Saudi Arabia due to work. But in my mind, I remembered that in his last e-mail, he said that he now lived alone. The tone of his voice was that they were separated by more than work. Sophie had also said that it was by his choice, and Renee said that they were nothing alike, and the marriage was in name only.

"I don't understand why he ever married her," Margie continued, "because they're such a mismatch. But he has the ability to marry women that he's not in love with. And he has!" she said with a laugh. "You were asking about his wife and that's a very, very strange relationship. It's not like a traditional marriage with give, take, living together, fighting together or any of that. For the last 18 months they haven't even really been connected, but they never really were connected to begin with. And how long have they been married? Just over two years? He has the ability to shut down his feelings for you, doesn't he? I think that he keeps himself busy and distracted so he doesn't allow himself to feel his love for you. It was like something he was trying to prove to himself by marrying her. I always felt that the man truly loved you, but I think it scared the hell out of him—and I think that it still does."

As she laid the tarot cards on the table she said, "The happiness and wish card is on your head, so be at peace. The unknown is still at work. You're getting ready to turn a corner." She turned several more cards before saying, "Karma, Karma, Karma. I don't know what this means, but between February and June of next year, you'll discover that no destructions are final."

As she pointed to the pictures on the cards, she said, "This is a girl with a blindfold, and this is a Capricorn [which Brayden is] and you don't know what to do with that. And this card is a rebirth and a renewal."

"Of what?" I asked, even though I knew.

"Of the old," she replied. "And you still don't know what to do about it. And choices to make. Lots of lots of choices, girl! And they come at you unexpectedly. You have lots of magic coming your way and you're either going to finish things out with Brayden so it leaves you alone and there's not that yearning, yearning, yearning and feeling of loss. Or you're going to reconnect. Or, you may find magic with someone else."

Her voice turned playful in a way to lecture. "Now—the first question you need to ask is if they're an airline pilot. And if they are not an airline pilot—then you may go out and have a drink with them. But say that your psychic said to stay away from airline pilots because they seem to be flakey. You could probably do an air traffic controller," she laughed.

By now I wasn't holding out much hope for anything. Then she said, "Julie, you're about to turn a corner in your life and there's real magic coming your way—it's so rare," she added with curiosity in her voice. "Are you doing spiritual work? You have mediumship abilities if you want to develop it. I think that you're going to be doing three things: helping people spiritually, publishing your book, and investing in real estate when the market turns around."

Margie had no knowledge of my thoughts of getting into spiritual work to help others who were struggling with similar experiences to mine, or of the angelic healing I had become certified in. Some of the detail she gave me was so accurate, that it gave me a glimmer of hope that she may be right about Brayden. He and I always seemed to reconnect around the first of the year. But I also knew that sometimes psychics picked up on the free will intentions of the recent past, and it was possible that she could be picking up the energy from Brayden's previous intentions.

She saw a pregnancy and it would be a girl, adding that it seems like everyone is okay with it. She didn't say who would have it, and when I told her that Brayden had just had a baby girl, she didn't hear me. As we ended the reading, I clarified the baby, but she shrugged and didn't think that the baby was enough to keep him in the marriage.

It made me think, so I called Sophie to ask if the child she saw in her dream was a boy or a girl.

"It was a girl," she replied. "Around two or three years old because it could walk."

That was strange, because several of my "connected" friends including Sophie and myself, were certain that I would have a boy, possibly two, or twins. But Sophie added that she felt that the child in her dream was mine. I believed that no child was accidental—they were all born with a purpose, and I tried to console myself by thinking that although not according to *my plan,* maybe this was what was destined to be, or a change of plans.

At the beginning of my quest to understand how the universe works in our lives, I had read several near-death experiences that said that a soul chooses the parents that it will be born to based on the lessons that it needs to learn. Although Sophie had previously told me that a child wouldn't be born to Brayden and Hilary's union, I wondered if his procrastination had caused my opportunity to have my own children to pass, so this soul was born to the two of them instead. It was only theory, but seemed like it may be a possibility.

I had that dream before he got married that the three of us were in a car and Hilary was driving. Brayden reached over and held my hand then leaned over and kissed me. We ended up at a drug store soda fountain and I was on the opposite side of the counter from them. When I told Brayden that it was time that we started having our children, Hilary said to him, "Aren't you going to tell her?" And Brayden got a mischievous look on his face.

I hoped at the time that it meant that the outcome would be in my favor, but now it was obvious that they were the ones who would have a child. Was this always the bigger plan for all of us revealed in riddles? And what if anything would happen from this point? Was I to go through all of this pain with no happiness for myself in the end? I was eager to meet with Renee so I could get her take on the situation.

The passing days were filled with news of celebrities and announcements on Facebook of people having baby girls. Suddenly everywhere I turned, I saw pregnant women, or other's carrying their newborn babies in fuzzy pink blankets. It was as if the reality of the situation wasn't sufficient enough, but I had to endure the constant reminders. Each time I saw someone with a child, my wound was ripped open, only adding to my deep pain and despair.

I met with Renee who had only mentioned "talk" of a pregnancy a few times in previous readings, including when Hilary became pregnant after our engagement and lost the baby once deposits were put down on the wedding.

"They say that he still wants out and he has a plan, but the baby would be a hook for him. It's like he's playing "hot potato." He's in, he's out, he's in, he's out. They also say that they're doing everything that they can to help but they can't affect his free will. This has become a fiscal relationship for him hasn't it? Because there's great concern about the money."

I knew that money had been the only reason keeping him in the marriage, and I felt anger and disappointment that he would trade the love and pain in my heart for the money in his bank account.

Renee continued by asking, "I don't normally go this direction, but has anyone ever suggested to you before that you may be cursed from being with each other? Because it's like he starts going in your direction, then hits a wall of energy and jumps into the volcano head first."

"Kris Campbell did," I replied, "She also thought that our relationship had been interfered with by a government in a past life; similar to what has happened with this Saudi connection now.

"Well, I'll give her kudos for that, and she may be right about the government interference too."

"She suggested that I do a Burning Karma prayer."

"Oh! She learned that from me."

"Do you recommend that I do that?"

"Yes, it couldn't hurt because it will get rid of any negative influences, but won't affect the positive connection of your relationship."

"I had thought about sending Brayden a message of congratulations and goodbye in a nice way. What do you think?"

"Yes, they're saying yes that it would be good. But you need to release your attachment to the outcome," she replied.

I cringed as the words came out of her mouth and I wondered how strong God could possibly ask me to be. How could I release my attachment and have belief too? It seemed an impossible thing to ask of me under the circumstances.

Renee continued by saying," I do see a soul mate in your life soon, and I'm not suggesting that it's not him, but he's been so wishy washy that you need to leave yourself open to other possibilities."

"'We will help your heart to heal,'" she said softly and melodically. "That was Raphael; he's standing right behind you," she said as she nodded her head in my direction. "They say that 'We are praying for you too.'"

I had complete trust in Renee and I had personally seen an angel myself, but there was something about the enormity of being told that an Arch Angel is standing behind you and helping you through your pain that is difficult to process. Why is it that we believe in angels, and yet we have difficulty believing that we are significant or worthy enough for them to give their time and attention to us? But at the same time, I wondered if they were going to help my heart to heal because it meant that Brayden and I wouldn't be together in the end.

"Will I still have a biological child of my own?" I asked.

Holding her palms slightly apart from each other, "They say that there is a short window."

Renee remarked on what a powerful family this was that Brayden had married into. "Would it be expected of her to have a child? Because this doesn't feel like they decided to create this 'love baby.'"

"Oh, I'm sure it probably would be. If not for her family in Great Britain, but for the Saudis who they both work for."

That night was spent dousing my pain with wine as I turned the situation over and over in my head, trying to understand how this could all be happening— just when I was led to believe that we were finally going to be together. I didn't know what day the baby was born, but by my calculations, Hilary would have conceived right before Brayden contacted me in January; an exchange between us that likely would have triggered his decision to make a plan to get out of the marriage. When I started feeling his anxiety a month or two later, he must have learned about the pregnancy and been struggling with what to do.

Although it was purely speculation on my part, Hilary was in her early 40s and with Brayden's flying schedule, it was quite possible that she was undergoing *in vitro* fertilization. Brayden didn't have to be present when she conceived. But even if that wasn't the case, if he hadn't fully committed himself to leaving and she wanted to get pregnant, then he wouldn't be able to avoid trying with her. Even couples who are going through the motions of a marriage still have sex. But why had the pregnancy not been revealed to me sooner? Why was I led to believe that everything was about to come together for us, and that he had a plan? Although Renee remarked that seeing someone pregnant and seeing a baby are two entirely different things, the guides had to have known that he would never jeopardize his parental rights once the baby was born—even I knew that.

Renee said that I needed to release my attachment to the outcome and trust in the higher plan for my life. That was easier said than done, but I knew that she was right. So many times before I thought that I knew what was best for me and was angry when it didn't happen, only to realize later that it was for the best. As a result of Brayden's marriage, I had grown in so many positive ways that I wouldn't have, had it not happened. But the baby.... How much more did I need to grow? This was more than I could bear any longer, and I still had a mild feeling of betrayal from God and from Brayden.

Renee had encouraged me by saying that Brayden seemed to come around when I started to give up on him. But how could I do that when I still loved and wanted him so deeply? I felt that it was yet another impossible thing to ask, but I knew that it was true and I had to try to change my mindset and let go of my hope, while still keeping my faith. Brayden and I had a stronger connection than most, but even when I had fallen in love in the past, it was like that energy was sent out into the Universe and all of my ex-boyfriends would come out of the wood work, as though they knew I was going off the market.

I thought about the events leading up to his wedding in Scotland when it was like the faucet had been turned on and I was experiencing all sorts of synchronicities and messages pressing me to go. I would have never gone if I thought he would go through with it, but he did. When I returned home, I asked Renee why I was guided to go. She said that the guides wouldn't tell her. The following year it was finally disclosed that I was guided to Scotland to show Brayden how much I loved him, because he struggled to believe that I truly loved him as much as I did.

For some reason, I had been guided to stay strong in my resolve that we were to be together. Just as I had been with the trip to Scotland, like they were just helping me to get to the next turning point so I wouldn't give up. By not knowing about the pregnancy sooner, I was spared months of pain and agony. But why? In Scotland, Brayden had the free will not to get married, but the baby?

For the first time, I no longer felt the conviction that we would be together as I had for so many years. This may be the final, tragic end to the beautiful love between us. He would never truly know my pain, and we would never again see each other.

Renee was no gypsy lady reading tea leaves, and neither were Sophie or Margie. She clearly communicated with angels and spirits on the other side. There were so many instances when she was dead accurate with information that she couldn't have possibly known. So when she used the word "curse," I was surprised that she even said it. She herself added that "she didn't normally go there." But now I had to wonder about the timing, and why after so many months she was bringing up the possibility, and suggesting that there may be some unseen force keeping Brayden and me apart. Maybe there had been a karmic agreement between him and me that we wouldn't be together until the baby was born. She had told me in one of our earliest readings that Brayden and I met before we were supposed to. That our energy was so drawn to each other's that we found each other anyways, adding, "It's so rare, like a shooting star."

I had dismissed so many things before, believing that they were fantasy, only to experience those things for myself first hand. I didn't believe in reincarnation for the longest time, and I wouldn't have imagined that there were Twin Flame soulmates who could have the synchronicities and psychic connection that Brayden and I did. I certainly wouldn't have ever thought that I would come face to face with an Indian shaman in the middle of a parking lot. As much as it pained me, Renee was right. I needed to do the Burning Karma, and pray that I could release my attachment to the outcome.

Several times in my past, I had seen that what I wanted was not always what was best for me. I never thought that I would love anyone the way that I loved Duff, and then I met Brayden. But I also believed that I met Duff so I would recognize the synchronicities between them so I wouldn't give up on Brayden. If that was true, then why would I lose Brayden now?

Although my disappointment with the way my life had gone for me was still tinged with anger for having been put through it, I had grown in positive ways that wouldn't have been possible without the experience.

Three years earlier, on October 10, I had proposed to Brayden. So in some sentimental way, I wanted that to be the day I said goodbye. Next to finding out about the baby—I knew it would the most painful experience of my life.

In some ways I felt a little silly, just as I had in the angelic healing class where my preconceived notions had been proven to be false. But no matter, the Burning Karma prayer was serious: it was an ancient three-day prayer ceremony in which I would be taking my case before Arch Angels and Ascended Masters to review my life path and Karmic records. They had the ability to rearrange and release anything in my life that wasn't serving my highest good, and it wasn't to be taken lightly. I wasn't asking for a shortcut, because I had already been through the pain and had clearly learned my lessons. I was only asking that if there was anything interfering with my relationship with Brayden that shouldn't be, that it be removed.

I had been given a lengthy prayer to say that would be followed by my request of specific issues in my life to be reviewed, which I printed on a page. There could be no ego or selfish motive in the requests, other than asking that anything that was hindering our highest good be released and cleared. The ceremony included the lighting of candles, which were of different colors and meanings. I was supposed to say the prayer at the same time each day and although it felt a little hocus pocus to me, there's much to the Universe that many of us will never understand. Prayers, ceremony, and the lighting of candles and incense are common practices in all of the world's religions.

My apartment was small and I didn't have the ability to create a true sacred space, so my meditations were done in my bedroom. I purchased plastic birthday candle holders and set them in small holes that I had pierced in a box, to keep the small candles upright. After printing the prayer and adding my request to the end, I carefully set everything out on my nightstand with an abalone shell that held a stick of Palo Santo wood (holy wood) I burned in place of sage to clear negativity and create a sacred space.

Imagining the enormity of what it might be like to physically go before the Arch Angels and Ascended Masters to ask that my request be granted, I prepared in the only way that I had time for. I washed my face, brushed my hair, and put my silk, violet robe on. Violet is the color of transformation, and that was what I was asking of them.

With my room dimly lit, I fanned the light, coconut-fragranced smoke from the Palo Santo wood around my body, sitting upright on my bed, just as I did when I prepared for meditation. Breathing colored light into each of my Chakras to clear and open them, I then imagined a beam of white, purifying light from the heavens, cleansing my body while breathing it in and grounding my energy to the earth.

I felt nervous and awkward that I may have not formed my request correctly, but there was no turning back and with one more deep breath, I lit the first small candle: white to represent purity, red for love, violet for transformation, green for the earth, blue for Brayden and pink for me. Imagining now that the angels were around me, I read the first part of the prayer from the page I had typed, asking that they look into my karmic records and everything about me, to assist me with my own divine plan, and that which would be for my highest good. I felt emotion well up in my voice and tears in my eyes as I read my final request:

I ask that any and all cords be cut, and karma and curses cleared, that are hindering Brayden Loch from taking action, and making the decisions that will bring us together as one with each other. I also ask that all vows and oaths between the two of us be cleared and healed, so we can begin our life in a way that is for our highest good. I revoke any and all agreements made in time and space, which are preventing and hindering this from happening.

I ask for these things with loving gratitude,

Julie Hopper

    As I blew the candles out one by one, I wondered if my request had been received. I didn't feel any different until I walked out of my bedroom. I paused mid step when I felt the strong impression of the word "Trust."

    Please let that be your confirmation and not my own hope! I prayed.

    I felt calm knowing about what I had to do next. I sat down at my computer to write the good-bye message that I would send to Brayden on the 10[th,] certain that I would anguish for hours over the right choice of words. Unless my request was granted and something changed, this would be the last message that I ever sent to him. My finger's typed the message effortlessly in one draft. I wanted to tell him how much pain I was in, but it wouldn't make any difference. And although the words were still difficult to say, I was surprised that I was beginning to shift to a more spiritual and accepting perspective of the situation, and less emotional. I was certain that the message was divinely inspired and the most heartfelt way to say good-bye.

    I experienced frequent moments when I sobbed uncontrollably, followed by my reminder of the word "Trust," which calmed me—it was all that I had. There was no longer any choice but to release it all and trust. The following night, I read the prayer and lit the candles, then I prayed some more. As I climbed into my warm, pillowy bed, I thanked God as I did every night, that I had a comfortable bed to sleep in and a roof over my head, when some would be grateful just to have food and water.

I often watched the women with their slicked back pony tails driving Cadillac Escalades and wondered why they had so much security and a husband to take care of them, when I had to struggle on my own. I lived my life with integrity, and was caring and compassionate to others. Why did the one thing that I wanted the most always have to be just beyond my reach? At times I felt that it was so unfair but then, the lesson that I was here to experience in this lifetime could have been one that was far more painful in other ways.

The next day, my mother and I would be driving to the Oregon coast to celebrate her birthday with family. I didn't know how I was going to excuse myself, or create a sacred space to pray. This night would possibly be the most important of my life, and I treated it with the degree of sacredness and reverence that it deserved.

7:00 pm was the hour I had chosen for the Burning Karma prayer each night, and I had nervous anticipation as I watched the clock for the hour to approach.

"Why aren't you having a glass of wine?" my sister laughed over her cocktail.

"Uh, well... I have a little meditation I need to do and I can't drink."

"Oh, come on!"

"No, really. I can't drink."

There was far too much commotion and lack of privacy at the house so at 6:30, I slipped quietly out the door, grabbing my niece's clam shovel from the garage as I headed for my car. My mother and niece, Mikala, knew what I was up to, but no one else seemed to notice me leave.

The ocean added increased energy and vibration, and the time of the full moon was growing near. I needed all the help that I could get, and whether it had an influence or not, I was grateful for the possibility. I prayed for my own guides to be with me as I searched the ocean front roads for a private place to park. I was nervous enough, but the idea of a cop knocking on my window while I had the equivalent of birthday candles burning inside of a box, wearing a violet, silk robe would be beyond humiliating! I laughed out loud as the picture formed in my mind.

I was running out of time and feeling a sense of urgency when I decided to drive further down the highway where there would be fewer houses. A big sand dune hid a parking place between it and the railroad tracks bordering the beach, and it had a big tree. *Perfect!* The Oregon coast is almost always cold, windy and frequently raining, especially near the beach. But this night was not only warm but unusually calm. The moon was nearly full and it cast an eerie atmosphere on the moment as it reflected on the ocean waves softly washing onto the shore.

In the driver's seat, I burned Palo Santo wood while grounding my energy and raising my vibration to the heavens. I imagined what it might be like to have the Arch Angels and Ascended Masters encircling my car to hear my final prayer. In a split second, I saw a flash of gold light in the corner of my eye reflect off my face. At the same moment, I was scared that I had been discovered by someone with a flashlight. My eyes darted in the direction of the light and I gasped to see forty or fifty feet away from me with the ocean in the distance, tall beings of intense, bright, white light to my right in a semi-circle around my car. There must have been at least twenty of them.

They were beautiful beyond description and, in the essence of their being, I could sense their absolute power and authority mixed with a beautiful calm of love and peace. Their presence felt more masculine in nature and the being in the center was taller and seemed to have more detail to his features, while the two on either side of him had fewer, but more than the others. They were clearly individual light forms, but the rays of deep, golden light cast from their sides connected them as if they were one. The image was only for a split second, but it was burned into my memory.

I asked myself if I had really just seen what I did, but I knew that it wasn't my imagination because unlike my other guides and the angel who I had seen in my mind's eye, these angels appeared in the physical before my eyes. The enormity of it humbled and frightened me at the same time it gave me hope and reassurance. It was difficult for me to absorb the concept that I would be significant and worthy enough for them to be there with me, but at the same time it made sense because they were the ones who I was addressing in my prayer.

Lighting the candles, I was still nervous that someone might see the flame and knock on my window at any moment. After reading the prayer, the first candle burned out and caught the little plastic holder on fire. I blew it out, and continued to wait for the others to burn down, hoping that I didn't somehow affect the meaning of it all. It was curious to me that the blue and pink candles representing Brayden and I hadn't burned down to half, while I had to blow the others out as they burned too closely to the plastic holders. I grew impatient, still nervous that I might be discovered at any moment, while reminding myself that it appeared to be a good omen.

When they finally burned down low enough, I stepped outside of the car, placing the page with the prayer onto the last lit candles to burn. The box contained the fire and ashes perfectly, but suddenly the rest of the plastic candle holders caught fire. *Oh my God! I'm going to screw this up!* As I poured my bottle water into the box to put out the flame, I laughed at the comedy of it all, while still trying to keep the moment sacred. The ashes that were supposed to be buried under a living tree, were now liquid and mixed with water. *Maybe my prayers will be delivered more quickly,* I reassured myself.

As I walked toward the tree with my box and shovel, the moon reflected serenely off of the dark, ocean waves and I paused for a moment breathing in the cool sea air. I took in the magnificent beauty of the evening as I contemplated whether or not my prayers would be answered. Setting the box down, I picked up the shovel and dug a hole into the firm sand below the tree, and poured the watery ashes into it before covering them up. *I'm sure this is meant to be buried in soil,* I thought with disappointment, but consoled myself with remembering that salt was a purifier.

It was done. And whatever mistakes I made—there was nothing that I could do to change it. This was my last effort. As I approached my car with the box and shovel, I paused mid-step as I felt myself surrounded by a wide circle of gentle energy. *Am I really feeling this?* I reasoned with myself, as I felt the energy lift up in swirl above me. I distinctly felt lighter, as if something had shifted. I was awestruck by the sensation, and paused for several moments to let the reality of it sink in. Something had lifted, or shifted. I didn't know what it meant, but I felt lighter and more at peace. It was mystical sense of being and although I've had so many other spiritual experiences, it was difficult for me to believe that it had happened; and that what I had just done might have some cosmic effect.

The feeling of peace and almost joy continued to grow as I returned to the party. My phone chimed with a notification less than an hour later and I checked my e-mail.

"Love Spell also commented on Delano Carson's photo." It was a notification from Facebook. *That's so weird!* The timing of it was far too strange to be coincidental: *I've just performed a prayer ceremony asking for intervention in my love relationship, and now I get a notification about someone who goes by the name Love Spell? I commented on that photo over a year and a half ago. What are the odds? This must be a positive confirmation!*

I returned home on the morning of the 9th, with the intention of sending Brayden my good-bye so he would receive it in Saudi Arabia on the 10th. The day was spent in quiet contemplation, knowing that this communication may be our last. My tears were often mixed with mild feelings of abandonment, as I thought about the last five years and the wedding dress that still hung in my closet.

It was never a competition, but she had won. She trapped a man into a marriage when he was in love with someone else, and although he was equally at fault, they had now brought a child into a marriage that was entered into for the wrong reasons. I had seen many couples stay in bad marriages to the detriment of the children, and although I knew that Brayden wouldn't be able to stay for any length of time, she had too much control over their daughter while in Saudi. If a marriage is going to end, it's better to do it before a child understands what's happening, rather than when they're old enough for a divorce to cause emotional damage. But that was up to him now, so I have to release it and move on with my life.

I had crossed oceans for him, giving him my heart and soul; defending his honor often at the demise of my own friendships and telling very few, including in my own family, that he had married. I loved and understood him like no other ever would. He was a beautiful person inside and out, and his actions would never change my belief in him. He would never fully know my devotion and pain, or the thousands of times I called his name when I needed his strength. I knew that he must have been getting the same guidance and messages that I had been, but he didn't understand or accept them enough to follow.

My peace had finally returned, and I knew that it was time for me to release what I had fought and struggled so hard to save for so many years; and hope that if not him, another love as great would come into my life. Brayden was safe and alive. Any widow who truly loved her husband would be grateful to know that—even if it meant that they could never be together again. Although my dreams for the future now felt empty and without direction, I would "Trust."

Speaking tenderly with my voice trembling and a heavy heart, I spoke the words as if he could hear me, "I'll love you for the rest of my life, Brayden Loch, and into the next."

To: Brayden Loch   *October 9, 2011*
From: Julie Hopper
Subject: A message from my heart ~

Brayden,

I sincerely want to congratulate you on the birth of your beautiful baby girl. I may have even felt love for her myself, as I saw your image in her.

I realized that three years after asking you to marry me, I was still watching someone else live the life that I yearn for with you ~ It's not right. So it's time for me to fully release you from my heart and mind before I break, and while there is still time to have a family of my own.

Please be kind to me, by not extending an offer of friendship; but know that through your daughter, you will experience the unconditional love that I felt for you. I wish you and your family continued joy and happiness throughout the years.

Love and light,

Julie

49231519R00235

Made in the USA
Middletown, DE
10 October 2017